LOCOMOTIVES OF THE ISLE OF WIGHT RAILWAYS

T. P. Cooper, J. C. H. Faulkner,
R. J. Maycock and R. A. Silsbury

crecy.co.uk

IWCR No. 8 in metallic crimson livery, at Newport shortly after delivery. *IWSR Archive, colour by John Faulkner*

First published in 2021 by Crécy Publishing

Printed in Bulgaria by Multiprint

ISBN 978 191080 9877

www.crecy.co.uk

Crécy Publishing Limited
1a Ringway Trading Estate,
Shadowmoss Road,
Manchester M22 5LH
www.crecy.co.uk

Front Cover: E1 W4 *Wroxall* at Newport in October 1933, showing the dark green livery adopted by the SR from 1925 onwards. Although intended mainly for goods traffic, the E1s were also used on passenger trains as required. *O. J. Morris ©Rail Archive Stephenson, colour by John Faulkner*

Title page: The preserved O2 class W24 *Calbourne*, newly outshopped in malachite green livery by the Isle of Wight Steam Railway on 30 March 2021. *John Faulkner*

Rear cover inset top: A post-First World War view of the IWR's *Sandown* in the yard at Ryde St John's. The high-level handrails are long gone and the loco has also lost the elegant polished brass dome and copper-capped chimney, while a patch has been installed along the bottom of the tank. The livery, now Midland red, is in the same style as the earlier Furness red. *RP1430, colour by John Faulkner*

Rear cover inset middle: O2 W36 *Carisbrooke* at Merstone soon after delivery in 1949. W35 and W36 were pull-push equipped for working the lightly-used Ventnor West branch. For fuller details see page 111.*©anistr.com*

Rear cover inset bottom: O2 W19 *Osborne* at Ryde St John's Road in 1936 wearing SR dark green and with the large 'MacLeod' bunker. Note that the buffer beam is bolted rather than riveted, the reason for which is not known. *IWSR Archive, colour by John Faulkner*

Rear cover main: W14 *Fishbourne*, W18 *Ningwood* and W17 *Seaview* in winter storage at Brickfields Siding, Sandown on 3 March 1963. For fuller details see page 120. *A.E. Bennett ©The Transport Treasury*

Contents

Introduction and Acknowledgements

It is in the nature of island railways that they differ in many ways from those on the mainland. In this, the railways of the Isle of Wight were no exception. Each company evolved separately with characteristics that survived both the takeover by the Southern Railway and nationalisation. This individuality was nowhere more evident than in the engines they owned.

As sources of information we have relied on the railway companies' minute books and related papers, the Beyer, Peacock and Manning, Wardle maker's records, together with news items and articles in newspapers and the railway press. We were fortunate to have access to the diaries of Thomas Smeaton and Charles Woodnutt covering much of the Southern Railway and post-nationalisation years, along with many other observations.

The book has been enhanced by extracts from a previous publication on the subject. In October 1982 the Railway Correspondence & Travel Society published *A Locomotive History of the Railways of the Isle of Wight* written by the late D. L. Bradley. He had unrivalled access to official documents that have since been dispersed or destroyed. Although a lot of Mr Bradley's information has been verified, we had to take on trust a few events, dates and proposed purchases not mentioned in the surviving records.

For consistency, a few terms have been used throughout the book that were not necessarily contemporary. A good example is the term General Overhaul, used by BR to describe the most extensive repairs, whereas the SR equivalent was an 'A' class Repair. Historic entries such as pre-decimal amounts and the twelve-hour clock have been left unchanged. Care should be taken with the dimensions as in some cases there were material differences in those quoted by the makers and other writers. There were also problems with certain dates during the 1920s and afterwards when engines were often laid aside at the end of a summer season but not officially withdrawn or sold for scrap until the arrival of a replacement the following year.

This book concentrates on a history of the steam and diesel engines. Consequently, we have not written in any detail about the Ryde Tramway cars and electric stock as they were not locomotives in the accepted sense, but needed to be included as part of the standard-gauge history. With well over 100 books about the Island's railways having been published, as well as numerous magazine articles, locating previously unpublished photographs has proved an almost impossible task. We have found a few, but the majority of the images have been chosen because they illustrate key features that we have endeavoured to interpret meaningfully. The descriptions of colours have been based on contemporary accounts, information gleaned from paint fragments and historic paintings. The colourised photographs provide a best guess at how the engines would have looked (See note at the end of Appendix 4). Any errors are our responsibility alone.

Numerous individuals have helped in making this work as accurate as possible. In particular, we thank the following for their observations, technical information and advice: F. Abraham, M. Brinton, A. Britton, M. Birkin, M. Downer, N. Felton, B. Francis, D. Gawn, T. Hastings, P. Hayward, the late M. Jacobs, the late J. Lock, R. Macdonald, J. Maskell, R. Newman, G. Peters, M. Prouten, A. Summers and J. Woodhams. Any royalties earned by the sale of this book will go to the Isle of Wight Steam Railway (IWSR). More information about the Railway can be found on the website *www.iwsteamrailway.co.uk*.

January 2021

The Story Behind the Book

This book would not have been created but for the existence of the Railway Correspondence & Travel Society (RCTS), an organisation that can trace its history back to 1928. The Society began arranging outings for groups of enthusiasts during the 1930s, including a visit to the Isle of Wight in 1939. The first locomotive stock book appeared in 1935 and during the war the Society was able to publish a book on LNER locomotives. It was the forerunner of more comprehensive multi-part histories of LNER and GWR locomotives. Meanwhile, the Society's long-running magazine, *Railway Observer*, recorded events on Britain's railways as and when they occurred.

In 1960 the Society published the first of a series of books concerning the locomotives of the Southern Railway and its constituent companies. The author was Donald L. Bradley, a member of the Society. Although not a railwayman, he was given unrivalled access to BR archives and the Drawing Offices at Ashford and Eastleigh Works. In his early books he acknowledged the considerable assistance given by J. E. Bell, the Ashford Works Manager, and his staff. (Mr Bell had been the Assistant for the Isle of Wight from 1934 until the onset of war in 1939.) Mr Bradley was able to see and make notes from a vast accumulation of paperwork, some of which dated back to the nineteenth century. This irreplaceable collection was soon to be dispersed following a series of major reorganisations and the end of steam working in 1967. A fraction of the documentation eventually passed to the National Railway Museum, York, and National Archives, Kew, but the remainder went into private collections, was 'lost' or simply destroyed.

Mr Bradley's research culminated in the publication of no fewer than ten books covering the London, Chatham & Dover, South Eastern, South Western, Brighton and Southern companies. He admitted that the more deeply the records were investigated, the more appalled he became at his lack of knowledge. Small wonder that the tenth book was not published until September 1976. The books were well regarded and soon became collectors' items.

In 1982 the RCTS published Mr Bradley's book about the Isle of Wight locomotives. By then Ryde Works was a shadow of its former self, key members of staff had retired and a great deal of paperwork had been destroyed or disposed of.

However, he was able to see some important documents that later passed into the hands of collectors and who have since refused requests by researchers to access them. They included the Isle of Wight Railway engine register, the Isle of Wight Central Railway boiler book and correspondence. The resulting publication was unfortunately a book too far for Mr Bradley, partly because of his limited knowledge of the history of the Isle of Wight's railways. Sir Peter Allen, President of the Transport Trust, wrote: 'I enjoyed reading it despite the numerous mistakes.' Railway historian Dick Riley added: 'Don did all this wonderful research, but then invented the bits he didn't know so blew the integrity of the whole book.' Despite this criticism, the book was a revelation simply because it contained a considerable amount of new and previously unknown information.

The Wight Locomotive Society was formed in April 1966 in response to a decision to close much of the Isle of Wight's railway system and end steam working. It achieved the aim of buying an LSWR class O2 engine and some carriages before moving to a permanent home at Havenstreet in 1971. Transformed into the Isle of Wight Steam Railway (IWSR), using a growing collection of engines and rolling stock, a passenger service now operates for much of the year to Wootton and in the opposite direction to Smallbrook Junction, where it connects with services on the last remaining commercial railway between Ryde and Shanklin. The whole railway is an Accredited Museum and an extensive collection can be seen at Havenstreet where there is an archive of material relating to the Isle of Wight railways. The IWSR produces its own magazine, *Island Rail News*, but has only rarely ventured into book publishing.

Attempts to revise Mr Bradley's book began soon after the original was published but were hampered by his death in 1986, the disappearance of his research notes and many of the documents he had examined. In 2012 the RCTS approached two of the authors to make available their research with a view to producing a revised edition. Unfortunately the RCTS was unable to fulfil its intention and in 2016 sold the rights to the original book to the IWSR. A small group then made a start on preparing their own version. Years later, this book is the result.

1

Historical Summary

Separated from Hampshire by the Solent and Spithead, the Isle of Wight extends 22 miles east to west and 13 miles north to south with a varied geology that epitomises the landscape of Southern England. Early trade with the mainland was largely shared between Ryde and Newport, the Island's capital, but Cowes grew in importance during the eighteenth century and became the main point of entry for travellers and merchandise, a position much prized by the inhabitants and one not seriously challenged until the London, Brighton & South Coast Railway opened to Portsmouth on 14 June 1847. The emergence of reliable ferry services saw the beginnings of a thriving holiday trade but travel was hampered by the poor state of the roads.

The railway mania of 1845 generated a proposal for a standard-gauge railway that was destined to fail. This was for an Isle of Wight Railway from Cowes to Ventnor with a branch from Newport to Ryde. Opposition was unexpectedly strong from the landed gentry, along with the publicans and shopkeepers who feared the swifter means of travel would encourage patronage of establishments of Portsmouth and Southampton. They did not appreciate that losses would be offset by the reciprocal flow of travellers from the mainland. Such was the level of opposition that the Bill in Parliament was withdrawn. Further early attempts to promote Island-wide railways were no more successful.

A less ambitious proposal put forward by the Cowes & Newport Railway (CNR) received Royal Assent on 8 August 1859 and the 4¼-mile line opened on 16 June 1862 worked by contract. At first business was brisk especially in the summer months and despite the need to use road transport for journeys beyond Newport. However, within a few years there was a decline following the opening of more convenient routes to and within the Isle of Wight.

The Isle of Wight Railway (IWR) was incorporated as the Isle of Wight (Eastern Section) Railway on 23 July 1860 to construct an 11¼-mile line from Ryde to Ventnor, with a goods spur and quay at Brading. When powers were granted for a branch to Newport in 1863 the words 'Eastern Section' were removed from the Company's title. That line was not built, nor was another to Yarmouth and Freshwater, while the main line to Ryde terminated at St John's Road, ¼ mile short of its authorised terminus at Melville Street. The railway opened from Ryde to Shanklin on 23 August 1864 and to Ventnor on 10 September 1866.

In isolation, the Cowes & Newport Railway had little chance of affluence but with no funds available for extensions the directors could only encourage other promoters to take on the task. In this they had some success for several proposals were soon before Parliament. The Isle of Wight (Newport Junction) Railway (IWNJR) obtained powers for a 9¼-mile line from Sandown to Newport on 31 July 1868. It was followed by the 7¾-mile Ryde & Newport Railway (RNR) on 25 July 1872. The two railways were to connect with the CNR at Newport, where a joint station was envisaged, and the IWR at Sandown and Ryde.

When the railway from Ryde to Newport opened on 20 December 1875, the CNR and RNR formed a joint committee to manage the operation of their lines from 1 July 1876. A modified agreement confirmed in an 1877 Act also authorised a branch to a jetty on the west bank of the River Medina. A siding to Newport Quay was built at the behest of the local council and the two came into use in November 1878. The Newport Quay siding was rarely used before its removal during 1892. Medina Jetty became the Island's principal point of entry for coal and minerals.

In the meantime, the IWNJR had been trying to complete its railway from Sandown to Newport. Permission to open from Sandown to Horringford was refused by the Board of Trade inspector on 24 June 1872 because the rails were second-hand. The line opened with some ceremony on 28 June but following a second adverse inspection the service was hurriedly withdrawn. After a delay caused by financial problems, the line opened from Sandown to Shide near Newport on 1 February 1875, a further ½ mile or so to Newport Pan Mill on 6 October and finally to the joint Newport station on 1 June 1879. It was worked by the IWR

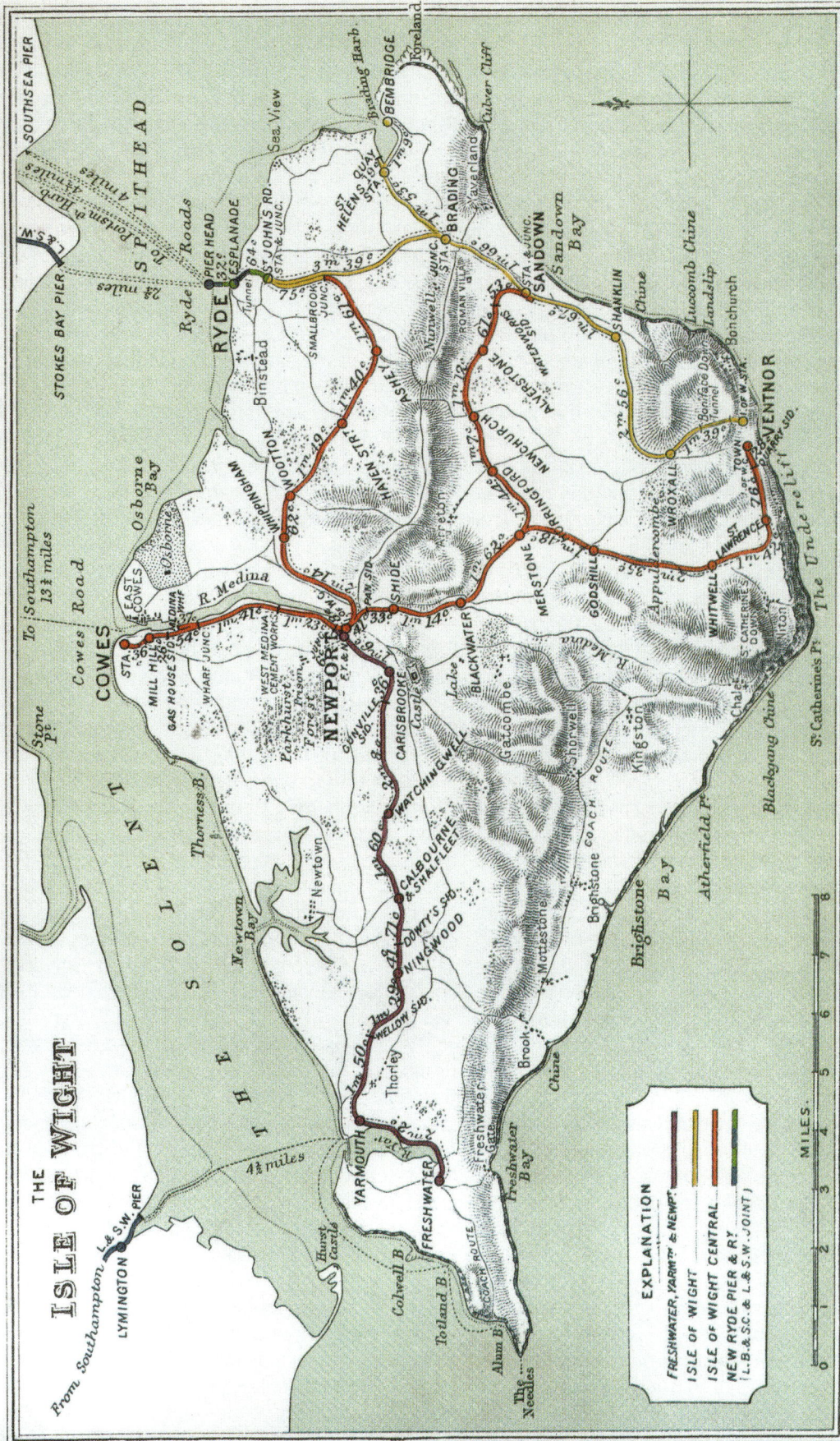

THE
ISLE OF WIGHT

The Railway Clearing House

prior to 1 April 1879 when the Joint Committee took charge. Operating as 'The Ryde, Newport & Cowes Railways', the three companies amalgamated to form the Isle of Wight Central Railway (IWCR) on 1 July 1887.

On 7 August 1874 the Brading Harbour Improvement & Railway Company (BHIR) was incorporated with powers to construct a mile-long embankment from St Helens to Bembridge, a harbour, a quay and a railway continuing from the IWR goods branch at Brading Quay to St Helens and Bembridge. A goods service began operating between Brading Quay and St Helens Quay on 1 August 1878 but passenger services over the whole 2¾-mile railway to Bembridge did not commence until 27 May 1882, worked by the IWR. After years in receivership, the Company's title was changed to Brading Harbour & Railway Co. in 1896 when powers were obtained to define the harbour limits and permit extensive dredging. This paved the way for several property sales including St Helens Quay and the railway, both of which were purchased by the IWR on 2 August 1898. A train ferry, using the former Granton to Burntisland vessel *Carrier*, commenced sailing in August 1885 between St Helens and Langstone Harbour but it failed to prosper and the service was abandoned in March 1888.

The railways eased travel within the Isle of Wight, although at no point did they offer a direct connection with the ferries to the mainland. At Cowes the station was reasonably close to the landing quay but at Ryde the terminus was at the back of the town well away from the shore. The Ryde Pier Company (RPC) had been incorporated on 13 July 1812 to construct a pier, the first section of which opened in May 1814, followed by extensions over the next twenty years until it was nearly half a mile in length. A horse tramway on a second pier alongside the original opened on 29 August 1864 and was extended to the railway terminus at St John's Road in 1871. The slow and uncomfortable tram was unsatisfactory and there were calls for a railway. The London & South Western (LSWR) and London, Brighton & South Coast (LBSCR) railways took an interest in the idea and on 23 July 1877 obtained parliamentary approval for a double-track railway. It opened for IWR trains from St John's Road to an Esplanade station on 5 April 1880. Ryde, Newport & Cowes trains began using the line when the terminus at Pier Head opened on 1 July. The tramway was cut back to its original length along the pier.

In the western half of the Island the Freshwater, Yarmouth & Newport Railway (FYNR) gained powers on 26 August 1880 for a 12-mile line from Freshwater to Yarmouth and Newport. The railway opened for goods traffic on 10 September 1888 and to passengers on 20 July 1889. It was worked by the IWCR until 1 July 1913, when the Freshwater Company took over operation of its railway.

Just one more railway was constructed, this being the 6¾-mile Newport, Godshill & St Lawrence Railway (NGSTLR). It opened from Merstone on the Sandown to Newport line to St Lawrence on 26 July 1897 and to the western outskirts of Ventnor on 1 June 1900. From the beginning the railway was worked by the IWCR and was absorbed by it in 1913.

Lines were single track with the exception of Ryde Pier Head to St John's Road and through Newport station. The one mile between St John's Road and Smallbrook were independent lines to Ventnor and Newport; the second track had been provided by the IWR solely for RNR use. The only crossing point between Ryde and Ventnor was at Sandown as passenger trains were not permitted to cross at Brading or Shanklin until 1892, when improved signalling and block working instruments were brought into use. Between Ryde and Newport there was a crossing loop at Ashey and a second at Whippingham was installed in 1912. On the Sandown to Newport line a crossing loop came into use at Merstone in 1895. Trains to Ventnor Town could cross at Whitwell and those between Newport and Freshwater at Carisbrooke and Ningwood. A loop at Yarmouth was so badly positioned that the Board of Trade refused to allow passenger trains to cross there.

The Railways Act passed by Parliament in 1921 forced 120 of Britain's railways to amalgamate into four regional companies. The Southern Railway (SR) came into being on 1 January 1923 and incorporated the London & South Western, London, Brighton & South Coast, South Eastern & Chatham railways along with several smaller undertakings. Negotiations with the Island companies were led by the LSWR and although the IWCR and IWR accepted the terms offered and were absorbed on 1 January 1923, the FYNR held out until the matter went to arbitration; it was taken over on 27 August. The RPC was purchased separately with effect from 1 January 1924. This gave the SR control of the Isle of Wight railways, Ryde tramway and railway piers, together with the Ryde to Portsmouth and Yarmouth to Lymington ferry services.

The SR inherited from the Island companies eighteen steam engines, 103 passenger carriages and vans, 571 goods vehicles and the tramway stock on Ryde Pier. In the interests of standardisation, and to reduce maintenance costs, the majority were replaced by engines and stock previously owned by the mainland companies. The workshops at Ryde were reorganised and that at Newport closed. Locomotive running sheds were retained at Newport and Ryde.

The increasing popularity of the Isle of Wight as a destination for holidaymakers was particularly evident on the line from Ryde Pier Head to Ventnor, where improvements were carried out to facilitate increased train frequency, starting in 1925 when a crossing loop was installed at Wroxall. In May 1926 a signal box and scissors crossing came into use at Smallbrook Junction so that the single lines between there and St John's Road could be operated as double track. The box closed in the winter months when they reverted to single-line operation. In 1927 the line was doubled from Brading to Sandown and a fourth platform was added at Ryde Pier Head in 1933. Elsewhere, a resited station and new crossing loop between Ryde and Newport at Havenstreet opened in May 1926 and redundant loops were removed at Ashey, Carisbrooke, Yarmouth and Whitwell. Ventnor Town station was more appropriately renamed Ventnor West on

1 June 1923. Goods traffic was not forgotten as both St Helens Quay and Medina Jetty were rebuilt, the latter as a wharf with additional storage capacity. Bridges were strengthened or rebuilt, flat bottom rails were replaced with second-hand chaired bullhead rails and the signalling brought up to date.

At nationalisation the 55 miles of Island railways became part of the Southern Region of British Railways (BR). During 1951 it became known the new organisation wished to dispense with much of the network. The Merstone to Ventnor West branch closed on 15 September 1952, the Newport to Freshwater and Brading to Bembridge lines on 21 September 1953 and the Sandown to Newport line on 6 February 1956. The closures did secure a commitment that the remaining lines would remain open 'at least until the beginning of 1966'.

The once extensive system was reduced to the Ryde to Ventnor and Ryde to Cowes lines but in 1963 the Beeching report recommended their closure. Notice was given that services would end on 12 October 1964 but the date was postponed after the County Council lodged objections. While the railways operated at a loss, they carried large numbers of visitors during the summer months, especially on Saturdays. Over 3 million people used the Portsmouth to Ryde ferries in the year ending September 1963 and most also patronised the Ryde to Ventnor line. After a lengthy public hearing before the Transport Users' Consultative Committee in June 1964, a report was sent to the Minister of Transport. His decision, announced in a press release on 28 July 1965, largely confirmed the proposals but a further delay ensued until alternative bus services could be arranged. The Ryde to Cowes line closed on 21 February 1966, followed by the Shanklin to Ventnor section on 18 April. The remaining goods yards closed for business on 16 May.

After establishing that Ryde Pier could not be adapted to accommodate buses, BR reluctantly accepted the continuing need for a tramway. Objections to an Esplanade bus station resulted in proposals for an extension to St John's Road but the Minister decided that the whole railway from Ryde Pier Head to Shanklin should be retained and modernised. Work to rebuild the railway pier began at the end of the summer timetable on 29 September 1963 and continued each winter for the next three years; during those months trains terminated at Ryde Esplanade. The last steam trains ran to Ryde Pier Head on 17 September 1966 and steam working ended altogether on 31 December. The 8½-mile line from Ryde Pier Head to Shanklin reopened for passenger traffic on 20 March 1967 after conversion to electric traction on the third-rail system, using second-hand London Transport tube stock. This allowed BR to close the tramway along Ryde Pier on 26 January 1969. Most of the tube cars lasted until replaced by newer stock in 1989–92. By then the railway was known as Island Line, a title that was retained when a franchise came into operation in 1996. The long-overdue transfer of newer replacements began in November 2020.

Meanwhile, there had been an attempt to reopen the Ryde to Cowes line. The Vectis Electric Railway (Vectrail) wanted to install overhead wires and operate second-hand German tramcars but later joined forces with the Sadler Rail Coach Co. when a change was made to diesel rail coaches. Sadler-Vectrail, the combined organisation, entered into fruitless negotiations to rent the track bed from the County Council and buy the permanent way from BR. The scheme was abandoned in 1970 after the enterprise's chief investor withdrew his support.

Despite some interest in the redundant steam engines, only the Wight Locomotive Society succeeded in purchasing one for preservation. Based temporarily at Newport, on 24 January 1971 the Society moved to a permanent home at Havenstreet (the station's name had been changed in 1958) and on 12 April steam trains commenced running during the summer months along the line towards Wootton. Passengers began using a new permanent station at Wootton on 7 August 1986 and an extension of the railway in the opposite direction to Smallbrook Junction opened on 20 July 1991; this provided a cross-platform connection with trains on the Ryde to Shanklin line. The halt at Ashey reopened on 2 May 1993. Although registered in 1972 as The Isle of Wight Railway Company Limited, we have used the title Isle of Wight Steam Railway (IWSR) to avoid confusion with its predecessor.

This is only an outline history of the Isle of Wight railways. A more comprehensive account can be found in other publications.[1-5] There is also a valuable record of interviews with some of the Island's railwaymen.[6]

2

Isle of Wight Railway

A contract for construction of the railway from Ryde to Ventnor was signed in December 1862 with Henry Bond. Construction began early in January 1863 with only twenty to thirty men, while at the end of the month a local newspaper reported that 200 'navvies' were coming to the Isle of Wight from Tewkesbury to join the labour force.[7] Work began on a ¾-mile tunnel under St Boniface Down but flooding in the shafts so delayed progress that the contractor concentrated on first completing the easier Ryde to Shanklin section.[8]

The contractor is known to have employed two engines. *Stuart* was one of two 2-2-0 tender engines delivered in January 1841 to the Glasgow, Paisley, Kilmarnock & Ayr Railway as 18 *Stuart* and 19 *Bute*. They were constructed by Edward Bury & Co. of Liverpool to the firm's distinctive design with forged-iron bar frames, 13in cylinders and a large spherical-topped copper firebox, known as 'haycock' or 'haystack'. Although among the best that could be bought, locomotive development was such that within ten years they were becoming obsolescent. The Glasgow & South Western Railway absorbed the railway in 1850 and rebuilt *Stuart* as a tank engine in July 1853.[9] The engine was later described as 'a 2-4-0 saddle tank with a haystack firebox, cast iron wheels and round coupling and connecting rods', square-topped tanks, 14in by 18in cylinders, 4ft 6in coupled wheels and weighed 18½ tons.[10] A Board of Trade inspector added that *Stuart* had 'a large amount of overhanging weight that renders it unfit for working passenger traffic'.[11] One of four old engines sold at auction on 20 June 1860, *Stuart* may have been employed by contractors building the Stokes Bay Railway opened on 6 April 1863. By then work on the IWR was under way so *Stuart* is likely to have reached the Island in May or thereabouts.

The second engine, named *Grafton*, was shipped to Brading from Hamworthy, near Poole, at roughly the same time. Like some of the workmen, it had been assisting in the construction of the Tewkesbury & Malvern Railway (there is a nearby village called Grafton). Three years later

the *Isle of Wight Times* for 11 April 1866 contained an advert for an auction of contractors' plant at Wroxall on 19 April. Lot 1 was 'a four-wheel locomotive with cylinders 18in stroke, by Hawthorns & Co. of Leith.' A footnote added that an engine would run from Shanklin to Wroxall on the day of the sale connecting with the 10.00am train from Ryde. Purchased for £465 by the contractor Frederick Furniss, in May *Grafton* was shipped by barge to Portsmouth for use on constructing the Hayling Island Railway.[12] After the line opened in July 1867, *Grafton* worked the services in a red livery as No. 1 *Brighton*. Sold in November 1871 for £240 to Isaac Boulton, a dealer of Ashton-under-Lyne, the engine was described as being 'an outside cylinder 0-4-2, with a 'haycock' firebox dome, and a saddle tank of the box type, the cylinders being 11in by 18in and the coupled wheels 3ft 6in. 0-4-2s with outside cylinders were rare in those days except in Scotland.'[13] The inference is that Hawthorns rebuilt it in August 1858 from a much older engine, possibly a Bury like *Stuart*. *Brighton* was hired out for various jobs before being sold to Brunner, Mond & Co.'s Chemical Works at Northwich in 1875 or 1876, where it ended its days.

Engines for working the line were first mentioned in a letter dated 21 January 1863 from Charles Beyer of Beyer, Peacock & Co. to his partner Henry Robertson concerning a meeting with John Fowler, the IWR Engineer:[14]

Peacock was in London last week and settled with Mr Fowler about 4 Tank Engines for the Isle of Wight, to be the same as Llangollen, but we have not received the official order from the General Rolling Stock Co. Price to the Isle of Wight Rw. £2,200 of which we shall get minus 10% off or £1,980.

Formed in May 1854, the firm gained a reputation as makers of well-built, reliable products and remained in business until 1966. The IWR directors discussed the matter on 16 June 1863, when the Engineer was asked to

Progress No.	Tried in steam	Dispatched
400	28.4.1864	17.6.1864 *Ryde*
401	5.5.1864	21.6.1864 *Sandown*
402	6.5.1864	22.6.1864 originally *Shanklin*. Sold to A. Albani, Italy
403	12.5.1864	28.6.1864 *Brading*, delivered as *Shanklin*
404	21.5.1864	26.1.1865 sold to Great Western Railway (GWR)

obtain quotes. No other makers were considered and on 23 July an order was placed for five engines. The maker's drawing office register contained the details for order No. 767 (*See* table above).[14]

Construction costs so depleted finances that on 2 March 1864 the IWR directors were forced to reduce the size of the order to three engines. Delivered to Portsmouth, George Pritchard of Southsea was hired to transport them by barge to Brading and according to the *Isle of Wight Observer* they were on the railway by 23 July.

This design of 2-4-0T had previously been used for West Midland Railway Nos 68 and 69 (maker's Nos 205 and 238, built 1861) and Swedish Government Railways *Edward Morgan*, *Jenny Jones* and *Blaida* (maker's Nos 258–260, built 1862). There were minor differences including side tanks 9in higher and a reduction in chimney height to 12ft 6in. They had Stephenson valve gear, feed pumps, copper-capped chimneys, large brass dome covers and balance safety valves over the fireboxes. A single weatherboard with two porthole spectacle plates was positioned at the front of the footplate. As was the norm at that time, a handbrake connected to wooden brake blocks acting on the coupled wheels. The livery was quoted as being dark chocolate with yellow and black lining.[12] (Bear in mind that early descriptions of colours were unreliable: 'light chocolate' was sometimes called 'dark maroon'.)[15] The polished brass and copper was finished off by brass nameplates on the boiler and oval maker's plates on the tank sides. One peculiarity unique to these nameplates was the insertion of a full stop after the name.[16]

Ryde at Ryde c.1864. As built, the first three Beyer, Peacock tanks provided no protection for the crew apart from a very small front weatherboard, one spectacle of which can be seen above the tank-top tool box. The square-cornered, single lining, in three panels, is faintly discernible on the tank-side. *IWSR Archive*

According to the maker's records, the three were sold to the IWR for £6,750 by quarterly instalments after having cost £4,522 4s 2d to build. Beyer, Peacock had little difficulty in disposing of the others. One was sold for £2,250 and sent to Newcastle for onward shipment to Signor A. Albani of Leghorn (Livorno), Northern Italy, his only purchase. The GWR took the last of the five engines at a reduced price of £2,150 as their No. 343 to assist similar 2-4-0Ts 225 and 226 bought on 1 August 1863 for the Worcester to Malvern Wells and Stratford-upon-Avon to Honeybourne services.[12]

Ryde headed the first passenger train from Ryde to Shanklin on 23 August 1864, assisted during the day by *Sandown*, but *Shanklin* missed the festivities, having been damaged a week earlier after losing control of a ballast train. Goods traffic began a few weeks later.[12] Other mishaps included one on 24 June 1865 when a train approached Ryde station too fast and collided with the stop blocks, an occurrence the driver repeated on 3 March 1866; he left the Company's service a month later. Within a short time it became evident that the passenger traffic was highly seasonal in nature and services had to be varied according to demand. Some maintenance could be deferred to the winter months but the lack of a steady income was a source of concern.[8]

Construction of the Shanklin to Ventnor section came to a halt in June 1865 when the contractor fell into financial difficulties. He arranged to be paid off by the Warrant Finance Co., the firm taking over his plant and contract to complete the line. Work had restarted by October, when a reporter from the *Isle of Wight Observer* was carried by a contractor's engine (*Stuart*) and ballast trucks from Wroxall to Shanklin. He commented on 'the neat and compact appearance of the engine, so beautifully clean we could almost fancy it was introduced to the drawing room after its day's work was done'. A few months later the engine collided with a cart on a level crossing, killing one of the contractor's men and a horse. After numerous delays, the first passenger train, headed by *Ryde*, ran to Ventnor on 10 September 1866. The financial position was so desperate that some creditors were suing the Company and to forestall action to seize its possessions, ownership of the engines and rolling stock was assigned to various parties including Beyer, Peacock. Fortunately, income increased following the opening to Ventnor so during 1867 a start was made on paying off the debts.[8]

At Ryde a two-road brick engine shed, wooden carriage shed, coal stage and water tank were erected on a plot bounded by the station, Monkton Mead Brook and St John's Road. Four engines could be accommodated under cover but there was a complete absence of machinery with which to maintain them. In 1870 an erecting shop was constructed in Ventnor stone alongside the engine shed with 'a furnace for resetting and adjusting springs and retyring wheels'. The engine shed became a machine shop after a corrugated iron running shed with room for six engines was erected on the opposite side of the

station. Other additions included a wheel lathe powered via a network of belts and overhead shafting from a small steam engine in a separate boiler house, gas lighting, a new water supply and an exterior hoist for use by engines needing attention to bearings or wheels. By the time these improvements were completed at the end of the 1870s, Ryde Works was largely self-sufficient and doing work for the other Island railways.[17]

During the 1867 summer season the railway operated an enhanced service using the three engines. Joseph Bourne, the Manager, explained that the timetable was designed so that they could manage with two should there be a breakdown. Despite this optimism, on 31 August he wrote to the directors warning that another was urgently needed for passenger work. Offers of four second-hand engines were discussed but two single-wheel tanks were immediately rejected, while the others were refused after inspection on account of their age and condition. They were:[12]

LSWR	Sharps 2-2-2 well tank No. 18 *Albert* built 1852, at £800
LBSCR	R. & W. Hawthorn 0-4-2T No. 17 built 1845, at £740
GWR	Dodds 0-4-2T No. 227 built 1854, at £830
South Eastern Railway	Nasmyth 2-2-2 well tank No. 90 built 1845, at £600

In May 1867 the Manager suggested that a quantity of contractor's plant lying at Wroxall might be of use to the Company. The IWR immediately purchased 709 sleepers for cash but other plant including rails, wagons and the engine *Stuart* could not be afforded. However, after lengthy negotiations, on 5 December they were bought from Warrant Finance Co. for a mixture of debentures, ordinary and preference shares with a nominal value of £1,100. *Stuart* was quite unsuitable for use on passenger trains but the directors were not sympathetic to more purchases and at a meeting on 19 December expressed the hope that 'the Warrant Finance Company's engine may be repaired more rapidly than a new one could be built'. On 27 February 1868 the Manager was 'directed to make necessary repairs in the locomotive engine purchased of the contractors to get it into working order for the summer traffic'.[8] Named *Brading*, loose tyres and wasted firebox plates delayed an entry into traffic until 14 April. It was used on goods trains, ballasting and ferrying stone from the quarry at Ventnor to various destinations along the line.[12]

Meanwhile, the Beyer, Peacock engines needed attention. On 4 November 1867 the makers received an order for twelve piston rings 'to be 15⅛in diameter instead of 15in … Wanted immediately'. Cast steel tyres were sought as replacements for the original iron variety, a decided improvement as they reduced wear and increased adhesion. The directors finally took Mr Bourne's requests seriously as a letter was sent to Beyer, Peacock &

Ventnor in original condition, with the addition of a rear weatherboard. Note also the wooden brake blocks and the tank filler at the cab end of the side tank. The livery is believed to be the 'dark chocolate' colour and the lining on the tank sides is in three panels with normal rounded corners. *NRM1804-52*

Co. inviting a tender for a fourth 2-4-0T. In a reply read out on 24 March 1868, the maker quoted £1,900 for materials or £2,250 for one the same as those previously supplied. Payment was expected in cash in three annual instalments plus interest. Even though the debt to Beyer, Peacock exceeded £5,000, on 23 April the decision was made to place an order. The manner of paying the £2,250 bill was rather convoluted. The first £62 10s 0d was due one month after delivery to Southampton, followed by monthly payments until £750 was paid, then a second annual payment of £750 was due in fourteen months and a third within twenty-six months of delivery.[8] According to the maker's drawing office register, the order number was S2259 and the engine itself was Progress No. 848. It was tried in steam on 12 October and dispatched on 19 October as *Ventnor*.[14]

Although the dimensions were identical to *Ryde*, *Sandown* and *Shanklin*, *Ventnor* was delivered with Bessemer steel axles and tyres, cast iron firebars and axleboxes with chilled faces. There was an additional weatherboard at the rear of the coal bunker to give the crew some protection when running bunker first. This followed a decision to cease running chimney first in both directions and remove the turntable at Ryde. The three 1864 2-4-0Ts subsequently acquired rear weatherboards, each with three spectacle plates. The brass nameplates on the boiler sides were typical of those fitted by Beyer, Peacock to their engines and measured 2ft 4¼in by 5in, the lettering being 3in high and the rectangular beading ½in wide.[18]

The maker's plates on the tank sides bore the annotation '& Owners' that was later chipped off.[16]

In April 1868 the Manager reported that an engine could be hired pending *Ventnor's* arrival but would cost £200 to transport to and from the Island. The directors decided to make do with the existing motive power but several mishaps disrupted services. On 10 April *Ryde* was approaching Smallbrook at 20mph with empty stock when the wheels left the track and so damaged the permanent way that the whole train became derailed, with the engine coming to rest at right angles to the direction of travel. No one was seriously injured and damage to the train was minor but it cost £290 to repair the track. The leading axle was found to be fractured, the flaw not being detectable by visual inspection. On 19 September *Ryde* derailed at Sandown, prompting a fresh look at the axles, and again on 5 November when passing over temporary points at Winstone siding while working a goods train. Wet weather played havoc with the permanent way that winter and on 23 December *Ryde* derailed yet again, this time at Brading. More incidents included one in March 1869 when *Ventnor* derailed in Ryde yard. By then improvements to the permanent way were under way.[12]

The need to spend money on the existing engines, workshops and permanent way precluded thoughts about a further purchase until the end of 1870. On 27 December the Manager wrote proposing to sell the former contractor's engine *Brading* for £500 and use the money as a down

Ryde c. 1880, by which time the dome had been repositioned on the boiler barrel, Naylor safety valve above the firebox and a rear weatherboard fitted but the brake blocks are still wooden. High rails have now been fitted above the tanks, which appear to have been strengthened by three double rows of rivets. The livery is now Furness red with the incurved corners to the lining and includes the sandbox cover. *NRM1803-52*

payment for a fifth Beyer, Peacock 2-4-0T, the balance to be paid by monthly instalments of £25. This was not acceptable to Beyer, Peacock so the directors intimated they would look elsewhere and instructed the Manager to seek alternative suppliers.[8]

Two accidents blighted the railway in 1871. On 13 February the 11.20am Ryde to Ventnor train came to a halt with a brake failure shortly after leaving Sandown. The engine from the next 12.10pm train was dispatched from Ryde to assist but collided with the rear of the disabled train at little less than top speed. A number of passengers were 'considerably shaken'.[7] When the directors heard about the accident three days later, they ordered 'That the driver of the Locomotive be dismissed and that the injured passengers be visited and attended to by the General Manager.'[8]

Alexander Beattie, the Chairman, visited the Isle of Wight on 14 April 1871 accompanied by his better-known relative Joseph Beattie, the LSWR Locomotive Superintendent, and toured Ryde Works, where satisfaction was expressed at their 'excellent condition'. Unfortunately, the next day there was a head-on collision between two trains north of Sandown station. A special train, conveying the Manager and directors to Shanklin for an inspection of the recently relaid loop, was due to leave Ryde after the arrival of a train from Ventnor hauled by *Sandown*. Unfortunately, instructions were given for the dispatch of *Sandown* and its train onto the single line from Sandown towards Ryde before a scheduled Ventnor-bound train hauled by *Shanklin* had cleared the section. Fortunately *Sandown*'s driver observed *Shanklin* approaching at 25-30mph so he applied

the brakes and sounded the whistle. Even though the trains collided at a walking pace, one passenger received severe head injuries and nineteen others suffered cuts and bruises, a modest number as the trains were carrying about 150 passengers between them. Repairs to the two engines cost £43, but one injured passenger was awarded damages of £1,250 and other claims totalled £244.[19] The directors agreed to give the drivers gratuities of 26/- and the firemen 5/-, while the Manager duly issued a lengthy notice concerning special trains that was later incorporated in the Company's Rules and Regulations.[8]

Revised terms for the purchase of a 2-4-0T from Beyer, Peacock were put to the directors on 5 October 1871. This time the £2,400 purchase price was to be met by the payment of £150 before dispatch from the maker's workshops and then monthly instalments of £40. As delayed payments attracted interest at 10%, the instalments were guaranteed personally by two directors, for which they received an allocation of £2,300 debenture stock as security.[8] An agreement signed on 14 December duly appeared in the maker's records as order 2802 and Progress No. 1141. The engine was tried in steam on 9 April 1872 and dispatched on 16 April as *Wroxall*.[14]

Landed at Brading Quay on 19 April 1872, *Wroxall* was similar to Seacombe, Hoylake & Deeside Railway Nos 3 and 4 (maker's Nos 2408, 2676) and East & West Junction Railway Nos 4-6 (maker's Nos 1238-1240) that were sold on to the Lancashire & Yorkshire Railway in May 1875, becoming Nos 517-519. The 2-4-0T differed in having the brass dome positioned on the rear boiler ring, wider firebox water spaces, pump and injector boiler feed, a cab enclosing the coal bunker, nameplates on the tank sides and 'Makers & Owners' plates on the bunker sides. The nameplates had a different font and were thinner than those carried by the other 2-4-0Ts.[16] The maker's records added: 'With this engine to be sent the same number of screw keys, fire irons, oil cans & c. as previously sent to this Rwy Co.'[14] Mr Bradley recounted a story that crews complained the cab interfered with the driver's lookout and impeded the fireman. Whatever the truth of this, the cab remained.

The Company now had an adequate number of engines for the summer season and heavy repairs could be undertaken in the winter months without fear of traffic interruption. Commencing with *Ryde* in February 1872, the livery was changed to Furness red with the same lining, black bands edged by fine yellow lines. The lining was laid out on the tank side in three panels but the curving in each corner was reversed.[12] Despite the existence of sandboxes, there were occasions when the fireman had to clamber to the front in poor weather to sand the rails. This was evidently the reason for the addition of prominent handrails above and at each end of the tanks on *Wroxall* and the other four 2-4-0Ts.

Ryde, *Sandown*, *Shanklin* and *Ventnor* were all plagued by severe priming. *Ryde*'s dome and balance safety valves were repositioned from the firebox to the boiler barrel in the same position as the dome on *Wroxall*. A Naylor safety valve in a small brass cover replaced the original dome over the firebox but was explosive in action and frightened horses; after the release pressure was raised to 135psi it was seldom activated. This work was probably done during the 1870s, not 1888-89 as suggested by Mr Bradley, but the fittings remained in place until *Ryde* was reboilered in 1900. Since the others were not modified, presumably the priming persisted.

Brading (alias *Stuart*) was hired to assist in ballasting the track on the Sandown to Newport railway and on 3 February 1872 made a trial run for about 2 miles. On 12 February the IWR directors were informed that *Brading* had been sold for £400 to a Mr George Wright, who

wrote to the IWNJR contractor on 30 April proposing to remove the engine from the line. He later asked that the IWR carry out some repairs but on 29 August the directors ordered: 'That the repairs be executed only at Mr Wright's expense and on his responsibility, and that the locomotive be retained by the General Manager until the costs of such repairs be paid by Mr Wright.' What then happened was not recorded. One possibility is that *Brading* passed into the hands of George Young, an IWR director and Chairman of the RNR, and was stored until needed on construction of the Ryde to Newport railway. This would explain why early in 1874 the IWNJR contractor hired an engine from the IWR that was needed back for the summer season. Even after the IWNJR line opened in 1875, worked as part of the IWR until 1879, there were frequent calls for the loan of an engine in place of the railway's unreliable possession.[8]

The first passenger trains between Newport and Ryde began running in December 1875. To help signalmen distinguish between IWR and Joint Committee trains, drivers were instructed to sound their whistle once or twice respectively when approaching Ryde station. When the railway to Ryde Pier Head opened in 1880 some visual indication was demanded. IWR engines had been fitted with a lamp bracket to the top of the smokebox door but the headlamps themselves seem to have been carried only at night. IWR trains began carrying a white headcode disc with a green centre during daytime and a lamp with a green lens at night. The Joint Committee's engines displayed one or two white lights at footplate level.[8]

On 14 March 1876 the Manager wrote that an additional 2-4-0T was needed for the growing goods traffic 'one third more powerful than those in present use'. He enclosed a quote from Beyer, Peacock offering one for £2,150 cash or £2,525 by deferred payments over five years. The latter option was accepted and on 1 June an agreement was signed, the terms being the same as those for *Wroxall*.[8] The maker's records for order S3450 noted the engine was Progress No. 1638. It was tried in steam on 7 December and dispatched on 22 December as *Brading*.[14]

Brading on Ryde Pier c. 1910. The Westinghouse brake equipment had been fitted, with the pump prominent on the front of the tank, although safety chains continue to be fitted. Lining does not show on the tank sides. *RP X1436*

The second *Brading* resembled *Wroxall* but had larger tanks, cylinders and firebox, spring balance safety valves and rectangular rather than round spectacle plates to the rear of the cab. The financial position had so improved that the debts to Beyer, Peacock were paid off in 1878 save for *Brading* and that was cleared in 1881. *Brading* was trouble-free until 17 August 1880, when a collision took place at Brading. The engine led a Ventnor-bound passenger train through points that had been wrongly set for the cattle dock before colliding with a rake of loaded coal wagons at 10mph. Damage was considerable but only thirteen passengers complained of any injury.[12]

In March 1877 a shortage of drivers arose so W. G. Beattie, the LSWR Locomotive Superintendent, was asked to ascertain whether three passed firemen would be willing to transfer to the Isle of Wight in time for the tourist season. Suitable rented accommodation would be made available at Ryde with £20 removal and out of pocket expenses being paid to successful applicants. When knowledge of the request reached the running shed lobbies there were a surprisingly large number of volunteers, including men who had been driving for years. Three Bournemouth passed firemen were offered and accepted the posts.[12] Their arrival greatly strengthened the driving staff but had repercussions as the men had been accustomed to working trains at higher speeds. As a result Joseph Bourne inserted the following notice in the Company's Rules and Regulations:[8]

Speed of Trains. – Trains are often driven down banks, especially Rowborough and Shanklin, at 35 or 40 miles per hour, whereas the speed should never exceed 25 miles per hour. No Train or Engine must pass a Station with steam on, or at a greater speed than 10 miles per hour. Enginemen are cautioned not to disobey this order under any circumstances.

At the half-yearly meeting of shareholders on 29 August 1878 the directors reported that the Brading Harbour Improvement & Railway Co. had opened the first section of its railway from Brading to St Helens on 1 August but omitted to mention that only goods traffic was being carried. Construction had begun in 1875 of sluice gates and St Helens Quay but a sea wall to Bembridge proved a difficult task and the tide was not finally shut out until 23 February 1880. Only then could progress be made on construction of the railway from St Helens to Bembridge.[7]

Two engines were employed on the work. *St Helens* was previously *Stuart* and the IWR's first *Brading*. Its arrival was not recorded but could have been any time from 1876 onwards; this is assuming it was used on construction of the Ryde to Newport railway. The second was *Stanley*, one of two 0-6-0 saddle tanks supplied by Manning, Wardle & Co. of Leeds to Scott & Edwards, contractors, of Melmerby, Yorkshire, to order No. 9130. *Stanley* (maker's No. 517) was dispatched by the makers on 5 March 1875.[20]

Manning, Wardle specialised in making tank engines for contractors and industrial users in Britain and abroad. *Stanley* was a member of the maker's class M, of which around 150 were produced between 1863 and 1914. With a distinctive wrap-over cab and saddle tank, *Stanley* carried a green livery when delivered to Stratford-upon-Avon in March 1875, where Scott & Edwards were constructing the 6¾-mile Alcester to Bearley line for the Great Western Railway.

The Manning, Wardle-built *Bembridge* is seen at Ryde St John's prior to 1911, with original chimney and cab. Wooden brake blocks are only fitted to the centre driving wheels. *IWSR Archive*

A Beyer, Peacock official of *Bonchurch* in photographic grey that clearly illustrates the design of the livery. Note that wooden brake blocks are still the norm, as are safety chains. The filler is now at the front end of the tank and an additional set of footsteps provided to aid access. *IWSR Archive*

Following completion of the contract in September 1876, the engine was employed on doubling the Clydach to Bryn Mawr section of the London & North Western Railway Abergavenny to Merthyr line. Scott & Edwards then took on the contract for the railway from St Helens to Bembridge and transferred it to the Island.[12] The *Isle of Wight Chronicle* for 31 July 1879 reported that *Stanley* was already working between Brading and St Helens.

According to Board of Trade returns, the two engines passed into the Brading Company's ownership, one by the end of 1879 and the second a year later. Said to have cost £650, *Stanley* later acquired a set of brass plates bearing the name *Bembridge* but it is doubtful whether *St Helens* was similarly endowed. The pair was housed in a substantial stone-built engine shed on St Helens Quay.

Following the completion of St Helens Quay, the IWR's own facilities nearer Brading fell into disuse, making that Company dependent for much of its goods business on the Brading Company. However, by June 1881 it was in the hands of a receiver, who gave notice that the goods service would be discontinued, probably because both engines needed repair. After negotiations, the IWR agreed to operate the line for 50% of the receipts provided the line to Bembridge was completed and opened to passenger traffic. *Bembridge* visited Ryde Works in August and services between Brading and Bembridge began on 27 May 1882.[8]

St Helens was steamed only when *Bembridge* was stopped for routine maintenance, usually on a Sunday. It visited Ryde Works three or four times between August 1882 and April 1888 for repairs that included cleaning out the tanks and turning the leading wheels. After a lengthy time in store, *St Helens* was sold in September 1893 to Westwood & Winley, the contractors for the Newport, Godshill & St Lawrence Railway, allegedly for £650.[10]

Meanwhile, the IWR directors had decided to buy an additional engine and some carriages, ostensibly because of their new commitments. On 16 October 1882 an order was placed with Beyer, Peacock & Co. for a 2-4-0T costing £2,100. The maker's records for order 6344 noted the engine was Progress No. 2376. It was tried in steam on 14 March 1883 and dispatched on 18 April as *Bonchurch*.[14]

Bonchurch travelled under its own steam to Southampton before being shipped to St Helens Quay aboard the barge *Nancy* on 26 April 1883. However, as the *Isle of Wight Times* reported, the usual tug was undergoing repairs and the less powerful *Mizpah* had to be employed. Time was lost and in rapidly deteriorating weather the engine broke loose and dragged the barge down. The Portsmouth Salvage Co. was commissioned to attempt recovery but little positive action was possible before the gale abated. On 29 April two hired Admiralty 'lumps' from Portsmouth Dockyard raised *Bonchurch* from the seabed near St Helens Fort and took it to the quay, where a landing was made the next day. The 2-4-0T was completely smothered in sand and had to be dismantled so that every part could be cleaned. Only entering service on 1 June, nevertheless a cheque in full payment was dispatched on 2 July.[12]

The new arrival was nominally the same size as *Brading* but had a more modern-looking cab with an exterior coal bunker, tanks with beading round the top, Ramsbottom safety valves over the firebox, larger cylinders and fewer tubes. The tank filler covers were located at the front of the tanks rather than adjacent to the footplate as on the other IWR engines. This was evidently not liked by the crews as

Boiler ordered	Maker	Cost	Engine	Date fitted	Mileage
14.2.1894	J. S. White & Co.	£609	Shanklin	12.1895	713,648
14.2.1894	J. S. White & Co.	£609	Ventnor	6.1896	642,252
14.2.1894	J. S. White & Co.	£609	Sandown	5.1897	739,004
1.9.1898	J. S. White & Co.	£704	Ryde	12.1900	820,125
1.9.1898	J. S. White & Co.	£704	Wroxall	6.1900	598,946
28.12.1900	Beyer, Peacock & Co.	£600	Brading	12.1902	576,893

additional filler holes were cut closer to the cab and sealed using wooden bungs. One unique feature was a handrail that ran across the rear of the cab roof. *Bonchurch* worked 67,449 miles before entering Ryde Works for heavy repairs in November 1886.[12]

Joseph Bourne resigned as Manager in 1884 after disagreeing with calls by the directors for economies. His replacement lasted only until 1886, when Henry Day was appointed Manager and Henry Brent took charge of the engineering side; both were existing employees and remained with the Company until 1923. These changes in management ushered in a more conservative policy towards expenditure that, in the absence of a renewals fund, had to be paid for out of income.[8]

Ryde Works was perfectly capable of carrying out overhauls, albeit not as swiftly as the larger and better-equipped workshops owned by the mainland companies. After *Ventnor* burst a cylinder in April 1883, replacements were purchased from Beyer, Peacock for the older engines. Other spares ordered in 1885–86 included three crank axles, four tube plates and new cylinders for *Wroxall*.[8] Although no more engines could be afforded, work began on bringing the older 2-4-0Ts up to the same standard as the newer arrivals. Those with weatherboards had them replaced by cabs but precisely when this happened is uncertain. They also acquired locally made front footsteps, as carried by *Bonchurch*. The lining on the tank sides was simplified to form a single panel; the nameplates were moved to the tank sides and maker's plates to the bunker sides.

The Regulation of Railways Act, passed in 1889 following a fatal accident at Armagh in Ireland, obliged companies to fit engines and stock used in passenger trains with automatic continuous brakes in addition to the existing handbrakes. IWCR 2-4-0T No. 4 and five carriages equipped with the Westinghouse brake were hired in October 1891 for trials between Ryde Pier Head and Ventnor. They were successful and on 24 February 1892 a tender was accepted for the supply of fittings, the work being carried out at Ryde Works. Starting with *Bonchurch* in April, by the end of the year eight engines and fifty-seven other vehicles had been equipped at a cost of £2,112 13s 7d. This quick-acting brake was a decided advantage on lines such as the IWR where stations were a short distance apart. The brake proved reliable and cheap to maintain, with only three minor failures in 1893. On the 2-4-0Ts the air compressor was located on the fireman's side attached to the front of the left-hand side tank; the reservoir was behind the rear wheels. The

opportunity was taken to replace the wooden brake blocks with iron brake shoes. Not only did they wear rapidly but the wood was said to smoulder on the downhill journey to Ryde and buckets of water had to be kept on hand in case of an emergency.[12]

The Company began running a fast train on 2 November 1891, leaving Ryde Pier Head for Ventnor at 3.15pm each weekday. Nicknamed the 'Invalids Express', the train was booked to cover the 12½ miles in twenty minutes but the first run was performed in nineteen minutes, twenty-two minutes faster than the ordinary trains. At first *Brading* and *Bonchurch* were rostered but it was soon found that smaller engines were more suited to the usual train of four carriages and a van. Speeds of up to 60mph were achieved on the level section between Brading and Sandown, and those through the stations were somewhat higher than management wished! A special white disc with a red cross was carried on the smokebox door. Running non-stop only in the Ventnor direction, the train began calling at Shanklin in 1903 but ceased operating altogether in 1908.

On 14 February 1894 the directors accepted a tender from J. S. White & Co. shipbuilders of Cowes for three replacement boilers delivered to St Helens Quay. It was the first of three orders (*See* table above).[12]

The boilers were pressed to 125psi and constructed in three rings of steel with the dome positioned centrally on the barrel. The Salter balance safety valves, brass dome covers and copper-capped chimneys were retained. On 25 March 1895 a steel firebox for *Brading* was ordered from J. S. White for £45, the copper from the old one being sold at a rate of £38 a ton; the boiler was later transferred to *Bonchurch*. Cylinders were purchased for *Wroxall* in April 1895 and *Ventnor* received a set in March 1899. At this period a pair of cylinders machined and prepared for fitting cost £93 delivered to Ryde. Steel fireboxes were cheaper but had shorter lives and, like a number of other companies, the IWR reverted to copper fireboxes when the next replacements were required. The spring balances on the safety valves carried by *Ryde* and *Ventnor* were side by side, whereas on *Sandown*, *Shanklin*, *Wroxall* and *Brading* they were wider apart at an angle of about 30 degrees. These positions were reversed on *Ryde* and *Shanklin* after they exchanged boilers in 1921. The 2-4-0Ts carried both screw and loose six-link couplings along with a second deep-toned whistle that was used to attract the goods guard's attention if braking assistance was required. The loose couplings and second whistle were removed after 1923.[21]

Sandown at Ventnor post-1897 after the fitting of a replacement boiler. Other features of note are the tank-top handrails, iron brake blocks, front foot-steps, the lining with inverted corners, the Westinghouse pump with associated reservoir beneath the bunker and the very large lumps of coal. Although the Westinghouse brake is connected, a six-link coupling is in use, resulting in a significant gap between the buffers of the locomotive and carriage. *RP 15572 IWSR Archive, colour by John Faulkner*

Shanklin is seen heading a Down train of mostly low-roof Oldbury carriages south of Wroxall. This higher angle view provides some useful details of the boiler, tank tops and cab roof. *IWSR Archive*

Ventnor at Ventnor. This photograph has been included to show the rear of the cab and the Westinghouse reservoir beneath the bunker, other features as fitted to *Sandown*; note also the six-link coupling on the main drawhook and a screw type at the left. The tank-side lining is a single panel with inverted corners. *IWSR Archive*

Bembridge remained in the Brading Company's ownership until October 1898, when the engine register recorded: 'Purchased for £430 from the Brading Harbour & Railway Company, stopped for patching firebox and renewing tyres and brake shoes.' One of the smaller 2-4-0Ts deputised on the Bembridge branch whenever it was out of service.[12] The purchase of St Helens Quay included four self-propelled steam cranes. Two larger cranes were purchased in 1904 and one of the older ones was later transferred to the harbour's dredger *Ballaster*. Most of the cranes disappeared during the 1930s.

The dangers of working on the footplate were highlighted in this report of an accident on 8 April 1901:[19]

Name	Miles worked	Coal burned per mile (lb)
Ryde	3,237	26¾
Sandown	1,867	27¼
Shanklin	-	heavy repairs
Ventnor	3,486	27
Wroxall	1,277	26½
Brading	4,439	28¼
Bonchurch	-	laid aside for reboiling
Bembridge	1,560	22½

Fireman James Henry Bannister was working with driver Rees on *Bonchurch* on the 9.00pm passenger train from Ryde to Ventnor. Upon applying the handbrake in Ventnor tunnel he slipped and fell off the engine receiving slight injuries. It was necessary for men to stand between the tank and bunker with one foot near the outer edge of the footplate. Unless there was a good hold of the brake handle there is nothing to stop a man falling off the engine. It is possible the driver tested the Westinghouse brake at the same time. This would have taken the strain on the brake causing Bannister's handbrake to spin and making him lose his balance. It is hardly possible to fit doors or bars to the locomotive but a ledge along the outer edge of the wooden covering was a suggested addition. Instructions were to be issued to drivers to test their brakes before entering Ventnor tunnel.

With a journey time from Ryde Pier Head to Ventnor of forty-two minutes and a return trip taking thirty-nine minutes, during winter months trains were timed so that one engine could operate the service, although two would generally be in steam with a third for the Bembridge branch. During the summer months, all available engines and carriages operated a service as frequent as the single-line sections allowed. The first Down train of the day was usually a mail and goods train that, with a return working as a goods train in the evening, avoided the need to provide overnight accommodation at Ventnor. Engines would only be steamed as and when passenger numbers justified, often at short notice.[8] This was because the price and availability of coal was more critical than for the mainland companies, particularly in the winter months when supplies could be disrupted by bad weather. Good-quality steam coal averaged 17s 11½d a ton landed on the quay at St Helens, this being approximately 2s 8½d more than the colliery charged the LSWR for delivery to Basingstoke. As a result, the Company was always coal conscious and in March and April 1903 conducted fuel trials. (*See* table top right)[12]

On 14 May 1903 Petroleum Products Ltd of Southampton wrote offering a free trial of their oil-burning system on one of the Company's engines. On 15 August *Bembridge* entered Ryde Works for conversion that took a week rather than the intended two days because of problems with the firebox burners.[8] No major problems arose during the month's trial but the saving of £5 6s 7½d was not enough to offset the costs of conversion and oil storage tanks at Ryde and Ventnor. *Bembridge* was reconverted to coal-burning on 16 October.[12]

The need to operate the railway more economically was not forgotten and while visiting North Tyneside in 1904 to inspect second-hand wagons, the Chairman and Mr Brent, the Engineer, took the opportunity to see a newly introduced electric motor car operating on the North Eastern Railway. A petrol motor was 'not at work or perfected'.[8] Although not mentioned in the minutes, in April 1905 Mr Drummond, the LSWR Locomotive Superintendent, was apparently commissioned at a fee of £150 to visit the Brading to Bembridge line and estimate the cost of operating the branch with a steam railcar of similar power to those provided for the Botley to Bishops Waltham service. Savings were found possible but insufficient to warrant the purchase of one from Beyer, Peacock & Co.[12]

Attempts were made to increase revenue by advertising holidays in the Isle of Wight throughout the Midlands, North of England, Edinburgh and Glasgow. Hoteliers were also encouraged to extend the tourist season by offering attractive terms for early and late holidays.[7] Revenue was increased but this highlighted the lack of modern heating and lighting in the carriages and the limited power of the engines, with the exception of *Brading* and *Bonchurch*. More powerful motive power, modern rolling stock and some track doubling were estimated to cost an unacceptable £31,000.[12]

Local politicians had for some time been agitating for improvements to the railways, including their acquisition by the County Council and electrification.[7] In April 1907 the IWR directors managed to rebut one speculative approach but in April 1908 decided to accept an offer from Siemens Brothers, which had converted the Ryde Pier tramway to electric power, to assess the railway's suitability for electric traction. The following figures were given in a report sent to the IWR in November:[12]

- Overhead traction for main line and essential sidings, five electric engines and existing carriage stock – £65,000.

IWR *Bembridge* stands at Brading with the branch train following the rebuild of 1911. The buffers appear to have wooden faces fitted. The stovepipe chimney and homemade cab did nothing to improve the loco's looks. *IWSR Archive*

- Overhead traction for all lines, five electric engines and existing carriage stock modernised – £73,000.
- Third rail traction for all lines and six multiple unit trains, each seating 308 passengers plus luggage – £87,000.

Additional work included a passing loop at Wroxall, simplifying the track layout at Ventnor and raising the maximum running speed to 35mph. Savings in working expenses were estimated at £9,000 to £11,000 a year provided trains were crewed by drivers and guards only. Inevitably, the directors decided that these modernisation schemes were beyond the Company's means.[12] The matter did not go away as on 21 July 1909 the directors were informed of correspondence with Philip Dawson, the LBSCR Consulting Engineer, and Allgemeine Elektricitäts-Gesellschaft (AEG) of Berlin, which was the principal contractor in the LBSCR's overhead electrification scheme. The Engineer was instructed to assist during a visit by Mr Dawson and the firm's representatives. It is not known what was discussed but on 30 December the Secretary was asked to inform Mr Dawson that the 'Board do not see their way to entertain the matter at present'.[8] After receiving several reports, in 1910 the County Council refused to commit any public money and the proposals faded away.

Routine purchases of spare parts in 1908 included twelve sets of steel tyres from Société Anonyme des Aciéries D'Angleur, near Liège in Belgium, they being cheaper than other suppliers. Cylinders were obtained from Manning, Wardle for *Bembridge* and crank axles from Beyer, Peacock for *Sandown* and *Bonchurch*. A start was made on removing the high handrails from the older engines (*Brading* and *Bonchurch* never had them) in response to the passing of more stringent safety legislation. After *Shanklin* broke a coupling rod when in service on 2 September 1910, Henry Brent, the Engineer and Locomotive Superintendent, submitted a report to the directors on 30 November:[8]

As instructed at the last Board Meeting a further very careful examination of all the remaining Side Rods has been made. Though not visible on an ordinary examination several rods under a magnifying glass show minute surface cracks which seem to confirm the report of the makers (after taking micro-sections) that the metal is permanently injured by 'fatigue' and has become crystallised. Three of these Engines are 46 years old and have run over one million miles each. The four small Engines have now been or are in process of being fitted with the new rods. These rods, now being made in accordance with modern practice, are 50% stronger than the old ones without increase of weight.

In November 1910 *Bonchurch* underwent an overhaul at Ryde Works when a new firebox was fitted. In June 1911 replacement motive power had to be provided for the Bembridge branch while *Bembridge* was taken in for repairs. It received a new firebox, stove pipe chimney and additions to the cab roof to give the crew more protection from the weather.[8]

The 1914 summer season passed by without incident despite a declaration of war against Germany on 4 August. That day, Britain's railways were placed under the direction of a Railway Executive Committee acting on behalf of the Government. In practice the existing management remained in place, albeit burdened with a significant increase in financial control and regulation. Within months there were difficulties in obtaining a regular supply of coal and other materials became scarce and more costly. The passenger service was scaled back and in December 1915 the Manager asked the Board of Trade for permission to operate mixed passenger and goods trains on the Bembridge branch.[11]

Inevitably, fewer engines were needed in service. In March 1915 *Ryde* and *Wroxall* were repaired and then tallowed down in store. The former returned to traffic in February 1916 and its place in store taken by *Bembridge*. Meanwhile, *Ventnor* underwent a prolonged overhaul that lasted from August 1915 to June 1916. *Wroxall* returned to traffic in May 1916 in place of *Brading*, which was stored until entering Ryde Works during the autumn.[12]

In April 1916 a circular was received from the War Office asking if any four- or six-coupled engines were available for sale. The matter was discussed by the directors at their meeting on the 26 April, when they decided to offer *Bembridge* for the sum of £750. It was examined on behalf of the War Department by the Eastleigh Works boilersmith who reported: '*Bembridge*, a six-coupled saddle tank built by Manning, Wardle in 1875, firebox (copper) new June 1911, 13⅜in by 18in cylinders new April 1908, boiler retubed April 1913, weight laden 23 tons. Boiler, firebox, cylinders and axles sound, main frames patched over driving boxes, attention required to tyres and blast pipe.' Minor repairs were executed by Ryde Works and on 21 June *Bembridge* became War Department property, although it was 27 July before the 0-6-0ST left Ryde Pier by barge. Landed at Portsmouth, *Bembridge* was towed to Eastleigh shed to have the boiler washed out and steam raised before departing for Dinton, Wiltshire, from where a two-mile military railway ran to Fovant army camp.[12] *Bembridge* was evidently what C. Hamilton Ellis described as 'a slatternly little Manning, Wardle from somewhere or other'.[22] By 1917 No. 15 *Bembridge* had moved to another military railway at Bulford, while in December repairs were received at Salisbury shed and in August–September 1918 at Eastleigh Works. Mr Lambert, a fitter at Ryde Works, claimed to have seen *Bembridge* on the quay at Basra, Iraq, in 1918–19 but Mr Bradley could not trace any record of foreign travel and reported its sale for scrap in October 1920.[23]

The IWR was one of several companies forced to make livery changes after a shortage of imported pigments used in paint mixes greatly increased prices. According to the engine register, in June 1916 *Ventnor* was the first to be painted in Midland red with black borders edged with fine yellow lines. The background to the name and maker's plates was emerald green, the inside of the frames and buffer beams bright red and the cab interior light brown with the pipe work painted blue. *Ryde* was stored in works grey and ran so painted until turned out in this livery in October. Difficulties continued as *Sandown*, *Shanklin* and *Bonchurch* appeared in an unvarnished reddish-brown colour late in 1917. During an overhaul *Brading* received a replacement cast iron tapered chimney supplied by Wheeler & Hurst of Newport. Copper and brass fittings, including the maker's plates, were removed or painted over.[12] The other 2-4-0Ts lost their finery as they passed through works, although *Bonchurch* retained its brass dome until reboilered in 1921.[10]

Following the end of the war a start was made on bringing the motive power up to an acceptable standard. A steady stream of orders placed with Beyer, Peacock & Co. during 1919 included motion parts, crank axles, tanks, whistles and smokebox doors. In October the directors were informed that *Bonchurch* required a steel boiler and copper firebox, cast iron blast pipe, valve spindles, cylinder covers and lubricator. A crank axle was ordered for *Brading* in December and new tanks were needed for *Shanklin* in April 1920. The engines were again being turned out in the Midland red livery.[24] New copper fireboxes and cylinders were purchased. (*See* table above)[25]

Such was the shortage of serviceable motive power that on 16 July 1919 the directors agreed to ask the Railway Executive Committee for the loan of a replacement for *Bembridge*. However, only large tender engines were available so the Company had to search the second-hand market. The following offers were considered:[8]

- September 1919, a Beyer, Peacock 2-4-0T similar to *Bonchurch* built in June 1884 for the Midland & South Western Railway as their No. 8 (later 29) and sold to J. F. Wake of Darlington in January 1918. The engine was refused on account of its £3,225 price and condition.
- April 1920, two engines being sold by J. F. Wake were 'unsuitable'.
- June 1920, two Great Northern Railway 0-4-4Ts Nos 660 and 762 at £1,640 each were inspected but refused.
- January 1921, a Metropolitan Railway six coupled Peckett saddle tank for £2,200 was rejected.

Name	Cylinders	Fitted	Boiler
Ryde	15in x 20in	5.1921	Reconditioned, ex *Shanklin* 5.1921
Shanklin	15in x 20in	7.1921	Ex *Ryde* 7.1921
Ventnor	16in x 20in	9.1920	
Wroxall	16in x 20in	11.1920	Reconditioned
Brading	16in x 24in	8.1921	
Bonchurch	16in x 24in	7.1921	New 160psi boiler 12.1921

Bonchurch at Ryde St John's after receiving a new boiler and locally cast chimney, somewhat shorter than the original. Note that LSWR-pattern lamp irons are now fitted; it is not certain when this occurred but seems to have been at the time of grouping in 1923. *O. J. Morris/©Rail Archive Stephenson*

No.	Name	Olive green*	Dark green
W13	*Ryde*	4.1924	10.1926
W14	*Shanklin*	1.1925	
W15	*Ventnor*	2.1924	
W16	*Wroxall*	5.1925	#3.1931
W17	*Brading*	11.10.1924	
W18	*Bonchurch*	4.1925	

*Removal dates of maker's plates prior to repainting.
Known overhaul date, the engine may have been painted in this livery previously.

According to Mr Bradley, in 1921 the IWR approached Beyer, Peacock & Co. for the supply of two 4-4-2Ts, one in four months and the other before the 1922 summer season, but delivery could not be promised before mid-1923. However, in May Kitson & Co. were able to offer two 0-6-2Ts for £4,160 each. They were similar to Furness Railway Nos 92–95 delivered in 1912 and 1914 with features such as steam sanding and braking, mechanical lubrication and Ross pop safety valves. A proposal to place an order was never put to the IWR directors as The Railways Act became law on 19 August.

Mishaps were evidently not recorded with the same vigour as previously and few details have survived. During 1920 *Ventnor* approached the terminus at Bembridge rather too quickly, collided with the buffer stops and put the turntable out of action for several days. *Bonchurch* was much admired by the men, who claimed that it was the most powerful engine in the Island. This was with some justification as on one Saturday in August 1921 *Bonchurch* was seen hauling a packed Ventnor to Ryde train consisting of seven ex-Metropolitan Railway eight-wheelers, two four-wheeled carriages and two vans. This was the longest train then seen on the line.[26]

After a period in store, *Sandown* was repaired between November 1920 and February 1921 when the boiler was retubed, the 15in cylinders reconditioned and frame fractures over the trailing coupled axle welded. *Sandown* was then sent to the Bembridge branch, where the poor condition could be lived with for a time. It was said to have been the last engine to be kept overnight at St Helens Quay before the shed was closed in October 1921. During a meeting in July 1922 the directors discussed the purchase from Beyer, Peacock of spare parts, including a replacement boiler for *Sandown*. Such matters had to be referred to Eastleigh Works, with the result that it never did get any repairs when laid aside at the end of the summer season. Eastleigh prepared drawings for certain spare parts that were apparently manufactured for the other 2-4-0Ts.[27]

The seven IWR engines entered SR stock on 1 January 1923. *Sandown* was towed to Ryde Pier Head on 4 May and loaded onto an Admiralty floating crane that had just delivered two LSWR class O2 0-4-4 tank engines. Taken to Eastleigh Works, *Sandown* was recorded in the LSWR locomotive register as broken up in September.[25] The

remaining six were allotted numbers and repainted in lined green. (*See* table left)[10]

The 'SOUTHERN' lettering, nameplate, 'W' prefix and number were all carried on the tank sides. Whether the nameplate background colour had been emerald green throughout their previous lives is uncertain but it does seem to have been early SR policy to paint the background black when applying the green livery. Brass number plates were later attached to the bunker back but, according to P. C. Allen, their background colour was green.[21]

During the summer of 1923 five Ryde-based engines were needed in traffic at peak times. In place of *Sandown*, W14 *Shanklin* was used temporarily on the Bembridge branch but derailed on 5 June when running round at Bembridge. The main cause was a defective wheel flange, although the worn condition of the points and crossings probably contributed to the mishap.[28] Ousted from Ryde by new arrivals, by May 1924 Newport shed was home to W14 *Shanklin*, W15 *Ventnor* and W17 *Brading*, the latter being used on goods work. W13 *Ryde* received axle repairs, an LSWR Drummond-pattern chimney and a repaint before joining the others at Newport. W16 *Wroxall* and W18 *Bonchurch* remained at Ryde and, although W18 *Bonchurch* fully lived up to its reputation when working alongside the O2s, the IWR 2-4-0Ts were on borrowed time.[10]

On 21 July 1924 W15 *Ventnor* was involved in a spectacular collision at a level crossing near Cement Mills halt, north of Newport. The engine was heading an afternoon train from Cowes when a lorry carrying 2 tons of cement stalled astride the track. At 10 to 15mph, W15 *Ventnor* crashed into the obstruction, flinging bags of cement high into the air, where they burst, showering the train and surrounding countryside with white powder. By good fortune, the locomotive stopped without leaving the track as the train was approaching the Mill Pond viaduct, where a derailment could have been disastrous. The only recognisable parts of the lorry were the chassis and front wheels. The owner threatened court action for damages but retracted when the SR's legal department discovered that the lorry was grossly overloaded and the 70-year-old driver did not possess a current driving licence. The accident was repeated on 16 September 1925 when a train collided with a horse-drawn cart loaded with cement; this time the cart driver was deaf.[28]

W15 *Ventnor* may not have seen much, if any use, after the July 1924 accident. Fit only for shunting duties, on 23 April 1925 the engine was lying at Ryde shed awaiting a decision on its fate. In July the boiler was exchanged with that on W16 *Wroxall* and after being stripped of spare parts the remains were sold to a local scrap merchant. By October W18 *Bonchurch* had been transferred to Newport shed for goods work in place of W17 *Brading*, usually a return trip to Sandown and Ventnor before some shunting at Newport. W17 *Brading* was withdrawn in April 1926 and W14 *Shanklin* returned to Ryde for occasional use on the Bembridge branch before withdrawal in November 1927. W18 *Bonchurch* had its frames arc welded but there were ample O2s and

IWR *Wroxall* repainted in early SR livery poses at Brading; now carrying *Ventnor's* boiler with the top of the Salter safety valves visible. The lining out even extended to the back-plates of the footsteps. *O. J. Morris ©Rail Archive Stephenson, colour by John Faulkner*

The 1931 rebuild of *Wroxall* quite altered its appearance, particularly the large cab from IWCR 8, the Drummond-pattern chimney and the replated tank sides now lacking the vertical rows of rivets. The smaller 'Southern' and SR-style nameplate leave the tank side less cluttered in appearance, although the number now on the bunker side sheet rather fills the space available. The locomotive is seen with a Freshwater train at Newport. *O. J. Morris ©Rail Archive Stephenson*

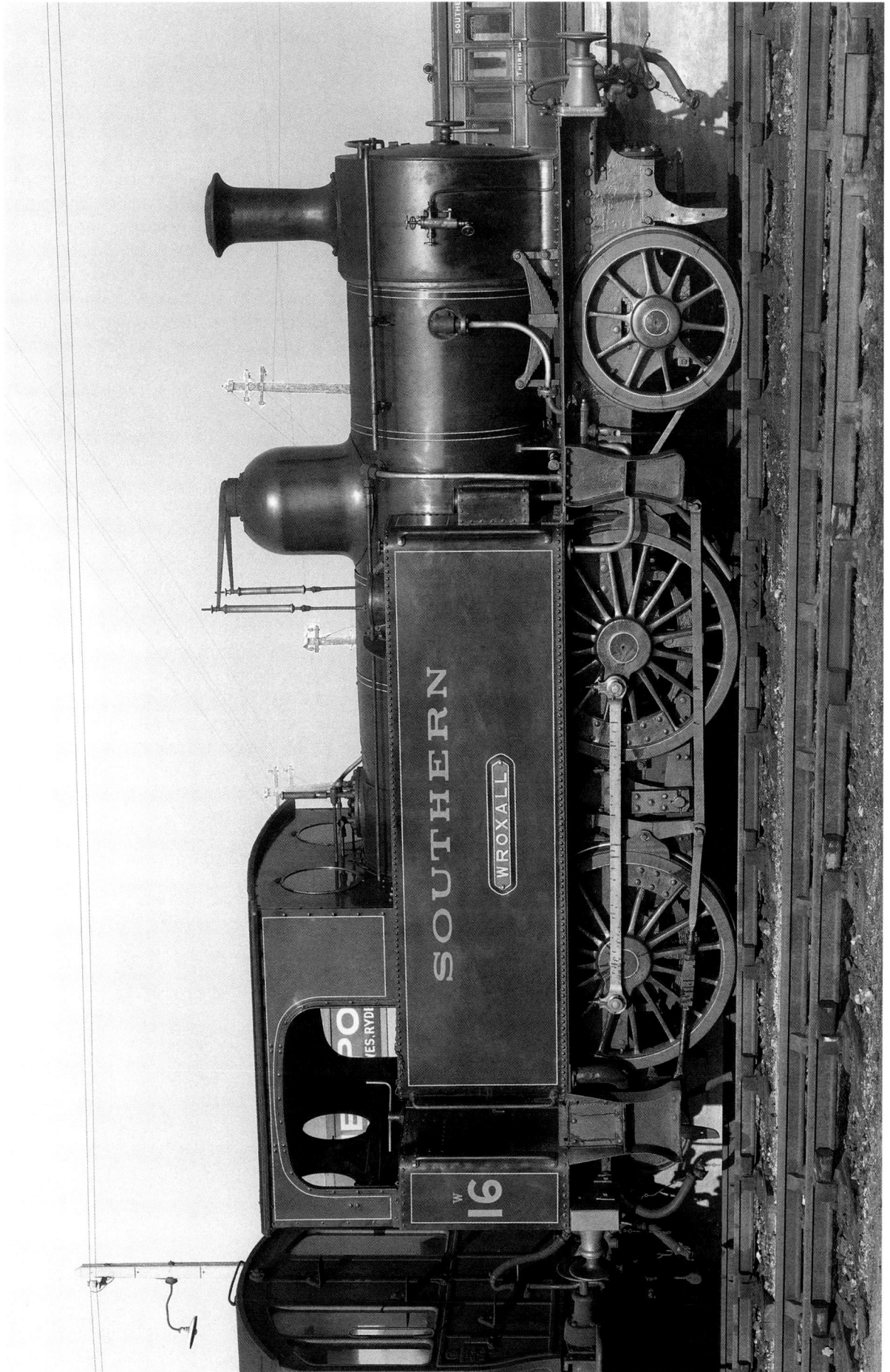

by April 1928 the 2-4-0T was lying idle at Newport. Sold for scrap, in September W18 *Bonchurch* was dismantled in Gasworks siding, south of Mill Hill, the nearest point to H. B. Jolliffe's scrapyard. The relatively new boiler was sold to a Ryde laundry, where it is thought to have remained until about 1937.[29]

The Bembridge branch had become a haven for the Beyer, Peacock 2-4-0Ts as engines weighing 35 tons or more were prohibited until the bridges could be strengthened and the track relaid.[30] By October 1926 W13 *Ryde* was at Ryde shed and taking turns with W14 *Shanklin* on the branch. A defective brake contributed to a mishap on 18 May 1929 when the trailing wheels derailed while running round at Bembridge.[28] In October that year W13 *Ryde* entered Ryde Works for a general overhaul, during which it received deeper cab-side sheets, steam carriage heating equipment and a hooter; a slender deep-toned organ pipe whistle. During a repaint, smaller and more appropriately sized 'SOUTHERN' lettering was used, SR design nameplates were attached to the tank sides somewhat lower than had been the case with the originals, while the running number and prefix were moved to the bunker sides. Returned to service in February 1930, a year was spent on the Bembridge branch prior to transfer to Newport for employment on the Freshwater line. It briefly returned to Ryde and was used on the Bembridge branch in August 1931. The nameplates were removed in April 1932 but *Ryde* remained serviceable until Saturday, 2 July, when four trips were run between Cowes and Ryde Pier Head. By then it was the oldest passenger engine in daily service in Britain. After withdrawal on 9 July W13 *Ryde* returned to Ryde and was placed in store with FYNR W1 *Medina* in the siding behind the coaling stage.[31]

In 1925 W16 *Wroxall* received W15 *Ventnor's* boiler and was then transferred to Newport shed. However, by August 1927 it was back at Ryde and taking turns on the Bembridge branch. In December 1930 a general overhaul commenced at Ryde Works, during which the cab was replaced by that from IWCR W8. Other additions included a Drummond-pattern chimney, reconditioned cylinders, new side tanks with front filler caps, improved sanding gear and steam heating. The IWR nameplates were replaced by the SR pattern following a repaint. Returned to service in March 1931, it was run in on the Bembridge branch and then transferred to Newport for service on the Freshwater line.[31] W16 *Wroxall* coped well with the heavier trains during the summer but the new cab was not liked during the winter as on 29 February 1932 Thomas Smeaton observed it with temporary side boards to keep out the draught. Laid aside at the end of that season, W16 *Wroxall* was not officially withdrawn until 25 March 1933. Within a month it had joined W13 *Ryde* and FYNR W1 at Ryde. The stay was short-lived as W16 *Wroxall* departed Medina Wharf for the mainland on 23 June and was broken up at Eastleigh Works on 22 July.[25]

Ryde remained in store at Ryde. In January 1933 the Railway Correspondence & Travel Society launched an appeal to save it for static display but this early attempt at railway preservation slipped away when the Society was unable to raise the £50 purchase price. Meanwhile, various fittings were replaced by those of an earlier pattern before a coat of grey paint was applied with black and white lining in the IWR style. In June 1934 W13 *Ryde* was towed to Medina Wharf, shipped to the mainland and taken to Eastleigh Works for storage in the paint shop alongside other aged engines. On 8 April 1940 it was taken outside to the dump and, according to the SR stock register, broken up on 14 August.[25]

Ryde as cosmetically restored was posed at Ryde St John's in 1933 and photographed from many angles. *A. B. MacLeod*

3

Cowes & Newport, Ryde & Newport and Newport Junction Railways

According to the *Hampshire Independent,* a local newspaper, at noon on Saturday, 15 October 1859 a ceremony was held to turn the first sod of the railway from Cowes to Newport at what later became Mill Hill station. Construction began soon afterwards of a nearby tunnel and within weeks work was in progress along much of the line. There was a mill pond to be bridged but otherwise the line followed a relatively level course along the west bank of the River Medina. Unfortunately, Mr Fernandez, the contractor, encountered large quantities of unstable clay that became liquid in wet weather. He withdrew after running into financial problems, leaving the Engineer Henry D. Martin to supervise the work until Jackson & White took on the contract. On 5 October 1861 the newspaper announced:[7]

> The first engines have commenced running on the Cowes & Newport Railway, though at present they are only employed with ballast wagons. Being the first engines in the Isle of Wight, they are a novelty, and hundreds run to see them.

After trial runs with workmen and their families, passenger services on the 4¼-mile line commenced on 16 June 1862. The *Hampshire Independent* wrote:[7]

> Long looked for, come at last! The Cowes & Newport Railway opened to traffic and transit on Monday morning 16 June, when the *Precursor* engine hauling three laurel and bunting bedecked four-wheeled carriages, reached Newport station in about ten minutes.

The line was worked by Henry Martin, who is said to have provided two engines and other stock for a monthly fee of £69 13s 6d. There were seven or eight return trips each weekday, starting and finishing at Cowes.[12] The *Isle of Wight Observer* reported that on 30 June 1862, the anniversary of Queen Victoria's Coronation and a public holiday in the Island, Cowes was swamped by an unprecedented number of visitors and five extra trains of four carriages were hauled by *Pioneer* carrying about 3,200 passengers.[12] Sadly this was an exception and many trains ran with an engine and a single carriage. While a parcels business soon developed, the railway lacked facilities to handle goods traffic, most of which remained river-borne.

The engines were *Pioneer* and *Precursor*, a pair of 2-2-2 well tanks purchased by Henry Martin from the long-established firm of Slaughter, Gruning & Co., Avon Street, Bristol, for £1,960 each. They were shipped by barge to Medham, about a mile south of Cowes, probably from Southampton, where the barge was grounded at high tide and at low water the engines and stock winched onto temporary track laid across the mudflats to the nearby line. Each had a large brass-covered dome over the firebox, an open footplate and wooden brake blocks to the driving wheels. A tall copper-capped chimney was complemented by brass beading that adorned the driving wheel splashers, rectangular brass nameplates attached to the boiler sides and oval maker's plates on the side sheets; no weatherboards were provided. In a letter to the *Isle of Wight County Press* in 1908, Percy Pinhorn of Newport, a grandson of Michael Ratsey who cut the first sod, described them as 'Painted a pretty blue tint, artistically lined out in white, black and red, with their shining brass domes and copper-capped chimneys they looked very smart.'[7] It is not known how long they kept this attractive livery.

Tank engines with single driving wheels were becoming obsolete by the 1860s because they lacked the traction of those with coupled wheels. This mattered little on the CNR with its short trains and few gradients, while at just over 19 tons they were not too heavy for the permanent way. Day-to-day working should have presented few operational difficulties but this proved a fallacy. The sidings and platform roads at Cowes and Newport were poorly ballasted and without fishplates, so derailments were frequent after periods of heavy rain or frost. It was 8 February 1864 before services were seriously affected when *Pioneer* left the track at Cowes while marshalling the stock for the first morning train. *Precursor* suffered the same fate when summoned to the rescue, so four horses had to be hired to haul the passenger carriages for the rest of the day. From correspondence with the Board of Trade it appears that the track deficiencies were rectified in May 1864.[12]

In March 1864 Henry Martin recommended the purchase of land adjoining Cowes station for engine and carriage sheds. By 1876 there existed a single-road shed for the engines and a second for carriages. Both were built in wood on brick footings with glass and slate roofing. Immediately in front of the engine shed was a wooden sheerlegs running on its own rails. On the opposite side of the line a small paint shop was served by its own siding.[32]

Timekeeping often suffered towards the end of a day. Passengers travelling to the mainland frequently missed the last ferry from Cowes giving connections at Southampton with train services to Bournemouth, Salisbury and London. Annoyed passengers demanded compensation, including payment for overnight accommodation. The departure of the last train from Newport was advanced ten minutes but this failed to solve the problem and an arrangement had to be made with the ferry company to coordinate the sailings and train services.[12]

Towards the end of the decade, *Pioneer* and *Precursor* required boiler repairs. According to Mr Bradley, the directors were informed in October 1869 that each would be out of traffic for three weeks but insisted that Mr Martin provide a relief engine. This resulted in the purchase in February 1870 of a small 0-4-2 saddle tank from Black, Hawthorn & Co. of Gateshead for £1,385. Shipped to Medham, the *Isle of Wight Observer* reported:[7]

On Friday 4 March as several men in the employ of the Cowes and Newport Railway were endeavouring to get a new locomotive on shore, which had just been received from the makers … the gear which they had trusted to get on shore proved too weak to sustain its weight and the engine was precipitated into the mud on the river side where the tide when it was high could flow completely round it. Efforts were, of course, made to get it out, but without avail and on Saturday and Sunday passengers by rail could see the engine on its side with the water up all around it.

No date was recorded for the rescue but it must have been about mid-month as the engine entered service on 24 March 1870. In other newspapers the arrival was identified as locomotive No. 3, but this was probably only because it was Henry Martin's third engine as in letters to the directors it was referred to as *Mill Hill*. It had been

The first locomotive, one of a pair, built by Slaughter, Gruning & Co. in 1861 for the Cowes & Newport Railway and named *Pioneer*. This builder's photograph, taken at Bristol in works grey, shows the livery style. Note the complete lack of protection for the crew and that wooden brake blocks were fitted to the driving and trailing wheels. The buffers appear to have wooden faces. *IWSR Archive/LPC*

CNR No. 3 in as-built condition but with no trace of lettering or livery discernible apart from the hint of lining on the cab-side sheet. Note how low the running plate is, requiring the buffers to be mounted partially above the wooden buffer beam with bracing behind. *L&GRP 28326*

built to a standard design of 0-4-0 saddle tank supplied by Black, Hawthorn to industrial users, the main additions being a pair of trailing wheels and a larger coal bunker. The 0-4-2ST had a primitive cab, copper-capped chimney and a small dome over the firebox. The livery was described as olive green with white lining and maker's plates on the cab sides. This unexpected purchase may have delayed Mr Martin's plans to overhaul the 2-2-2WTs. On 4 April 1872 the directors were informed that he was 'about to erect two engines for his own use' and in the following September was 'about to put up further machinery on the Company's property for repairs of rolling stock in use on the Company's line'.[32]

Construction of the IWNJR's line from Sandown to Newport should have been straightforward as the route followed the valleys of the Eastern Yar and Medina rivers for much of its length. Work began at Sandown in 1871 but made slow progress because of a lack of finance and wet weather. Henry Jackson, the contractor, hoped to open the line from Sandown to Horringford on 28 June 1872, Queen Victoria's Coronation holiday. According to local newspapers, the IWR engine *Brading* (formerly *Stuart*) and some 'proper' wagons were hired for ballasting and on 3 February 1872 conveyed the Chairman and Secretary over the line for two miles. On 13 April the contractor and his guests travelled from Horringford to Sandown and back, while on 22 May the engine ran to Horringford in eleven minutes hauling a first-class carriage and brake van loaned by the IWR. *Brading* is thought to have left the line soon afterwards.[32]

At a meeting of the Newport Junction directors on 9 April 1872, the Secretary was instructed to approach the LSWR for the loan or sale of a six-wheeled tank engine suitable for hauling passenger trains. In a reply read out a week later, one was offered for sale at £1,000 or for hire at £2 a day exclusive of the accompanying driver and stoker's wages. A plate was to be carried stating 'This engine is the property of the London and South Western Railway'.[32] W. G. Beattie, the LSWR Locomotive Superintendent, is said to have offered

In the absence of any known photograph of the contractor's locomotive *Bee*, we offer an engraving taken from a Hughes letterhead to illustrate this locomotive.
IWSR Archive

two 2-2-2 well tanks, *Firefly* and *Comet*. *Firefly* was a Nine Elms rebuild of an 1847 Rothwell single. The IWNJR preferred the newer *Comet*, one of the Company's earliest tank engines when built in June 1852 at Nine Elms Works for £1,830. One of seven 'Sussex' class 2-2-2 well tanks designed by Joseph Beattie, a new firebox, smokebox and cylinders were fitted in November 1863. The engine was laid aside in April 1872 with a mileage of 403,217 after being replaced by a new 2-4-0 well tank carrying the same number and name. The older *Comet* was shipped by barge to Brading on 8 June 1872 and steamed the next day before running to Sandown, where a wooden engine shed had been erected. There was a crew of three (presumably a driver, fireman and fitter), 10 tons of coal, 25 gallons of oil, 46lb of tallow and an assortment of spare parts. It probably carried the LSWR livery of chocolate brown with white lining.[15] *Comet's* dimensions are summarised in Appendix 2.[33]

The Board of Trade inspector refused permission to open the line from Sandown to Horringford but the *Isle of Wight Chronicle* reported that on 28 June 1872 a 'train consisting of a sturdy-looking engine, appropriately named *Comet* (gaily decorated with bunting and bouquets) attached to three carriages' made a number of trips for shareholders and friends.[7] Although the contractor briefly operated a daily passenger service, it had ended by 27 July when the *Isle of Wight Express* announced 'the train service has ceased, and no work is being done to complete the line'. This was followed by a letter from the Secretary to the Board of Trade on 23 September stating that: 'The Company's engine and carriages have been housed for protection against the weather.'[11] *Comet* was reclaimed by the LSWR and sold in December 1872 to the Hoylake & Birkenhead Rail & Tramway Co. for £325. Taken out of service in May 1878 with a collapsed tube plate, on 17 February 1879 *Comet* was sold to J. Lever, a Warrington soap manufacturer, for just £142.[33] The IWNJR's debt of £1,698 14s 6d to the LSWR for rent was eventually written off.[12]

Meanwhile, construction of the Ryde to Newport railway began without ceremony in July 1872 when its Act of Incorporation became law. Unlike the CNR and IWNJR, the RNR had to traverse higher ground before falling steeply from Wootton to Newport. The line then crossed the River Medina on a viaduct containing an opening section for vessels before entering a new joint station near to the CNR terminus. The contractors Barnett & Gale made good progress until they met the infamous clay subsoil and in March 1874 J. & G. Taylor took on the task. In May the *Isle of Wight Times* mentioned that a start had begun at Smallbrook on laying the permanent way, nineteen ballast wagons had been shipped from the mainland and an engine was expected in '4 or 5 weeks'. Described in another press report as 'the *Dorothy* engine', this was probably *Stuart*, the IWR's first *Brading*. In May 1875 it ran down and badly injured a labourer at Havenstreet.[12]

Driver Barrett, whose father worked on the line, said the contractors employed a second engine named *Bee*.[34] Built by Henry Hughes of Loughborough, this small 0-4-0 had a rounded saddle tank and a front spectacle plate

RNR No. 4 at the builders in 1875 prior to delivery, unnamed and with brass numerals attached to the side of the chimney. Although the colour is uncertain, lining has been applied on the tank side only, which appears as incomplete double lines either side of a darker colour. Note that the buffer beams are timber with radiused, lined ends; also the couplings with hooks. *BP Official*

in lieu of a cab. The outside cylinders were 10in by 16in, coupled wheels 2ft 5in diameter and the wheelbase was 5ft 0in. Its date of arrival is unknown, possibly early 1875 (but see also Chapter 6).[35]

Completion of the line was delayed by a dispute between the RNR and IWNJR about payment for the viaduct and bridge at Newport and months elapsed before the *Isle of Wight Observer* reported that George Young, the RNR Chairman, and the Engineer had made the first trip by rail from Ryde to Newport on 22 October 1875. Earlier that day one of the contractor's engines hit and killed eighteen sheep while working a ballast train.[12] Heavy rain then caused earth slips that delayed the line's opening until 20 December.

The acquisition of engines for working the railway did not go smoothly. A letter from George Young to the LSWR was read out at a meeting of its locomotive and stores committee on 17 June 1875 asking whether they had two suitable tank engines for sale.[36] The matter was referred to W. G. Beattie, the Locomotive Superintendent, who offered two outside cylinder 2-2-2 well tanks for £785 each with delivery to Southampton or Portsmouth. They were 9 *Chaplin* and probably 34 *Osprey* (the third member of the class, 10 *Aurora,* had been withdrawn in 1871). Built in July 1856 by Nine Elms Works for £1,540, *Chaplin* was similar to *Comet* albeit with smaller 3ft 1in trailing wheels. The engine received new cylinders and a firebox in 1866–67 and had clocked up 496,711 miles. When inspected on 23 June 1875 by Francis Holt, the Midland Railway's Derby workshop superintendent, he reported them to be in good mechanical

order and only after they reached Southampton was it realised that the cylinders fouled the loading gauge. The purchase was duly abandoned, a lucky escape as *Chaplin* and *Osprey* were worn out and remained in LSWR service only until August 1877.[33]

Left without any motive power, 'Mr George Young Isle of Wight Extensions' ordered two 2-4-0 tank engines from Beyer, Peacock & Co. for £1,765 each on 14 July 1875. The maker's records for order 3370 contained the following details:[14]

Progress No.	tried in steam	Dispatched
1583	16.11.1875	25.5.1876 as 4 *Cowes*
1584	18.11.1875	25.5.1876 as 5 *Osborne*

The pair were built to a design first supplied in 1866 to the Kristianstad to Hässleholm Railway (maker's No. 733). Smaller than the IWR 2-4-0Ts, they had Beyer, Peacock's standard features including a three-ring iron boiler, raised firebox, Allan straight link motion and injector boiler feed; wooden brake blocks acted on the driving wheels. The plain cabs had a pair of round spectacle plates to the front and rectangular lookouts to the rear. Conflicting statements say they were painted dark chocolate or green (a situation made worse by the lack of any consistent descriptions of colours at that time).[15] The maker's records contained instructions that 8in brass figures be riveted on both sides of the copper-capped chimney, the nameplates placed on the tank sides, a 'Makers & Owners' nameplate to the sides of smokebox and that they 'be provided with the usual set of screw keys, oil cans, fire irons & c'. Some of these features appeared in a Beyer, Peacock photograph of No. 4 but early views of the pair at work show a nameplate on the tank side and no numeral on the chimney. The brass nameplates were similar to those carried by the IWR 2-4-0T *Wroxall*.[14]

The Beyer, Peacock engines were ready for dispatch by December 1875 but there were problems in funding their purchase as George Young lacked the ready cash. Eventually payment was made by quarterly instalments of £220 over five years, Mr Martin having been prevailed upon to act as guarantor. Sadly, details of the financial arrangements between the two men have not survived. It cost a further £85 17s 4d to transport the 2-4-0Ts to the Island.[32]

George Young had hoped that the IWR would operate the CNR and RNR but its shareholders refused to sanction any agreement. Henry Martin agreed to an extension of his existing operating contract but that proved costly as his charges from December 1875 to June 1876 totalled £199 10s 0d. Small wonder RNR shareholders were later told that 'large items of locomotive expenses have arisen from temporary arrangements for hire of engines, which the Company were compelled to make in order to carry the traffic'. These costs continued as the Joint Committee had to rent Mr Martin's engines and stock. The minutes suggested he initially charged 10% of their value each year but a later bill was for a more modest 7½% a year based on a valuation of £1,194 12s 8d by Mr Bourne, the IWR Manager.[32]

The Joint Committee began operations on 1 July 1876 with *Pioneer*, *Precursor* and *Mill Hill* hired from Henry Martin, and the Beyer, Peacock 2-4-0Ts *Cowes* and *Osborne*. That was barely enough as four were needed in steam during the summer months and three in winter. There was a sixth engine as in November 1876 Messrs Guy and Hunter were paid £3 for repairs to 'No. 6 engine'.[32] This is likely to have been *Bee*, apparently acquired by Mr Martin as part of his deal with George Young. The 0-4-0T was employed completing the spurs to Medina Jetty and Newport Quay. The latter was reached by a low-level lifting bridge that was so lightly built that only *Bee* could run over it. *Bee* had a pull-out regulator that tended to open too readily. One day at Medina Jetty the engine started off with only the fireman on board and driver Barrett was fortunate to catch and stop *Bee* before it could get away. Too small for general use, *Bee* was not taken into IWCR stock and is understood to have left the Island in June 1888 via Newport Quay after being sold to Robert T. Relf, a contractor of Okehampton, Devon. The other contractor's engine *Dorothy*, assuming it was *Stuart*, went to assist on the works at St Helens.[36]

Construction of the Sandown to Newport railway halted after the contractor was declared bankrupt late in 1872. A replacement was appointed but financial problems so delayed progress that months elapsed before thoughts returned to motive power. George Sheward, the Chairman, was also a director of the London & North Western Railway (LNWR) so he turned to that railway for *Comet*'s replacement.

No. 10 *Queen Mab* was a 2-2-2 well tank built in January 1861 by R. & W. Hawthorn & Co. (maker's No. 1128) for the Whitehaven Junction Railway at a cost of £1,850. On 1 December 1866 the engine entered LNWR stock and was allocated No. 1553, then 1580 in April 1867, 1262 in July 1867 and 1825 in January 1872 before being laid aside in December 1873. The 2-2-2T was purchased for £750 on 17 June 1874 by Mr Sheward's English & Foreign Credit Co. and later that month was landed at Brading before running over the IWR to Sandown.[12] The engine is said to have arrived carrying a sandy brown livery and the name *Newport*.[35] Naturally the IWNJR was charged rent for the use of *Newport*, something of an impertinence as it was not a good investment. A trial run from Pan Lane to Sandown and back took place on 25 November 1874 and the 2-2-2WT may have been serviceable when passenger services began between Sandown and Shide on 1 February 1875, managed by the IWR. Maintenance was entrusted to the driver, who often made matters worse, and staff from Ryde Works were frequently called upon to assist. The IWR accounts recorded numerous payments for repairs and engine hire, which was hardly surprising as *Newport* failed on no fewer than nineteen occasions in 1875-78, twice with broken crank axles and once with a hairline fracture in the firebox.[12] During one visit to Ryde Works it was said that a cab with three spectacles in the back sheet and two in the front was fitted, not that this did anything to improve performance. (The drawing of *Newport* shows it with a more primitive cab and a nameplate, neither of which may be accurate).[2] Such were the problems with *Newport* that there must have been a collective sigh of relief when the Joint Committee took over operation of the line in April 1879. Herbert Simmons, the Joint Committee's Assistant Manager, wrote to the IWNJR directors on 1 July 1881 reporting that the engine had burst its boiler and 'should be substituted by another'.[32] He met with no response so *Newport* was stored and passed into IWNJR ownership after the English & Foreign Credit Co. was wound up.[37]

Board of Trade returns showed that the small quantity of goods carried by the Joint Committee in 1876 grew slowly until 1879, when there was a sudden increase following completion of Medina Jetty and the railway to Sandown. Most traffic was coal landed at the jetty and taken forward from Newport in mixed passenger and goods trains. The Joint Committee gained a reputation for bad timekeeping as wagons would be attached and detached at any station, much to the frustration of passengers. This was not helped by frequent mishaps caused by the poor condition of the engines, rolling stock and permanent way. In September 1879 two wagons ran away from Ashey quarry into the path of No. 4, which was hauling a passenger train bound for Newport. George Young, the quarry's owner, was sent a £125 bill for the damage but the incident was repeated a few months later.[32]

On 13 August 1879 Mr Simmons broached the subject of an additional engine but no decision was made. By the next meeting on 14 January 1880 he had inspected and rejected one offered for £600 by Frimin, Hill & Co..[32]

RNR No. 5 *Osborne* at Freshwater c. 1889. The nameplate is fixed to the tank-side but the maker's plate is not seen. By this date the loco has acquired handrails to the tank tops and a front footstep, although the wooden brake blocks remain. Note also the different appearance of the front buffer beam, possibly a replacement following an accident? The headcode consists of a single disc. *RP 36122*

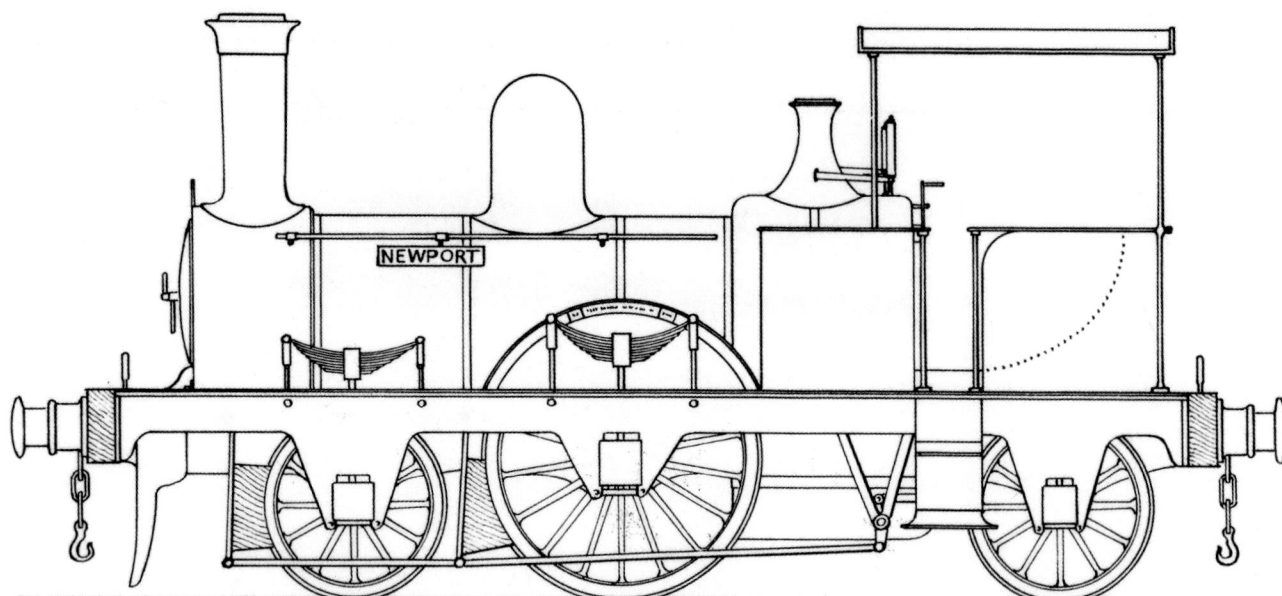

No photograph of the sole locomotive owned by the IWNJR is known so this side elevation is included to give an ndication of its likely appearance. *IWSR Archive*

Henry Martin, who had become the Joint Committee's 'Consulting Manager', reported that an engine from his old employers, the North London Railway (NLR), was for sale. The 4-4-0T, on offer for £750, was inspected at Bow Works on 28 January and purchased by Mr Martin on 25 February.[12]

This engine was one of eight designed by William Adams and constructed by Slaughter, Gruning & Co. (maker's No. 443) in October 1861 at a cost of £2,650. Becoming NLR No. 35, later 35A, the 4-4-0T was rebuilt at Bow Works by John Park in March 1875 with a larger boiler, cylinders, cab and other modern features such as iron brake shoes. The boiler was domed with Salter balance safety valves and carried a large sand canister between the chimney and dome. All the other members of the class were sold: No. 30 to Cannington, Shaw & Co., glass bottle manufacturers of St Helens, Lancs, Nos 31, 32 and 34 to Bute Docks, Cardiff, and Nos 33, 36 and 37 to the Girvan & Portpatrick Junction Railway.[12]

Becoming No. 7 *Whippingham*, the 4-4-0T is said to have retained the NLR livery of black with red lining until 1888.[35] The engine was purchased by the Joint Committee for £800 in instalments at a rate of £18 12s 6d a month, its ownership being emphasised by a cast iron plate that was affixed to the frame stay saying 'H. D. Martin – Owner'.[36] Presumably the payments were underwritten by the RNR as in December 1880 its directors were told about correspondence from Vincent J. Barton, who wanted

commission on the sale of the engine to Mr Martin. This was refused as 'they did not purchase one of the engines he recommended and that moreover, commission is usually paid by the vendor'. A month later they reluctantly decided to pay him £7 10s 0d to avoid litigation! Mr Barton was well-known as in June 1875 the IWNJR had refused his offer of two second-hand engines each costing £850.[32]

At 36 tons, *Whippingham* was heavier than the Joint Committee's other engines and there were numerous derailments, particularly on the Sandown to Newport line. On 1 February 1884, when hauling the 3.42pm train to Newport, the right-hand leading bogie wheel left the rails and landed on the sleepers some 620 yards east of Blackwater station. At this spot the line passed over soft peat that had sunk under the weight. The Board of Trade inspector concluded that the permanent way was too weak, worn out and needed to be renewed.[19]

The Joint Committee established its headquarters at Newport station but the engines and rolling stock were still being maintained in cramped facilities at Cowes. There was space for little more than basic repairs and it is known that some work was done by the IWR at Ryde Works.

While the Joint Committee did reduce operating costs, the continued existence of three separate companies made no sense. Proposals to amalgamate all the Island companies foundered in 1885 but a more limited scheme to merge the CNR, RNR and IWNJR succeeded two years later.

The only locomotive purchased during the Joint Committee period was this 4-4-0T dating from 1861 when it was built for the North London Railway and which arrived on the Island in 1880. Reportedly named *Whippingham*, no photograph in this condition is known so here it is seen at Newport sometime during the 1890s wearing IWCR 'Metallic crimson' livery and displaying the number within the Central Railway garter. The lining shows well with the outside single yellow line wholly on the tank side; note also the lined out bogie-side frames and tool box. *RP 36100*

4

Isle of Wight Central Railway

The Isle of Wight Central Railway came into being on 1 July 1887, formed by an amalgamation of the Cowes & Newport, Ryde & Newport, and Newport Junction companies. Mr Simmons was appointed Manager and for the first time there was sufficient capital to purchase Henry Martin's engines, rolling stock, tools, plant, etc. On 26 October he was given debenture stock to the value of £10,000 paying 3% per annum and a month later a cheque was issued for £594 6s 2d, that being the balance owed for the NLR 4-4-0T. Mr Martin still had some influence over the railway's affairs as he served as a director until his death in 1898.[38]

Perhaps the most visible change was in the engine livery although whether it predated the amalgamation is not at all clear. Described as 'metallic crimson lake', the black lining was edged with yellow (a specification appears later in the chapter). Each year in early March the boilers were inspected for insurance purposes, they being identified by name or number, and it is from these lists that the removal dates of the names have been surmised. The early disappearance of those on Nos 3 and 7 suggests they were only painted on.[12]

Name	No.	Railway of origin	Name removed
Pioneer	1	CNR	1893
Precursor	2	CNR	1895
Mill Hill	3	CNR	1888
Cowes	4	RNR	1893
Osborne	5	RNR	1892
Newport	6	IWNJR	
Whippingham	7	Joint Committee	1888

Newport is said to have had the name painted on the boiler and never bore a number; the engine lay in store for a considerable time, first at Sandown and then in a carriage shed at Newport. In September 1892 the Manager produced tenders for the disposal of a quantity of scrap including the 'old locomotive' but was instructed

that it be retained and advertised separately. The directors finally agreed on 24 October 1894 that the relic be broken up and the remains sold for scrap, an event that took place a few months later.[38]

In 1886 the CNR and RNR directors had signed a provisional agreement to operate the railway from Freshwater to Newport, then under construction. When the time came to honour the undertaking, the IWCR had come into being and its directors, none of whom was party to the original discussions, were reluctant to take on the commitment. The obligation was only honoured after lengthy and acrimonious correspondence that delayed the line's opening to passengers until July 1889.

The IWCR estimated that one extra engine, six carriages and eleven wagons were required to operate the FYNR at a cost of £4,000, money that was badly needed elsewhere. Tenders were sought for a new tank engine but the cheapest from Manning, Wardle & Co. at £2,540 was considered too expensive. Second-hand examples were then sought and on 28 August 1889 the following were considered:[12]

LBSCR	0-6-0 wing tank No. 395 built 1868, new firebox 1885, at £495
	Kitson 0-4-2 saddle tank 496 *Bognor* built 1869, new firebox in 1888 at £950
LSWR	Beyer, Peacock 2-4-0 well tank No. 0251 built 1867, with vacuum brake, at £750
	Manning, Wardle 0-6-0 saddle tank 458 *Jumbo* built 1862, steam brake, at £600

After inspection, these well-worn specimens were rejected and fresh tenders for new engines were requested. On 30 October 1889 the following replies were read out:[38]

Robert Stephenson & Co.	£1,790
Black, Hawthorn & Co.	£1,845
Kitson & Co.	£2,225
Neilson & Co.	£2,550

IWCR No. 6, the Black, Hawthorn 4-4-0T, was an elegant machine and shows the fine lines to advantage in this view at Newport shortly after delivery in 1890. The details of the livery show particularly well, and note that the outside line applied to the side tanks continues around to the front; also the elaborately lined out buffer beam. *O. J. Morris collection ©Rail Archive Stephenson*

Black, Hawthorn had offered a 4-4-0T with completion promised in six months. No other manufacturer could match such early delivery and this proved the deciding factor provided the driving wheel diameter was reduced and the cylinders enlarged. Although ready on 19 March 1890, delivery to Medham was delayed until 7 June because of a strike at the maker's works.[12]

Becoming IWCR No. 6, this large 4-4-0T had outside cylinders, a three-ring iron boiler, Ramsbottom safety valves, single slide bars and a sizeable side-windowed cab. It was an odd mixture of old and new with obsolete buffer beam safety chains, iron brake shoes and the Westinghouse brake. Delivered in lined red livery with maker's plates on the bunker sides, the tank sides were noticeably bare of other adornment apart from the lining. The rapid acceleration was much appreciated but the engine had a reputation for rough riding and would hunt from side to side, causing some damage to the track. The Company had sufficient funds to pay the £1,900 purchase price but the directors could not resist sending only £1,000 on 6 August 1890. Black, Hawthorn promptly asked for the balance so a cheque was reluctantly dispatched on

27 August. Delivery from Southampton to Cowes cost another £41 14s 7d.[38]

The local newspapers reported a continuing litany of mishaps. On 13 August 1889 the axle of a coal wagon attached to the 2.40pm Newport to Ryde train fractured after leaving Ashey, causing several other vehicles to leave the rails and severely damaging 55 yards of track. No one was injured and the engine, No. 4, was able to proceed with the two leading carriages after a forty-five-minute delay, although it was the following day before normal traffic was resumed. On the evening of 15 October 1891, No. 2 was drawing six coal trucks onto Newport drawbridge when a rail gave way and the 2-2-2WT sank up to its axles into the decking. Only the existence of a longitudinal girder prevented a descent into the river.

The 1889 Regulation of Railways Act obliged companies to equip vehicles running in passenger trains with continuous brakes and the two principal manufacturers of braking equipment immediately made offers to railway companies of free or cut-price fittings for trial purposes. The Westinghouse Air Brake Co.'s representative visited Newport on 26 February 1890 and persuaded the directors to have 2-4-0T No. 4 and seven carriages equipped at a cost of £150, payable only if the brake was not adopted by the Company. Evidently the trial was satisfactory as on 25 April Black, Hawthorn & Co. were instructed to fit the brake to No. 6 before delivery.[12] Even so, the Board of Trade had to send several strongly worded letters before more of the Company's motive power was equipped: Nos 1 and 5 in March–April 1892, No. 7 in December 1893 and No. 2 in January 1894; No. 3 was not done until 1901. Most had their wooden brake blocks replaced with longer-lasting iron shoes, much to the relief of the fitters, and No. 6 lost its safety chains.

A priority for the Company was the provision of a new running shed, workshop and stores building at Newport to replace the inadequate facilities at Cowes. The directors prevaricated and even considered an offer to share the use of Ryde Works with the IWR. In the end Herbert Simmons, the Manager, provided convincing evidence that the money had to be spent. Constructed by local builder T. Jenkins at a cost of £1,798 10s 0d, the buildings were in wood with iron supports on a concrete base and with slate and glass roofs. The two-road running shed had accommodation for eight engines and came into use on 2 February 1891. A fitting and machine shop, ready a month later, was followed by paint and carpenters' shops. Water tanks were erected to serve the fitting shop and running shed. Additional machinery was purchased second-hand from Nine Elms

Works in London at a time when, conveniently for the Company, the LSWR was moving its own workshops to Eastleigh. In addition to the usual inspection pits and work benches, the fitting shop contained five forges, a steam hammer, planing, slotting and grinding machines, and several lathes including a wheel-turning lathe of 5ft capacity. Power was supplied by a small steam engine housed in a separate boiler house.[39] Six men and three boys were the normal staff in the workshop, barely enough to keep pace with demand, and much of the skilled repair work had to be contracted out. Engines frequently spent months out of service waiting for the directors to sanction purchases of spare parts.

On 16 December 1891 the directors accepted a tender of £321 from Avonside Engine Works for repairs to No. 1 that included a new boiler, firebox and cylinders; at the same time a cab and gravity-fed sanding gear from a box on top of the boiler was fitted, plus a tapered stovepipe chimney. No. 1 was then put to work on trains between Sandown and Newport. No. 2 later received similar attention, albeit without a new boiler but with a straight-sided stovepipe chimney, and then worked on the Freshwater line. It was the turn of Nos 4 and 5 at the end of the 1894 season when they received new tubes, tyres and cylinders.[12] The pair acquired high handrails above the tanks so the fireman could reach the front of the engine when in motion.

CNR *Precursor* at Newport following provision of a square cab, boiler-mounted sandbox, stovepipe chimney, smokebox handrail and assorted fixtures and fittings in 1886, but prior to the fitting of the Westinghouse brake in 1894. The builder's plate is still on the cab-side sheet and the lined livery shows up well, but the colour is impossible to determine and there is no number or company indication. Also noteworthy is the large headlamp and what appears to be a disc headcode board. *IWSR Archive*

They were removed after the practice was outlawed by safety legislation in 1900. No. 3 was left on Medina Jetty, where its condition steadily deteriorated. If a writer in *The Locomotive Magazine* is to be believed, it kept the olive green livery until withdrawn for an overhaul at the turn of the century.[35]

On 18 April 1893 a ceremony was held at Merstone when the first sod was cut of the railway from Merstone to Ventnor but it was another year before there was any significant progress. The line was not easy to build as it climbed from Merstone to a summit at the north end of St Lawrence tunnel before falling through the tunnel and along a shelf cut in the Undercliff to approach Ventnor from the west. The contractors are known to have employed three engines; they had enquired about one of the IWCR's antiques but could not agree on a price.

St Lawrence was previously *St Helens*, the first *Brading* and *Stuart*. Purchased in September 1893 by Westwood & Winley from the Brading Harbour railway, there is a persistent story that *St Lawrence* ran over the public highway from one work site to another. Rails were in place by November 1896, when the engine ran daily from its base at Whitwell to assist in the construction of the tunnel. Desperate for motive power, in 1897 the IWCR hired *St Lawrence* for shunting at Medina Jetty. Driver Barrett described the engine as 'a real antique' that can have been of little practical use since the boiler pressure was only 60psi.[34] After being dumped in a siding at Whitwell utterly worn out, the IWCR tried to buy it for use as a tar tank but their offers of £10 and then £15 were rejected. Broken up in June 1898, according to local legend, the remains were tipped into the formation somewhere in the Undercliff, a not improbable possibility as old ferrous metal was virtually worthless once any copper and brass had been removed. By then *St Lawrence* was possibly the oldest working engine in the British Isles and a truly historic relic.[38]

Godshill was a small 0-6-0 saddle tank built by the Worcester Engine Co. in 1863 or 1865, rebuilt by Kerr, Stuart & Co. (maker's No. 81) in 1893 and employed with the name *California* at the firm's Stoke-on-Trent works. Sold in May 1897, the purchasers were C. J. Westwood & Co., who had taken over construction of the line after the previous contractors became bankrupt. With square-topped tanks similar to *St Lawrence*, unusually for a contractor's engine, the dimensions for *Godshill* are known (see Appendix 2).[40]

Godshill was hired by the IWCR on several occasions during 1898, including one period of forty-five days. C. J. Westwood contracted to build the remaining section of railway to Ventnor but also became bankrupt so it passed into the hands of the next contractor, J. T. Firbank. After the line opened from St Lawrence to Ventnor Town in 1900 *Godshill* was returned to the mainland and used on one of Firbank's contracts in London, probably the Great Western & Great Central Joint Railway south of Northolt, before being disposed of for scrap in 1904.[12]

Weaste was an 0-4-0 saddle tank built in June 1888 by Hudswell Clarke & Co. of Leeds (maker's No. 302) for

Views of contractor's locomotives on the Island are rather rare; although of poor quality, this image of *Weaste* is included to illustrate one of the type and was believed taken on the Basingstoke to Alton line. *IWSR Archive*

The contractor's locomotive *Godshill* used on the construction of the Ventnor extension of the NG&StLR, seen at Kerr Stuart's works prior to transfer to the Island.

T. A. Walker, a contractor working on the Manchester Ship Canal. Described as 'diminutive', it had a cut-down chimney, the outside cylinders measured 8in by 15in and the wheels were 2ft 6in diameter.[41] During an inspection of the works in July 1895 the construction methods in the tunnel were criticised and more plant was called for. *Weaste* probably arrived sometime after C. J. Westwood took over the contract. It was used mainly to remove spoil from the tunnel but was also hired by the IWCR for a brief time shunting at Medina Jetty.[42] *Weaste* passed into the hands of J. T. Firbank and was taken back to the mainland. It was employed during 1901 on constructing the Basingstoke & Alton Light Railway but then disappeared from sight until 1918, when the Weston-super-Mare Gaslight & Coke Co. were the owners. *Weaste* was sold for scrap in 1922 or thereabouts.[12]

The operation of mixed passenger and goods trains continued to cause much dissatisfaction. One local doctor complained the Company operated goods trains to which it attached a couple of carriages.[7] The two 4-4-0Ts 6 and 7 could easily manage these trains but whenever one was unavailable separate passenger and goods trains had to be run using the older and weaker engines. This resulted in an accident on 8 January 1895 involving the 7.50am Newport to Sandown passenger train. The Board of Trade inspector discovered that a four-wagon goods train hauled by No. 3 had been dispatched ten minutes ahead of the passenger train but stalled on the gradient approaching Sandown station. The train was then divided with the two leading wagons being taken to the sidings while the remaining two were left with the brakes applied. However, a wagon containing oil in casks destined for Newport was allowed to run back against them. Although the oil wagon was stopped, the other two set off downhill at ever-increasing speed towards the approaching passenger train headed by No. 1. In the resulting collision, two passengers were seriously injured and thirteen others required medical attention to cuts and bruises. The Board of Trade inspector criticised the operation of goods trains without brake vans but he was more scathing about the running of the passenger train before the goods train had reached Sandown. A derailment on the Freshwater line two months later (see Chapter 5) only added to the Company's woes.[19]

Alexander Hindmarsh, who had driven the first train on the CNR in 1862 and later became Locomotive Foreman, died on 13 January 1894 at the age of 76. Nothing was done about a replacement until November, when several engineering firms were asked if they had anyone suitable. After an interview with the directors in January 1895 John Seymour, who worked for Kitson & Co. in Leeds, was appointed Locomotive Superintendent. Six months later the directors interviewed applicants for Mr Simmons' job as Manager, a 'resignation' being submitted in September, following which he went abroad. His replacement, Charles Conacher, had worked for the Cambrian and Great Northern railways. The combination of a new Manager and Locomotive Superintendent did much to lift the Company from its wretched state and it is noticeable that most of the complaints faded away. One of Mr Conacher's first tasks was to preside over the opening of the railway from Merstone to St Lawrence. The 4-4-0T No. 6 was used with some LBSCR carriages dressed with flags and fronted by a large board proclaiming 'Success to the Newport, Godshill & St Lawrence Railway'. Ordinary services on the line were left to the smaller engines.[38]

On 30 January 1895 the IWCR signed an agreement with the owners of Cement Mills to provide motive power for trainloads of chalk from Shide to Cement Mills using the firm's wagons. Despite the size of the business, about 30,000 tons a year, no special provision was made for their working in the timetables. Instead, the loaded wagons were merely pushed in front of the engine of the daily goods train with the rest of the train trailing behind. It was not until SR days that separate chalk trains were operated. The agreement lasted until cement production ended in 1944.[38]

The need for additional motive power was acknowledged on 21 October 1896 when the directors decided to seek tenders for an engine similar to the Black, Hawthorn 4-4-0T. Five manufacturers responded:[12]

Robert Stephenson & Co.	£2,395
Black, Hawthorn & Co.	£2,260
Kitson & Co.	£2,395
Neilson & Co.	£2,400
Beyer, Peacock & Co.	£2,300

Beyer, Peacock also offered a 2-4-0T for £1,950. No doubt the cheaper price was a deciding factor as an order was placed on 16 December 1896. The maker's drawing office register for order 8206 noted that the engine was Progress No. 3942. It was dispatched on 11 May 1898 as No. 8.[14]

Essentially a modernised version of RNR Nos 4 and 5, this attractive 2-4-0T had a steel boiler, increased working pressure, steam sanding, 4 tons more weight and greater coal and water capacity. The cab was larger with deeper sides, while the rear of the coal bunker was flared back; at some later date the top of the bunker was enclosed. The Beyer, Peacock records contained the following instructions:[14]

The engine to run 3,000 miles on the I. W. C. Ry. Co. system with average trains accompanied by a B. P. & Co. mileage runner. All repairs and breakdown attributed to defects in the construction of engine to be carried out by and at the entire cost of B. P. & Co. until the trial mileage (which will be the first 3,000 miles run by the engine in steam) is completed.

The IWCR expected delivery in time for the 1897 season but the maker was overwhelmed by business and construction was delayed. After No. 2 broke down, *St Lawrence* and *Godshill* were hired in succession but failed and in January 1898 *Sandown* had to be hired from the IWR.[12] No. 8 was delivered in May but so great was the need for motive power that it ran for twenty-seven weeks and covered 28,050 miles (1,050 a week) before being stopped for a single day. That was not unusual as in the year ending 30 June the Company's engines each ran an average of 48,900 miles (940 a week), an underestimate for most as two were employed full time in shunting.[43]

The Company was in no position to pay for No. 8. Anticipating this, in August 1897 two directors set up the Southern Counties Rolling Stock Co. to buy engines and rolling stock before selling them on to the IWCR on easy terms. No. 8 cost £21 17s 0d in 120 monthly instalments made out of the traffic receipts. These payments took priority over the debenture interest. The final bill was:[38]

Beyer, Peacock & Co.	£1,961 0s 0d
Rail charges to Southampton	£28 12s 0d
Shipment to Medham	£43 17s 9d
Total	£2,033 9s 9d

Among the correspondence with Beyer, Peacock was a livery specification:

Smokebox and chimney to be primed over and filled up with best filling and after rubbing down to receive two coats of Griffiths Bros. quick drying Black Enamel and

The builder's official photograph of IWCR No. 8 at their works in photographic grey livery, which clearly shows the updated features compared to RNR Nos 4 and 5. This also provides a useful template for the lining. *RP 15577*

two coats of varnish. Firebox to be treated in similar manner. Remainder of engine to be prepared, and afterwards receive two coats of Red Oxide as ground for Metallic Crimson Lake then two coats Crimson Lake, the surface to be picked out and fine lined to pattern sent by I. W. C. Ry. Co. Two garters also supplied by I. W. C. Ry. Co. to be transferred on centre of tank sides the figures to be painted inside the garters in 4in figures with 1in black shading and gilded to match garter. Three coats of varnish to be given. The first and second coats to be flattened when dry. Buffer beams painted vermilion with 1in black border and ⅝in picking out line 1in from inside of border line. A yellow fine line between the black lines equidistant from each, and one outside of black picking out line ½in from inside edge. All accessories to be blacked. Top of cab inside, painted white and varnished.

The maker's photograph of No. 8 shows the lining arrangement to good effect. The IWCR may not have been quite so scrupulous when it came to repainting its engines. Samples taken from one in preservation (No. 11) showed a dull brick red, cheap paint made from red oxide. The garter device came from a batch of transfers purchased from Messrs Tearnes in 1893. There were two sizes, one 12¾in wide by 14¾in high, the other 9½in wide by 11½in high. The words 'CENTRAL RAILWAY' were around the edge, the body of the garter was vermilion and the remainder gilt. The running number in matching shaded lettering was usually placed in the centre of the garter.[44]

There remained a dire shortage of useable motive power as Nos 1 and 2 were worn out and No. 5 needed a replacement boiler. When the matter was discussed by the directors on 14 September 1898 they asked whether a second-hand engine could be purchased that would suit the Company. The following offers were received:[12]

LSWR	Manning, Wardle 0-6-0 saddle tank 392 *Lady Portsmouth* built in 1862 at £550.
	'Ilfracombe Goods' 0-6-0 tender engine No. 282 built by Beyer, Peacock in 1873 and reboilered in 1889 at £750 with tender or £685 without.
LBSCR	Class A1 0-6-0T 75 *Blackwall* built by Brighton Works in December 1872, new 14in cylinders and firebox in June 1897, at £800 (mileage 580,982).

On 12 October 1898 Mr Conacher, the Manager, was authorised to spend £431 on a new boiler from Beyer, Peacock and have *Blackwall* inspected by a qualified engineer. When examined by J. M. Budge of Doncaster Works (Great Northern Railway) on 2 November he found it to be in good mechanical order. His report was presented to the directors on 30 November but they then ordered that a quote be obtained from Beyer, Peacock & Co. for a new engine. The reply read out on 25 January 1899 offered one with delivery in seven months for £1,900. The directors preferred to purchase *Blackwall* for £800.[38]

Designed by William Stroudley, fifty LBSCR class A (later A1) 0-6-0 tank engines were constructed at Brighton Works between 1872 and 1880. No. 75 *Blackwall* was one of the first six to be completed. Going by the nicknames 'Rooter' or 'Terrier', they were intended for use

The first of the LBSCR 'Terriers' was purchased in 1899 and was repainted in the metallic crimson livery with garter prior to shipment, although still retaining wooden brake blocks. The gentleman on the footplate appears to be in uniform but does not look like a locomotive crew member. *IWSR Archive*

on inner suburban services with lightweight carriage sets running over poorly maintained track. Improvements to the permanent way and the drafting in of heavier engines and carriages during the 1890s made many surplus to requirements. They were among the first of Stroudley's LBSCR engines to have his classic design of cab with brass-edged spectacle plates, round-topped tanks, copper-capped chimneys, 13in diameter inside cylinders and combined dome and spring balance safety valves. The frames were slotted to save weight, while the footplate was so low that the buffer casing projected above running plate level. The older members of the class, including *Blackwall*, had wooden brake blocks, but later batches had iron brake shoes and the Westinghouse brake. All still carried their original boilers, albeit with new copper fireboxes, and new cylinders.[45]

Brighton Works gave *Blackwall* an overhaul and a repaint in lined red livery, the running number 9 being placed inside the garter device on the tank sides; the ornate LBSCR lining on the front buffer beam remained untouched for several years. Delivered in March 1899, the wheelbase caused some initial problems when shunting in sidings at Cowes and Ryde St John's Road but otherwise No. 9 was well liked. That year the LBSCR decided to dispose of more of the class and, perhaps prompted by the sale of *Blackwall*, began advertising them in the engineering journals at prices between £500 and £700 according to mileage and mechanical condition. Sadly, the majority suffered from defective fireboxes and cylinders, precisely the problems purchasers did not want, so they went for scrap. Nevertheless, the IWCR eventually owned four.

No. 9 was paid for by the Southern Counties Rolling Stock Co. and resold by hire purchase at £9 8s 10d per month over ten years. Prompted by the purchase of Nos 8 and 9 in this fashion, on 14 June 1899 the directors agreed to sell Nos 1 to 7 for £4,000 and buy them back for £44 8s 4d per month over ten years. The detailed valuation was: 1 – £110, 2 – £90, 3 – £150, 4 – £800, 5 – £1,100, 6 – £1,450, 7 – £300. The monthly payment for the nine was £75 14s 2d, a sum that could be afforded even during the winter months. The only disadvantage arose when the breaking up of Nos 1 and 2 had to be deferred as they were no longer IWCR property.[12]

On 22 November 1899 the directors considered a letter from the Manager warning that No. 3 required extensive repairs and No. 2 was 'quite unserviceable'. However, LBSCR class A 0-6-0T 69 *Peckham* was available for purchase at £700. Completed in August 1874, it received new 14in cylinders in April 1899 and had clocked up 576,292 miles. Like No. 9, the wooden brake blocks were still in place but the Westinghouse brake had been fitted. Mr Drummond, the LSWR Locomotive Superintendent, carried out an inspection and recommended some minor work that was made a condition of purchase. On 7 February 1900 a decision was made to buy *Peckham* 'through the Southern Counties Rolling Stock Co.' and on 25 April it was reported that transport to the Island had been arranged. Prior to delivery, Brighton Works repainted the engine as IWCR No. 10.[38]

The arrival of No. 10 coincided with a change in livery intended prominently to advertise the IWCR following the opening of the railway to Ventnor. According to Mr Bradley,

The second 'Terrier' arrived in 1900, by which time the IWCR had decided to have the company's name, instead of the garter, emblazoned in full on the tank sides, the number now being placed on the bunker side. Apart from the two exhaust steam domes atop the front of the tanks, No. 10 appears identical to No. 9. *LocoPub*

the first engine to leave Newport Works carrying this style was No. 7 in May 1901 and Nos 4, 5, 6, 8 and 9 were similarly painted by the end of the year.[12] The red colour and lining remained unchanged but the garter on the tank sides was replaced by the Company's name spelled out in unshaded 'gold' block lettering (note the use of a full stop). The running number in matching numerals was placed on the bunker sides and repeated on the buffer beams, e.g. 'N⁰ (coupling) 10'. The tank sides were lettered as follows:

Isle of Wight
Central Railway.
(Nos. 3, 9, 10)

Isle of Wight Central Railway.
(Nos. 4, 5, 6, 7, 8)

RNR No. 5 at Newport post-1901 carrying the livery with the company name spelt in full and showing the lining well. Note the Westinghouse brake pump fixed to the front end of the side tank, the cylinder lubricator on the side of the smokebox and the large screw jack bolted onto the running plate to assist with the not infrequent requirement for rerailing! Other alterations include the removal of the nameplates, fitting of iron brake blocks and furled canvas weather sheets to the cab. *IWSR Archive*

Mr Seymour, the Locomotive Superintendent, was an army reservist and in 1899 volunteered for service in the Second Boer War, where he remained until May 1901. He was sorely missed and upon his return the directors immediately asked for a report on the condition of the engines:[46]

- No. 1 was working on Medina Jetty pending the return to service of No. 3 'but is in a deplorable state consequent on old age. Its framing is broken and its cylinder and motion parts generally are completely worn out.'
- No. 2 had been out of service for two years after a cylinder broke. Many 'minor parts' had been removed to keep its partner in use.
- No. 3 had been employed on Medina Jetty until incapable of further use. A new firebox ordered in December 1899 for £200 was fitted during heavy boiler repairs along with a larger cab salvaged from No. 2 and the Westinghouse brake. The 0-4-2ST was still in the works.
- No. 4 was in need of an overhaul. The boiler pressure had been reduced to 110psi but running costs compared unfavourably with its sister No. 5.
- No. 5 with its new 150psi boiler was described as 'in excellent condition'. The boiler had been modelled on that supplied by Beyer, Peacock with No. 8.
- No. 6 was in works stripped and awaiting a first major repair since purchase in 1890. The wheels, axleboxes and springs had all caused problems in the past, the firebox needed extensive patching and almost every other part required an overhaul.

- No. 7 was described as in good condition. After a recent overhaul the 4-4-0T was handling the heaviest trains in the absence of No. 6.
- No. 8 had been stopped on 10 June for wheel turning after running 140,000 miles in the three years since arrival and was in good condition.
- No. 9 had 'done some hard work during the two years it has been running'. Although in good condition, there were minor cracks in the boiler's back tube plate.
- No. 10 was in good condition after a year's service and had 'given general satisfaction'.

Given the condition of No. 1, on 30 August 1901 the Manager was authorised to enquire about another second-hand engine. He discovered that LBSCR class A 0-6-0T 40 *Brighton*, built in March 1878, was available for sale at £700 (mileage 522,583) but Mr Drummond reported that it was worth no more than £600. The lower price was accepted on 14 November and payment was made by the Southern Counties Rolling Stock Co. The LBSCR supplied reconditioned 13in cylinders and repainted the engine in red livery for an additional charge of £35 16s 0d. Leaving Brighton Works on 13 December, IWCR No. 11 was shipped to the Island on 8 January 1902.[38] A few days later the *Isle of Wight Guardian* announced:[7]

The Isle of Wight Central Railway has just added a powerful new engine to its rolling stock. For the purpose of landing it from a Southampton lighter, a temporary line was constructed to the water's edge, where a platform was erected. The engine was conveyed on the

CNR No. 3 shunting at Newport soon after 1900. CNR No. 3 shunting at Newport soon after 1900, fitted with larger cab and Westinghouse brake, but still with wooden brake shoes. The livery displays the company's name in full on the saddle tank side. *IWSR Archive*

This photograph of No. 12 by now rebuilt as an A1X was taken at Newport c. 1920 and is included as it shows clearly the lining and where the bunker extension joins the original. *RP36108*

metals off the lighter across the field to the permanent way at Medham, about a mile from Cowes. The plan adopted for the engine was simplicity itself, and it worked admirably. A gang of men were employed for a week making the necessary preparations.

During 1902 the IWCR was able to raise more capital and start paying off the rolling stock company. However, in October Mr Conacher wrote that No. 7 required new cylinders but the need to make new patterns before casting the cylinders kept it out of service for many months. More bad news was given a few weeks later after No. 3 broke a crank pin, while No. 10 broke a crank axle and was found to require other repairs costing £120.[38]

The purchase of a fourth class A 0-6-0T from the LBSCR was proposed in June 1903 but an offer of 71 *Wapping* for sale at £700 was rejected by the directors on 22 July because of the condition of its boiler and age. Like No. 9, it was one of the first six members of the class built in 1872. No. 71 was later sold for the same amount to the Kent & East Sussex Railway and ran in service as 5 *Rolvendon* until the 1930s. After further enquiries, on 26 August the Manager was authorised to offer £700 for 84 *Crowborough* built in September 1880, with 14in cylinders fitted in March 1892 and a mileage of 614,090. Agreement was reached on 23 September at £725, the price to include new tyres. After a repaint, IWCR 12 left Brighton Works for the Island on 20 November. This time payment was made by the IWCR.

Beyer, Peacock 2-4-0T No. 4 had been out of service awaiting a decision whether to spend £445 on a new boiler, firebox and cylinders from the makers. The directors again hesitated and on 15 June 1904 were informed that the Midland & South Western Junction Railway (MSWJR)

had potential replacements priced between £800 and £1,000, while the LBSCR could offer class A 0-6-0T 648 *Merton* at £750. They opted for the new boiler, etc. There was such a shortage of motive power that trains had to be cancelled or run so late that passengers travelling to the mainland missed their ferries at Cowes or Ryde. Mr Seymour prepared another report: [12]

- No. 1 was laid aside worn out on 30 August 1901, mileage 548,314.
- No. 2 was laid aside worn out on 17 January 1900, mileage 594,769.
- No. 3 was back in service on Medina Jetty, mileage 297,611.
- No. 4 was stopped at Newport awaiting a new boiler and cylinders, mileage 498,968.
- No. 5 received a new boiler in May 1899 and new cylinders February 1903, mileage 506,755.
- No. 6 had been repaired during the winter of 1901-02 when the frames were patched and the boiler retubed, mileage 389,687.
- No. 7 received new cylinders in May 1903, mileage 846,034.
- No. 8 underwent heavy repairs in the winter 1903-04, mileage 187,289.
- No. 9 received new tyres in March 1904, mileage 661,322.
- No. 10 received a new crank axle in April 1903, mileage 647,924.
- No. 11 was fitted with bunker coal rails in October 1904, mileage 601,004.
- No. 12 received a new blast pipe in October 1903, mileage 633,197.

The IWCR Rail motor No. 1 as built, and photographed at Sandown. Interestingly the locomotive carries a Central Railway garter, while the carriage has the company name in full, both styles by then having been superseded by the initials IWCR. Note the locomotive builder's plate on the cab door, the trellis entrance gate above the rear bogie and the curtains dressed at the windows. *O. J. Morris collection ©Rail Archive Stephenson*

The Southern Counties Rolling Stock Co. wanted £500 in exchange for permission to break up Nos 1 and 2 but the directors decided to hand over No. 12 in lieu. After an agreement was sealed in September 1904, they were dismantled and the remains sold for scrap. The boiler from No. 1 was kept back and used to power machinery in the Newport workshop but was evidently placed outside the building as in 1906 a 'house' to cover it was belatedly erected. When the workshop was converted to electricity in 1918, the boiler was sold for £200 to a laundry in Bournemouth.[38]

Several mainland railways were experimenting with steam and petrol-engine motor carriages. This reached the ears of the IWCR directors, who on 23 December 1903 instructed Mr Conacher to make enquiries about their working costs. The matter was raised repeatedly until 23 March 1904, when letters were read from Avonside Engine Co. and H. F. Stephens, Engineer and Locomotive Superintendent of the Kent & East Sussex Railway (KESR). Anxious to see some in operation, the Chairman and Manager visited the GWR's Swindon Works on 22 June and the LSWR's Basingstoke & Alton Light Railway on 13 July. They were pleased with their visits as on 21 December Mr Conacher produced a letter from R. Y. Pickering & Co. offering to build a car similar to one supplied to the KESR for £400. After enquiries the car was rejected as too small for the IWCR's needs. On 3 May 1905 the directors decided to ask for quotes for between one and three 'steam motor cars' seating twelve first- and forty third-class passengers but later opted to reduce the first-class seating to six and seek fresh tenders from Hurst, Nelson & Co., Birmingham Carriage & Wagon Co., Metropolitan Carriage & Wagon Co., and Kitson & Co. The directors then concentrated on the appointment of a

Locomotive Superintendent in place of Mr Seymour, who resigned in July to take up a similar post in Jamaica. Sadly he was killed in an earthquake on 14 January 1907 at the age of 41. His replacement, Robert Guest, worked for the LSWR, latterly as Bournemouth shed foreman, and was an enthusiast of motor cars.[38]

On 25 October 1905 the directors decided to purchase a steam motor car from Hurst, Nelson & Co. for £1,450, to be delivered by 1 March 1906. The makers replied that delivery was unachievable before June but after considering offers from other firms the order was allowed to continue. The carriage was constructed by Hurst, Nelson at their Motherwell Works but the engine portion was supplied by R. & W. Hawthorn & Co. of Newcastle upon Tyne and did not reach Motherwell until 24 September. To save time and expense the motor was worked in steam from Motherwell to Southampton Docks, where it was run along a temporary track and onto a barge prior to shipment to St Helens Quay on 4 October.[47] A description of the engine portion was given in the *Railway Magazine*:[43]

The engine and boiler are of the ordinary locomotive type, carried on a four-wheel bogie. These wheels are coupled and power is transmitted from two high-pressure outside cylinders to the trailing axle. The valve motion is of the Walschaert type, which is particularly adapted to this form of engine. Coal and water are carried in bunkers and side tanks on either side of the boiler, and dry sand is applied to all four-wheels of the engine. The boiler is fitted to the frames in the usual manner, and has been fitted with a pair of Crosby's Patent Duplex Safety Valves.

There was a neat cab, side tanks extending from the footplate to the smokebox front and a copper-capped chimney. The pivot pin for the carriage was located at the rear end of the frames. As with 4-4-0T No. 6, it arrived fitted with the obsolete safety chains on the buffer beams. Control of the regulator from the driving position in the far end of the carriage was by means of a longitudinal shaft under the flooring with a universal joint at the engine end worked by endless cables round pulleys at either end; the Westinghouse brake was fitted. The livery, described as metallic crimson lake, was carried on the engine and the lower carriage panelling, the upper portion being cream. The tank sides were adorned with the garter, arranged 'No. (garter) 1'. It was described in correspondence and the minute book as 'No. 1 Motor'. The carriage portion had to be kept away from the dirt of the running shed, so a separate shed was erected for it at Newport.

Trials were run between Merstone and Ventnor Town on 5 October 1906 with the manufacturers' representatives in attendance, followed by visits to other parts of the railway system, including Ryde Esplanade where a photograph was taken for publicity purposes. The Manager wrote to the directors on 29 October stating that the engine's axle bearings were overheating, possibly because of the lengthy run on the mainland. The maker agreed to supply a free replacement and by 21 January 1907 the motor was in use. A series of comparative tests were held with No. 11 hauling three four-wheeled carriages and a brake van, details being: [12]

| No. 1 Motor | Cost per mile 1.4 d. | Coal burned per mile 13.2 lb |
| No. 11 and train | Cost per mile 1.9 d. | Coal burned per mile 17.8 lb |

The directors were impressed by this reduction in operating costs and instructed Mr Conacher to investigate the possibility of working the Sandown to Newport services in a similar manner. When this proved practicable, on 12 February 1907 they decided to obtain quotes for a motor seating sixty-five and having one third more power than No. 1 Motor. Hurst, Nelson & Co. responded with a price of £2,040 but that was considered too expensive. However, on 25 March Mr Conacher wrote proposing to utilise engine No. 3 with a new carriage, apparently

Mr Guest's idea. Further quotes were requested for one seating eight first- and forty third-class passengers with a guard and luggage compartment[38] and on 27 May Mr Conacher submitted the following offers: [12]

Bristol Carriage & Wagon Co.	£2.398
Metropolitan Amalgamated Carriage & Wagon Co.	£1,630
Hurst, Nelson & Co.	£1,125

The asking prices were again too high, so the matter was deferred until the autumn. On 25 September 1907 Mr Conacher reported that the Midland Railway had offered a bogie composite carriage for sale at £130, its conversion, including fitting the Westinghouse brake and lighting, would increase the cost to about £250. He was authorised to proceed with the purchase, subject to inspection, and spend another £300 on the engine. The carriage had arrived by 20 December.[38]

Instructions were issued for No. 3's conversion to be completed before Easter 1908 but repairs to Nos 9, 6 and 8 intervened. In the meantime, the carriage and an LBSCR 0-6-0T worked the Merstone to Ventnor Town line whenever No. 1 Motor was unavailable. The cab, smokebox, boiler and tanks were neatly encased in steel sheet and the whistle moved to the cab roof. It was said that mechanical pull-push gear was fitted along with some means of communication between the engine and carriage. Painted red, there was a garter on the cab sides, inside which was the number 3 and small shaded lettering on the bodysides spelling out 'Isle of Wight Central Railway'. The carriage was altered to create a driver's compartment in one end. The pair were not truly a rail motor, although always considered as such by Newport Works. As No. 3 Motor, the engine and carriage entered service together on 18 April 1909, having cost a total of £437 9s 5d.[39]

Early in 1908 No. 1 Motor sustained damage to its springs when crossing Towngate viaduct, near Newport, on a run to Freshwater. The engine makers agreed to pay half the cost of replacements, the balance being shared between the IWCR and FYNR. One axle was again overheating but a replacement did not arrive until August and another month elapsed before

IWCR Rail motor No. 3 between St Lawrence and Ventnor Town. On the waist panels, in addition to the class designations on the doors, are the words 'Isle of Wight' between the second and third compartments, 'Central' centrally and 'Railway' between the corresponding second and third compartments at the far end. *L&G*

the motor entered service on the Freshwater line, where the many curves, gradients and lightly ballasted track made for a lively ride at anything more than a slow speed. In October 1909 the firebox and tubes received attention and the carriage lighting was altered from oil to acetylene. After another summer season, the motor was laid aside in November 1910 and during the winter divided into two units. The engine received a small exterior coal bunker before being used spasmodically for light shunting and ballasting duties.

No. 3 Motor proved to be a dismal failure. The engine struggled with the heavy carriage and by February 1911 was unserviceable. The pair were split up in June 1912, after having travelled just 6,892 miles. It remained in store until May 1913, when the casing was removed from the boiler prior to a return to shunting on Medina Jetty.[12] Thus ended the IWCR's dalliance with rail motor cars. As other railways found, savings gained from their operation were illusionary as they cost more to build and maintain. The motor cars also lacked flexibility, an important factor on a railway the size of the IWCR where an engine might have to work both passenger and goods trains during the course of a day's work.

Returning to the conventional engines, the NLR 4-4-0T No. 7 had been repaired during the winter of 1902–03 but within two years was suffering from leaking tubes and a fractured steam chest. At the time no suitable second-hand replacements were available, so £59 was spent on minor repairs. The end came when a tube burst while working the 9.30pm Ryde St John's Road to Newport goods train on 23 July 1906. The local scrap merchants were given the task of dismantling the engine at Medina Jetty during January–February 1907, following which the remains were shipped to the mainland for melting down. The driving wheels were kept back for possible use on No. 6 but thankfully never needed. A replacement was sought and on 31 October 1906 the following offers were considered:[12]

LBSCR	Class D 0-4-2T 11 *Selhurst* built 1874, new boiler 1892, at £995
	Class E 0-6-0T 99 *Bordeaux* built 1874, new boiler and cylinders 1901, at £940
MSWJR	Beyer, Peacock 2-4-0T No. 6 built 1882, new copper firebox and cylinders 1902, at £695

An offer of £650 for the Beyer, Peacock 2-4-0T was refused but the MSWJR did agree to renew the brick arch and remove the vacuum brake before delivery to Southampton Docks. Purchased for the asking price of £695, it reached the Island on 2 December 1906 and began work as IWCR No. 7 five days later.[12]

IWCR No. 3 in 1914 following disbandment of its use as Rail motor No. 3. The cladding surrounding the boiler and smokebox has been removed but the incongruously large cab remains. Traces of round-cornered double lining are just visible on the saddle tank side, as is the company name in full, while a square-cornered, single line may be discerned on the cab complete with the Central Railway garter. *LPC/RP 36105*

2-4-0T No. 7 at Cowes soon after purchase, showing clearly the extent of the lining applied with the I W C R lettering style. Of interest are the inverted, rounded corners on the tank and bunker sides, and note also lining to the driving wheel bosses and the ends of the buffer beams. *O.I. Morris ©Rail Archive Stephenson*

The 2-4-0T had been ordered in March 1882 with two others from Beyer, Peacock & Co. (order 6219) by the Swindon, Marlborough & Andover Railway and delivered on 7 July at a cost of £1,995. Generally similar to the IWR 2-4-0T *Brading*, the driving wheels and bunker were larger, the tank capacity less and the braking was steam. The cab had two large round lookouts to the front and two rectangular ones at the back. It was the first to carry 'I. W. C. R.' in shaded lettering on the tank sides, with matching numerals on the bunker sides and 'No. 7' on the rear.

Despite the introduction of a less prominent livery, Mr Conacher continued to take every opportunity to publicise the IWCR's existence to the general public. In an interview for the *Railway Magazine* he disclosed that summer 'passenger trains cover a distance of 5,000 miles weekly, and the service is not much less in winter'. He did not mention difficulties caused by a lack of working capital. In July 1908 the directors refused permission to spend £220 on buying a second-hand wheel lathe from the LSWR but agreed to pay £46 for a wheel press from Loudon Bros. Delays in the Newport workshops, caused mainly by work on the rail motors, aggravated a shortage of useable engines and the directors were pressed to sanction the acquisition of additional motive power.[39]

On 26 May 1908 the IWCR directors discussed a report from Mr Guest recommending the purchase of an engine from the Metropolitan Railway for £500 but were 'unable to contemplate the expenditure'. According to Mr Bradley, LSWR Metropolitan-type 4-4-0T No. 0319 was inspected that month but was refused as the firebox could only be guaranteed for 10,000 miles. One of six built in January 1875 by Beyer, Peacock & Co. (maker's No. 1355), it was withdrawn in January 1909.[33] Unlikely as it may seem, on 9 July an offer was apparently made to buy LSWR class O2 0-4-4T No. 209 (later W24 *Calbourne*) for £750. The IWCR minute book is silent on the matter but it may have been an initiative by Mr Guest, who knew it to be a better proposition than the Metropolitan engines. Mr Drummond, the LSWR Locomotive Superintendent, was supposedly prepared to sell No. 209 for £1,285 including an overhaul, spare parts, the Westinghouse brake and delivery to St Helens or Ryde, but wanted payment in advance and broke off negotiations when this was not forthcoming.[12] More offers were considered by the IWCR directors on 12 August and written into the minute book. The asking prices differ from those quoted elsewhere and the engines concerned were not always identified.[38]

LBSCR	Class D 0-4-2T 23 *Mayfield* built 1875, at £1,000
Metropolitan Railway	Beyer, Peacock 4-4-0T at £480
MSWJR	Beyer, Peacock 2-4-0T at £800
GWR	Sharp Stewart 2-4-2T 1304 *Plynlimmon* built in 1891 for the Manchester & Milford Railway as their No. 2 at £800

After further correspondence from Messrs Conacher and Guest, on 26 September 1908 the directors agreed to ask the Cambrian Railways Engineer to inspect *Plynlimmon* with a view to offering £700 if found satisfactory. However, by the time the report was received the summer season had ended, so the purchase was deferred. When a fresh enquiry was made in February 1909 the GWR replied tersely that *Plynlimmon* was no longer for disposal.

A fresh list of offers from the MSWJR, LBSCR and LSWR was put to the directors on 28 April 1909, none of which was considered acceptable. Mr Guest then wrote on 25 May recommending the purchase of a 0-4-4T from Frazer & Co., locomotive dealers for £875. Since the engine had not been used for eight years, the directors offered £700 but that was rejected so the Manager was authorised to raise the offer to £850 'as the matter was pressing'. After Mr Conacher wrote reporting success on 28 June, it was towed by rail from the North East and shipped by barge to St Helens Quay on 11 July.

With a marked similarity to the NER Fletcher class BTP, the 0-4-4T had been built at Seaham Works to the design of George Hardy for the Marquis of Londonderry's Railway. Construction of No. 21 probably began in April 1895 but, given the modest size of the workforce, would have taken several months to complete. The engine was employed on a passenger service between Seaham and Sunderland but on 7 October 1900 the Company was taken over by the NER. Soon afterwards it was renumbered 1712 before being laid aside in store at Percy Main with a mileage of 84,217.[12]

The IWCR directors and management evidently failed to appreciate the size and weight of what they had purchased as the new arrival was tight to the loading gauge, spread the track and caused other damage. To bring the weight down to 40 tons, various handrails and fittings were removed, the tanks shortened to reduce capacity to 600 gallons and the coal capacity limited to 1½ tons. It was also necessary to lower the track under a few bridges between Cowes and Ryde. Equipped with the Westinghouse brake and painted in lined red livery, IWCR No. 2 performed reasonably well in service but suffered badly from priming and was less sure footed than Nos 6 and 7. Trips to Freshwater resulted in complaints of track damage but it did see some use on the Merstone to Ventnor line.

Between Newport and Cowes, a private level crossing to Cement Mills was the location of numerous accidents. In July 1907 one of the Isle of Wight's first motor cars was wrecked by a train and in October 1909 a cart was smashed when struck at speed by the 11.45am train from Cowes. On both occasions the directors denied any liability. Warning boards were erected at the crossing, engine drivers were instructed to sound their whistles and the cement company was issued with padlocks and keys for the gates, not that this stopped them from being left open.[48] On 23 October 1909 4-4-0T No. 6 was being prepared for the 3.20pm Newport to Ryde train when at 2.55pm its driver was ordered to remove five coal trucks from a goods train arriving from Medina Jetty and fly-shunt them into the 'long siding'. This he hastened to do

Illustrations of IWCR 0-4-4T No. 2 on the Island are rare. This retouched view shows it being readied to be hauled off the barge at St Helens in July 1909. Note the deep buffer beam and the two holes where a lower pair of buffers had originally been fitted to be compatible with chaldron wagons. *IWSR Archive*

but forgot about other wagons, which rebounded towards No. 6. A swift brake application would probably have avoided serious trouble but the driver panicked and opened the regulator, causing a collision so violent that the leading coal truck was crushed against the engine.[12]

The Company's lack of capital precluded any thoughts about electrification or other more efficient operating methods. However, in December 1909 the Manager had a meeting at Newport with a Mr Marshall, who represented the Electric Railways Syndicate and was seeking support for the amalgamation and electrification of the Island's railways. Any notion that the IWCR would have anything to do with the proposals was quickly scotched.[38]

Charles Conacher left the Company in 1910 for an equally thankless task managing the Cambrian Railways. His departure came not a moment too soon as in 1911 Harry Willmott and other shareholders engineered a takeover of the directorship and Willmott got himself appointed Chairman. An experienced railwayman, he persuaded the directors to commission an independent report into the condition of the engines and rolling stock. Written by Mr Thom, who occupied a senior position at Doncaster Works, it contradicted one from Mr Guest and made unpleasant reading:[46]

- No. 1 had just returned to service following repairs and alterations lasting six months. The water spaces in the front and back of the boiler were dirty and full of sediment. About thirty boiler tubes needed replacement.
- No. 2 had spiral springs to the leading axleboxes that caused the engine to hunt and roll when running. A new arrangement was suggested and various faults with the boiler needed correcting. (The springing was later modified.) The copper boiler tubes were in poor condition, so it was recommended they be sold, the income more than covering the cost of buying and fitting steel replacements.
- No. 3 had a broken left cylinder and crank pin. The crank axle and coupling rods were bent, while several of the mixed brass and steel tubes needed renewing. New cylinders had been ordered and the wheels sent to Hawthorn Leslie & Co. for attention. The 0-4-2T was worth repairing only because some expenditure had already been incurred.
- No. 4 had not been in the workshop since 1905. The boiler tubes needed replacement but, more seriously, the firebox was so unsafe that the engine had to be stopped for a thorough overhaul.
- No. 5 had last been in the workshop in 1906. The boiler tubes and firebox were little better than No. 4 but temporary repairs were made so the engine could continue working for another three months.
- No. 6 was in the workshop for repairs. The copper back plate was so thin that it could not carry any pressure.
- No. 7 had not been in the workshop since purchase in 1906. The main frames were broken, the engine

was riding badly on the springs and the firebox was in a poor condition.
- No. 8 had been in the workshop in 1907 and was in fair condition. However, the boiler tubes were in a poor state and needed renewing.
- No. 9 had not been in the workshop for eight years. Surprisingly, the boiler tubes were in fair condition although due for replacement. The springs and axleboxes and other motion work were worn and needed an overhaul.
- No. 10 had returned to service in February 1911 after spending twelve months undergoing repairs. Parts of the copper firebox were thin and the manner in which the boiler and firebox had been repaired was unsatisfactory.
- No. 11 had spent 1909 in the workshop but already the axleboxes were worn, while the firebox was so thin that the engine was dangerous and unfit for use.
- No. 12 had never been overhauled since its purchase in 1902. The brakes, springs, axleboxes, boiler tubes and firebox were all in a bad state. To keep the engine serviceable, repairs were needed to the firebox and the boiler pressure reduced from 140 to 120psi. No. 12 was mainly employed shunting on Medina Jetty.
- Four self-propelled steam cranes on Medina Jetty were in an even worse condition, two of which required replacement boilers. (The cranes disappeared after a new concrete wharf came into use in 1931.)

The report was quickly followed by the resignation of Mr Guest. However, the employment of Mr (later Colonel) H. F. Stephens to oversee engineering matters on a part-time basis lasted only a couple of months and by the end of the year Harry Willmott's son Russell had been appointed Manager, Engineer and Locomotive Superintendent. Together, father and son greatly improved the management, operation and profitability of the Company.[38]

Russell Willmott's arrival in January 1912 was followed by a change in the livery to black with vermilion lining edged in fine white lines; the buffer beams were vermilion as previously, No. 2 apparently had the footplate valance painted red and some engines had red coupling rods.[24] The lettering was abbreviated to 'I. W. C.' in gilt with brown shading and a matching running number on the cab side. The number was repeated on the buffer beams to the right of the coupling in yellow shaded black.[10] This livery had been carried by engines on Mr Willmott's previous railway, the Stratford-upon-Avon and Midland Junction Railway. Several staff came across to the Isle of Wight to help bring the IWCR up to an acceptable standard, additional workshop machinery and tools were purchased and progress was made in reducing the arrears of maintenance. Normality had been achieved by 1914, when a replacement firebox was ordered for No. 8 and new injectors and brake gear for No. 7.

Early in 1912 the winter passenger service was cut back drastically and the number of engines in steam reduced. Economies in shunting were achieved following the

IWCR No. 11, the third 'Terrier', was given two coal rails in 1904 to increase its coal capacity. This view at Newport is post-1912, when black livery, lettered I.W.C. and with simplified lining, was applied. Note also that iron brake blocks are fitted; also the 'Newport' destination board. *H Gordon Tidey*

construction of additional sidings at Newport and Medina Jetty and more savings were made after the FYNR went its own way in July 1913. The working agreement obliged the Freshwater Company to buy engines and stock used on the line and although Nos 4 and 6 were offered, a price could not be agreed. This left the IWCR with a distinct surplus of motive power, so it was hardly surprising that at the end of the 1913 summer season Nos 1 and 2 were put into store in the rail motor shed, soon to be joined by No. 3.

Bob Glassey joined the Company as locomotive foreman at Newport on 13 July 1914. At one time an engine driver on the Caledonian Railway, he came from the Lancashire, Derbyshire and East Coast Railway, for whom both Harry and Russell Willmott had worked in the past. Remaining at Newport well into SR days, Mr MacLeod described him as 'a real character'. His main claim to fame was the introduction of Caledonian type hooters on the IWCR; only the LBSCR engines kept their original whistles. They helped the signalmen at Ryde distinguish between approaching IWR and IWCR trains.[41]

Unlike a few of the Company's purchases, the four LBSCR class A 0-6-0Ts proved to be excellent investments. Nos 11 and 12 had arrived fitted with iron brake shoes, an advantage that was eventually extended to the older pair. All four acquired replacement chimneys supplied by the Newport foundry of Wheeler & Hurst. The limited coal-carrying capacity was a handicap on the IWCR, where they were running close to 800 miles a week. No. 11 had the coal bunker fitted with two coal rails in 1904 but they blocked the view from the lookouts. Nothing more was

done until December 1912, when the bunker on No. 9 was extended in place of a rear toolbox at a cost of £9.[38] The other three were later similarly modified.

The provision of new boilers for the LBSCR 0-6-0Ts had been suggested in the 1911 report but several years elapsed before it was acted on. On the mainland many of the class found a fresh lease of life following the introduction of pull-push working on the LBSCR in 1905. To allow for their continued use, twelve engines were turned out by Brighton Works between 1911 and 1913 with replacement boilers; another went to the Newhaven Harbour Co.'s *Fenchurch*. Designed by D. E. Marsh, the Locomotive Superintendent, the barrel was constructed in one ring while the dome and spring balance safety valves were sited further forward than previously. A new cast saddle was fitted to support a longer circular smokebox, along with separate splashers and larger steam-worked sandboxes under the footplate. Engines with these boilers were designated class A1X (the unaltered examples became class A1).

Two additional boilers were built by the LBSCR for the IWCR at a cost of £1,195 each. One was fitted to No. 12 in July 1916 and the second to No. 11 in August 1918. The old boiler from No. 12 was repaired by Brighton Works at a cost of £184 and transferred to No. 9. The LBSCR supplied new 14in diameter cylinders for Nos 9, 10 and 12 fitted in March 1917, June 1915 and March 1916 respectively, while No. 11 gained a 13in set in May 1918. The Island engines retained the existing combined splashers and sandboxes with gravity feed. When fresh from Newport Works, Nos 11 and 12 had lined boiler bands and scarlet coupling rods.

This image depicts IWCR No. 11 as cosmetically restored at Havenstreet in 1975 and, apart from a replica chimney, represents her post-1918 appearance. Photographic evidence of No. 11 in late IWCR days shows a wooden cab door, possibly the driver's personal embellishment as it has not been recorded on other Central Terriers. *John Goss*

0-4-4T No. 2 was sold in 1917 'as it stood' to Armstrong Whitworth & Co., Elswick, for £1,200 and departed by barge from Ryde Pier on 17 July. The factory at Elswick was mainly concerned with armaments and went into decline after the Great War. No. 26, as it became, is understood to have been scrapped there in 1921 or 1922.[38] Encouraged by the high prices, on 30 October 1917 Russell Willmott recommended the sale of Nos 1, 3 and 4. Nos 1 and 3 had been stored for upwards of five years, while No. 4 was laid aside with worn out cylinders. The directors were informed on 14 February 1918 that 1 and 3 had been sold for £950 and £750 respectively to Holloway Brothers Ltd, London, who had a government contract to lay out the yards of the Furness Withy Shipbuilding Co. at Haverton Hill on the north bank of the River Tees opposite Middlesbrough. Both kept their existing liveries, although No. 1 had the tanks sides inscribed with the buyer's number 8 before departing for the mainland. On completion of the contract later that year, Robert Stephenson & Co. carried out some repairs prior to No. 1's sale to William Benson & Sons Ltd of Fourstones Quarry, Hexham, where breaking up took place sometime after the end of the war. No. 3 was sold for use in Plenmeller Colliery, near Haltwhistle. It was still there in 1930 but probably went for scrap when the colliery closed in May 1932. No. 4 remained unsold in store at Newport.[35]

On 1 March 1919 an 'Appendix to the Working Time Tables and to the Book of Rules and Regulations' was issued to staff. The document brought together existing instructions on a range of operational matters including whistle codes, lamp positions and the working of mixed trains. There was even a lengthy list of tools that each driver was expected to have with him. For haulage purposes, engines were placed in one of three classes and allocated maximum loads: class A Nos 6 and 7, class

B 9–12 and class C 4, 5 and 8. Engines were required to carry the following headcode 'Head-Lamps'.

Passenger and mixed trains	one white light over the left-hand buffer
Light engines	one white light over the right-hand buffer
Goods and coal trains	one white light over both buffers

Those working passenger trains also carried small red-painted destination boards on a spare lamp iron. Owing to the prevailing gradients, IWCR engines faced towards Ryde but there were exceptions as during 1920 No. 6 was seen running chimney first to Cowes.[49]

According to Mr Bradley, Kitson & Co.'s order book contained a copy of a letter from the IWCR dated 16 July 1919 asking for the cost of two six-coupled tank engines having a maximum axle loading of 13½ tons, a bunker capacity of 70cu ft and the ability to work 170-ton trains between Cowes and Ryde. The reply on 24 September proposed two 2-6-0Ts with 17in by 24in outside cylinders, 5ft 3in coupled wheels and a weight of 41 tons, priced at £4,175 each. Although apparently suitable, they were refused on 20 November as it was cheaper to repair the existing motive power.

Beyer, Peacock 2-4-0T No. 7 underwent an overhaul at Newport between November 1919 and April 1920. The boiler was reconditioned and the firebox renewed, Ramsbottom safety valves and a closed dome were fitted along with a shorter cast iron chimney courtesy of Wheeler & Hurst's Newport foundry. No. 4 received an overhaul that included a new chimney, cylinders and extended cab sides to match No. 5.

The final IWCR livery is shown well in this view of No. 7 ex-works at Newport in 1920. Corners have now reverted to being normal rounded. *IWSR Archive*

No. 8 was the first IWCR locomotive to be repainted in Southern colours and is seen here at Ventnor West c. 1925. This rear end view shows the enclosed bunker fitted by the IWCR and the SR cast bunker number plate in addition to the painted numerals on the buffer beam. *RP 4183*

On 3 July 1920 No. 11 was hauling the 1.24pm Saturdays only passenger train from Ryde Pier Head when the trailing axle broke as the train approached St John's Road, damaging about 45 yards of track and delaying services for an hour. The 0-6-0T had received an overhaul the previous January but a flaw in the axle had not been detected. Brighton Works supplied replacement axles, the first of several.[12]

No.	Olive green	Dark green
W5	5.1924	
W8	4.1924	
W9	8.1924	
W10	by 4.1925	5.1930
W11	5.1924	12.1927
W12	5.1925	8.1927

July 1921	New driving and leading axles for No. 11
February 1922	New axles and wheels for No. 12
February 1923	New driving axle and wheels for No. 9

The IWCR suffered a major tragedy when Russell Willmott died from cancer on 25 June 1920 aged only 40. He had overseen an improvement in the Company's fortunes since his arrival in 1912 and this was nowhere more evident than in the condition of the motive power. Proposals for the grouping of Britain's railways were being considered so it was hardly surprising that his successor, George Newcombe, made no significant changes before the SR took charge.[38]

Nine engines entered SR stock on 1 January 1923 and were allocated Nos W4–12. W4, 6 and 7 remained in IWCR livery until withdrawal although a SR number plate was carried by W6 (and perhaps W7). Six were repainted in lined green:[21]

For the 1923 summer season Newport shed rostered six engines for the former IWCR services, an increase of one compared with previous years, plus a further one when responsibility was taken back for the Freshwater line. There were no motive power changes until early in 1924, when there was an influx of IWR engines. After undergoing repairs and repaints, W9 went to the Freshwater line while W11 took charge of the Ventnor West branch. W5 was transferred to Ryde for the Bembridge branch, with W6 for the Ryde to Ventnor line. The Ryde crews complained that W6 lost time consistently and the brakes were inferior to those on the IWR 2-4-0Ts; it was probably the engine whose failure at Wroxall on 2 August greatly disrupted the evening passenger service. Consequently, W6 was confined to shunting at Ryde because, as reported on 4 May 1925, it could not be used elsewhere:[10]

The Engineer has recently debarred Engine No. 6 from working on any part of the Island, except Ryde and

Preserved A1X W11 currently carries early SR olive green livery as applied during the 1920s and, correctly, does not carry a nameplate. Seen at Havenstreet on 14 September 2014. *John Faulkner*

Ventnor. It would be considerable assistance to us if he could see his way to withdraw this restriction in view of the fact that this Engine originally belonged to the IoW Central Railway and had therefore been constantly employed upon the Newport and Ryde services. Further, we think it is doubtful whether the weights approach those of Diagram No. 22 Class [class O2], which Engines are allowed on the Ryde, Cowes and Sandown services. In other words, it is necessary for No. 6 Engine to take up the same working as Diagram 22 Class.

The plea was in vain as the restrictions remained in place until its withdrawal. W6 was not the only IWCR engine to have its workings restricted as W7 was not permitted to run over the Freshwater line and latterly W8 was allowed on the Ventnor West branch only one day a week 'for relief purposes'.[30] By May 1924 W7 and W12 were said to be badly in need of a refit but only W12 benefited from repairs before the workshop at Newport closed in May 1925. W4 was withdrawn in July 1925, W6 was laid aside later that year, while W5 and W7 were withdrawn in April 1926; all were sold for scrap.[10]

Beyer, Peacock 2-4-0T W8 lingered on for several years. Unable to handle the heavier trains, it was soon relegated to a spare at Newport, deputised on the Freshwater and Ventnor West lines, but saw little use following the introduction of pull-push working on the latter. In August 1925 P. C. Allen noted the 2-4-0T's presence at Ryde but its charms were not appreciated and within months a return had been made to Newport shed. Alistair MacLeod, who took charge of the Island's motive power in 1928, noted that W8 was in relatively good condition but the boiler was too small for it to be of any practical value. An overhaul might have helped but that was not forthcoming.[10] Early in 1929 the 2-4-0T went back to Ryde for employment on the Bembridge branch. Although allocated the name *Bembridge*, the nameplates were never fitted and withdrawal took place in December. When seen lying at the back of Newport shed on 22 February 1930 the cab had been removed for reuse on the IWR 2-4-0T W16 *Wroxall*. Breaking up by Messrs W. Hurst & Son began a month later.[29]

Of the four LBSCR A1 and A1X 0-6-0Ts, W9 lasted only a short time. It was equipped with pull-push gear in February–March 1926 but remained in service on the Freshwater line until 19 October, when the two leading wheels left the track near Watchingwell. The driver was blamed for exceeding the 30mph speed limit when running downhill on the lightly laid track.[28] In January 1927 the engine entered Ryde Works for an overhaul but the general condition was found to be so poor that it was withdrawn as beyond economic repair. Sold to a local scrap merchant, W9 was broken up in the gasworks siding at St Helens Quay.

W10 and W12 acquired pull-push gear in February–March 1926 followed by steam-heating fittings in October 1927. W12 underwent an overhaul in December 1929 and received the boiler fitted to W11 in 1918 but discarded in 1927. *Ventnor* nameplates were attached prior to a return to service in May 1930. W10 was overhauled in February 1930 and given the 1916 boiler taken off W12, an LBSCR Marsh chimney and the name *Cowes* before leaving works in April. By then the 1916 and 1918 boilers had a lower working pressure of 140psi and one register noted them as A1 pattern. LSWR Drummond-pattern chimneys were fitted during 1932. W10 *Cowes* and W12 *Ventnor* were returned to the mainland in May 1936, withdrawn and stored in the Eastleigh paint shop. The pair were moved to the works dump on 8 April 1940 and, although the boilers were never reused, other spare parts were recovered. They were eventually broken up in the week ending 2 April 1949.[31]

W11 is the last survivor of the IWCR's engines. It is believed to have been one of the first to be equipped with pull-push gear in 1924 for service on the Ventnor West branch with two sets of newly transferred LCDR carriages; certainly it was a favourite on the line. An LBSCR A1X-pattern boiler was sent from the mainland and fitted during an overhaul lasting from October to December 1927. As with the other Island rebuilds, the combined splashers and sandboxes were retained and steam-heating equipment was added. The nameplates for *Newport* were fitted following a repaint in June 1930 and further overhauls included one in 1939, when the boiler was again changed. W11 remained active until cement production ceased at Cement Mills on 30 June 1944 but was rarely used thereafter. Following removal of the pull-push gear and Westinghouse brake, the engine was shipped back to the mainland on 22 February 1947 still in the pre-war dark green livery. It was taken into Eastleigh Works in July to receive repairs, the vacuum brake and a repaint in unlined black with the mainland number 2640. After a week spent shunting at Winchester, 2640 was transferred to Fratton for the Hayling Island services, where it remained apart from a short visit to the Kent & East Sussex line in mid-1948. Returned to Eastleigh Works in March 1951, this overhaul was accompanied by a repaint in BR lined black as 32640. The boiler carried since 1939 was changed during the next overhaul in February 1956 and another was fitted in November 1958. After many years spent working on the Hayling Island branch, 32640 was transferred to Brighton as coal stage pilot in May 1963, from where withdrawal took place in September. Although scheduled for breaking up in February 1964, it was one of three members of the class to be sold to Sir Billy Butlin. The engine was painted in an approximation of the LBSCR Stroudley livery at Eastleigh Works and put on display at the Pwllheli holiday camp. Rescued for preservation, it was returned to the Isle of Wight in January 1973.

Following closure of Newport Works the building was used for the dismantling of old locomotives. At some period in the latter half of 1925, RNR No. 4 is being stripped of any useful parts, while behind is IWR W15 *Ventnor* undergoing the same treatment. *IWSR Archive*

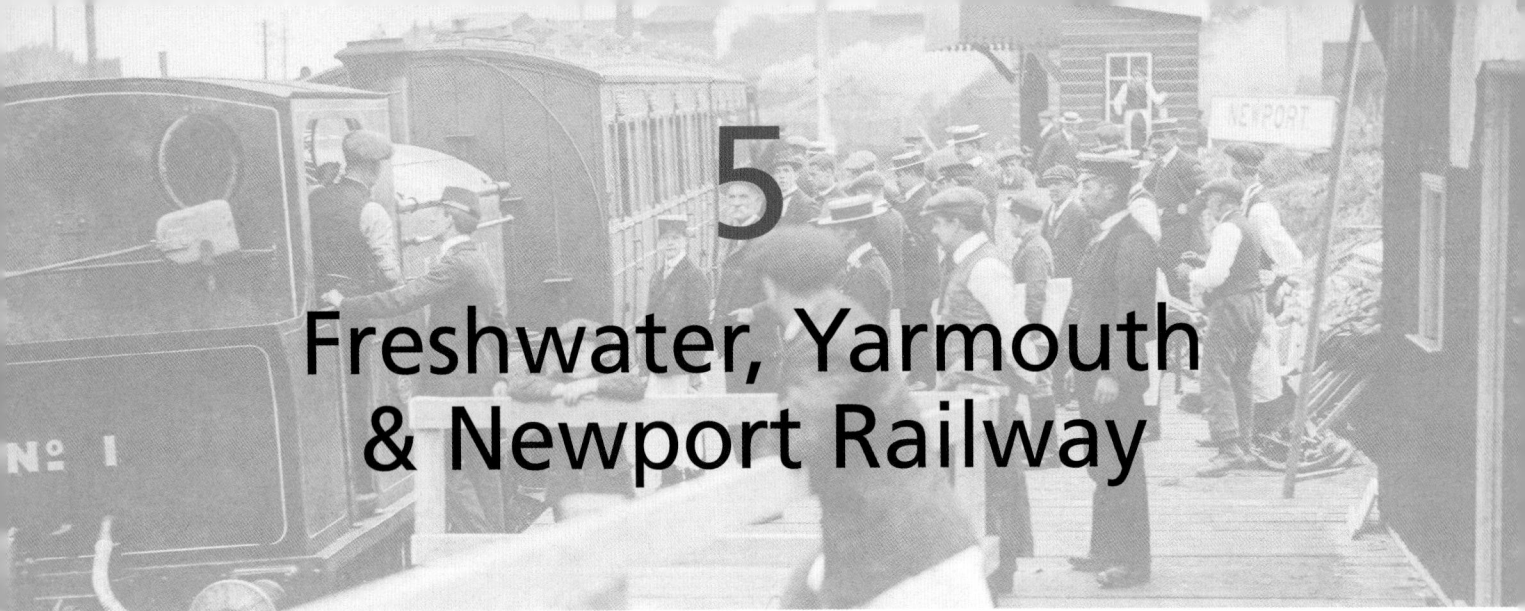

5
Freshwater, Yarmouth & Newport Railway

A contract with William Jackson to construct the 12-mile Freshwater to Newport railway was sealed on 10 March 1886. Work began later that year near Yarmouth at a point beside the River Yar where materials could be landed. The line was constructed cheaply by following the contours, avoiding major earthworks and tunnels but creating a series of switchback gradients and 6¾ miles of curves. There were two engineering features of note, a brick and iron trestle viaduct at Town Gate, Newport, and a second trestle viaduct near Calbourne. The lack of a direct connection to Newport station meant that engines had to run round trains each time they arrived from and departed for Freshwater. It was not until 1911 that the Board of Trade authorised the propelling of trains into the station.[50]

One engine is known to have worked on the construction of the railway. *Freshwater* was a compact 0-6-0T, one of a class of four built by Robert Stephenson & Co., two in 1876 (maker's Nos 2309 and 2310) and two in 1885 (maker's Nos 2383 and 2384). According to the general arrangement drawing, construction of No. 2383, later *Freshwater*, began on 13 April 1885 but whether it was for an order that was later cancelled is not known. Certainly there was delay before the engine was sold to Mr Jackson.[51] According to Mr Bradley, it was dispatched by the maker on 6 June 1887 and landed at Yarmouth eight days later.[12] *Freshwater* was painted green with lining to the tank side, cab side, cab rear sheet, running plate and wheel centres. The name was in shaded lettering on the tank and maker's plates were carried on the rectangular sandboxes. (Known dimensions are in Appendix 2.)

Freshwater was set to work hauling materials as construction progressed towards Freshwater and Newport. The 0-6-0T was also called upon to work a number of special trains. The first took place on the occasion of Queen Victoria's Golden Jubilee (20 June 1887), when several journeys were run between Yarmouth and Freshwater for local residents. On 12 May 1888 the *Isle of Wight County Press* described a second trial run from Betty Haunt Lane,

near Carisbrooke, to Freshwater and back when two contractor's wagons, dressed for the occasion, carried the Island's deputy governor. A further journey took place on 10 August when a single wagon, equipped with padded seats and lined with green baize, accommodated the Engineer, contractor and six other worthies. Goods traffic began on 1 September when *Freshwater* hauled two wagons of coal from Newport to Freshwater. The line was not ready for passenger use but on 9 October a fourteen-carriage excursion ran from IWR stations to Newport, from where the excursionists were conveyed free of charge to Yarmouth and Freshwater. At Newport three more carriages were added for local dignitaries, their families and friends. Another ten-carriage train was hauled to Ryde and back on 30 April 1889 for the Ashey races.[36]

A Board of Trade inspector visited the line on 2 May 1889, during which two IWCR engines, Nos 5 and 7, were utilised for testing the bridges while *Freshwater* ran on the IWCR. Approval was given after a second visit on 3 June but the IWCR was reluctant to work the line and delayed opening until 20 July. The IWCR provided motive power, rolling stock and operating staff in return for 45% of the gross receipts, while the FYNR had responsibility for maintenance of the permanent way, fencing and signalling. Engine and carriage sheds had been constructed at Freshwater but were rarely used as trains started and ended their journeys at Newport. Constructed in wood and corrugated iron, one of the buildings blew down during high winds in January 1890 and had to be rebuilt at the insistence of the IWCR, even though they had no use for it.[50] The FYNR directors were disappointed if they expected to see any new engines on the Freshwater services as trains were usually hauled by one of the elderly 2-2-2 well tanks. At busy periods during the 1890 summer 4-4-0T No. 7 was employed but had to be forbidden following damage to track on the curves.[12]

On 24 December 1889 William Jackson 'surreptitiously' removed *Freshwater* to the IWR's Ryde Works for repairs and negotiated its sale to the London & St Katherine Dock Co.

The contractor's locomotive *Freshwater* believed to have been photographed at Newport c. 1889. The cleanliness and polishing pattern suggests that it was being used for an official occasion, although that has not been recorded. Note the wooden brake blocks. *IWSR Archive*

The FYNR's Manning, Wardle 0-6-0T No. 1 is seen at the new FYNR Newport station still in the course of erection during July 1913. This view shows the livery clearly, with the number prominently on the bunker. *IWSR Archive*

On becoming aware of this, the FYNR took court action to regain possession on the contention that the materials and machinery became the property of the Company following completion of the contract. The case came before Mr Justice Kay in the Chancery Division of the High Court of Justice on Tuesday, 14 January 1890 but was adjourned while the plaintiffs gathered evidence. Jackson became bankrupt before this could happen and, although *Freshwater* was in FYNR hands by 28 March, two of the directors had to find £300 in cash to get it. This probably included the cost of the repairs as the IWR, in the absence of any payment, chained the engine to the rails in the workshop and guarded it day and night to pre-empt clandestine recovery. Only after the money was received was *Freshwater* released.[50]

Freshwater then passed into the hands of Henry Jackson, William's brother, who took over maintenance of the permanent way. The engine left the Island in about October 1891 and with the name *Longdown* was used by James and John Dickson constructing the Exeter to Christow line until work halted due to a lack of funds.[12] Similar difficulties were experienced by Henry Jackson, who in 1891 contracted to build the Weston, Clevedon & Portishead Light Railway. When he gave up the contract in 1897, the engine was on site at Weston-super-Mare and subsequently purchased by the Company. Employed as a 2-4-0T with the name *Portishead*, it reverted to an 0-6-0T when sold in April 1900 to the Renishaw Iron Co. for £950. Withdrawn in 1937, breaking up took place following the outbreak of war.

Income never reached expectations and the FYNR was soon being managed by a receiver. Henry Jackson did as little as possible to maintain the permanent way and that became obvious when the heavier Beyer, Peacock 2-4-0Ts began working the line in 1895. On 30 March, No. 5 and the leading carriage of the 1.00pm Newport to Freshwater train derailed shortly after leaving Newport. The line at this point was on a sharp curve and a large number of decayed sleepers had allowed the gauge to spread by 1⅜in. The incident came to the attention of the Board of Trade, whose inspector caustically commented 'a heavy responsibility will rest upon all concerned if the admitted defects are not remedied, and a very different state of maintenance ensured in the future'. Within weeks a new receiver had been appointed and Henry Jackson dismissed. Money was found to fund permanent way improvements that finally put the railway in a satisfactory condition.[19]

The arrival of Charles Conacher as IWCR Manager ushered in a more harmonious period. When the IWCR purchased a steam rail motor in 1906 the FYNR directors requested that it run on their line as part of an increased frequency of trains during the summer months. They got their wish in 1908 when the disused carriage shed at Freshwater was renovated prior to the introduction of an early morning departure to Newport. However, the arrangement was unpopular with crews, who had to lodge overnight, so the working ended at the end of the summer season. Old animosities re-emerged following Mr Conacher's resignation in 1910, especially after Harry Willmott took over as IWCR Chairman.[50]

On 4 June 1912 the FYNR directors noted that the working agreement was due to expire at the end of the year and agreed that a 'gentleman experienced in railway matters' be asked to advise on future working of the line. That person was Sam Fay, Manager of the Great Central Railway (GCR). His advice was that the existing and proposed agreements were so adverse to the Company that they would be better off working their own line. The directors were loath to sever links with the IWCR and an attempt was made to gain an amicable arrangement but without success. Matters came to a head on 19 November when it was agreed to extend the working agreement for six months but give formal notice that the agreement would end following the arrival of the last train at Newport on 30 June 1913. The directors agreed to purchase some second-hand carriages but two engines on offer by the LBSCR were rejected because both required heavy boiler repairs. They were:[12]

Class A1 0-6-0T 637 *Southdown* built in May 1878, priced at £725

Class E1 0-6-0T 688 *Rhine* built April 1883, at £970

The working agreement obliged the FYNR to purchase engines and stock used on the line whenever the agreement ended. According to the IWCR, that consisted of two engines, six carriages and thirty-three goods trucks. Nos 4 and 6 were declined after inspection as too expensive and in poor mechanical order but five carriages and thirty-one wagons were purchased for £1,400. Instead, Sam Fay negotiated the purchase and loan of two engines from the mainland.[50]

No. 56 *Northolt* was an 0-6-0 saddle tank built by Manning, Wardle & Co. of Leeds, one of two supplied as order No. 50700 in 1902 to the contractors Pauling & Co. A member of the maker's class Q, it was a more modern version of the IWR's *Bembridge* with a roomy cab, steam brakes and small driving wheels that gave good traction on adverse gradients. Having been built to a robust industrial design, the engine was simple and easy to maintain. *Northolt* was delivered to Uxbridge and employed on construction of the Great Western & Great Central Joint Railway from Northolt to High Wycombe, a substantial contract on which Pauling & Co. used thirty-four engines, including some LBSCR class A 0-6-0Ts. After the line opened in 1906, it assisted on work to extend the Great Western Railway Camerton branch to Limpley Stoke, completed in 1910, but then disappeared from sight until purchased by the FYNR on 4 June 1913 for £725.[12]

Before delivery *Northolt* apparently visited the GCR workshops in Gorton, Manchester, where it was repainted in the GCR passenger engine livery: emerald green with a black border edged in white to the tank side, cab side, bunker side and rear. The tank side was lettered 'F. Y. & N. Rly' in gilt shaded black and the rear of the bunker '№ 1' in plain figures; maker's plates were carried on the cab side. Equipped with both the Westinghouse brake and a vacuum ejector, FYNR No. 1 was taken by barge to St Helens Quay in June 1913.[50]

The second engine was an LBSCR class A1 0-6-0T on loan from the LSWR. Built in December 1876, 46 *Newington*

FYNR No. 2 at Newport c1920 painted in FYNR livery. The lining to the cab front could not be carried round the spectacle plates. *P. C. Allen*

(later 646) was sold to the LSWR in March 1903 with 668 *Clapham* for £500 each. Becoming LSWR 734-735, they were used on the 6¾-mile Lyme Regis branch constructed under a Light Railway Order and opened on 24 August 1903. Although adequate for most of the year, the summer trains taxed them to their limits and in 1907 adapted class O2 0-4-4Ts took over the task. Shunting duties were performed until 1911, when both were laid aside until No. 735 was overhauled in June 1912, followed by 734 in September. They received new Drummond-pattern boilers with dome-top lock-up safety valves, new 13in cylinders, steam-heating equipment, coal rails and reconditioned crank axles purchased from the LBSCR. The boilers were not as free steaming as the Stroudley version and suffered from priming if not carefully handled. No. 734 soon made its way to the Isle of Wight, while 735 was employed on the Lee-on-Solent Light Railway and survived until December 1936.[12]

The loan arrangements seem to have been rather hurried as No. 734 retained the LSWR Drummond lined green livery and did not visit Eastleigh Works prior to its arrival at St Helens Quay on 25 June 1913. According to Mr Bradley, the hire charges were £1 6s 8d a day. However, on 18 December Herbert Walker, the LSWR Manager, informed the Locomotive and Stores Committee that he had written on 13 December agreeing to sell the engine to the FYNR for £900. He expected payment the following spring and was charging interest at 5% from 1 December. LSWR records suggest the sale was formally agreed in March 1914, with payment spread over three years; no hire charges were paid. Lacking the Westinghouse brake, No. 734 was unable to run with the former IWCR carriages.[36]

In addition to the two 0-6-0Ts, the FYNR became the owner of a four-wheeled rail motor car. Ordered on 25 March 1913 from the Drewry Car Co., several hundred of these type B vehicles were supplied to foreign railways as inspection cars and two went to the LBSCR. The firm lacked their own workshops and sub-contracted construction to Baguley Cars Ltd of Shobnall Road, Burton-on-Trent. The rail motor was demonstrated to the GCR at Bulwell, Nottinghamshire, on 25 June before being partly dismantled for the journey. Landed at Newport Quay, the rail motor was loaded on a cart and towed by a traction engine to Carisbrooke, where it was put on the rails.[52]

The body of the rail motor was teak with a roof and glass end screens with roll-down weather sheets to cover the open sides. The woodwork was varnished and lettered 'FRESHWATER RAILWAY'. Capable of being driven from either end, there were three reversible upholstered bench seats accommodating twelve people including the driver. The engine and gearbox were carried on an inner frame of steel angle such that the whole unit could be removed for maintenance. The Baguley 20hp water-cooled engine was powered by benzol, rather than petrol. The four cylinders measured 90mm by 130mm with interchangeable valves all on one side and radiators at each end. The crankshaft ran in phosphor-bronze bearings lined with white metal, lubrication was by a gear driven pump and ignition was by magneto, accumulator and coil. There was a reversible three-speed

gearbox and double chains connected the transmission with the driving axle. The Hadfields 2ft diameter cast steel wheels and forged steel axles were carried in railway type axleboxes fitted with phosphor-bronze bearings and wick lubrication. A pedal brake worked on a drum on the countershaft supplemented by a handbrake acting on the wheel tyres. There were no buffers, drawgear or any means of coupling to conventional railway vehicles. The rail motor weighed 1ton 15cwt.[52] The men called the rail motor 'The Lurcher' because of an unfortunate tendency to lurch along the track at any sort of speed. Whatever passengers may have thought of the ride, or its use in poor weather, this was the Island's first rail motor worked by an internal combustion engine and a pioneering innovation.

The FYNR took over the operation of its railway on 1 July 1913. To avoid incurring fees for the use of Newport station, contractors hurriedly erected a separate station on FYNR land with a wooden platform, buildings, run-round loop and sidings. Goods vehicles were exchanged between the two railways but passengers had to walk along a narrow footpath, a great burden for those with luggage. After correspondence involving the Board of Trade, some trains began running into the IWCR station on 11 May 1914, for which a 'nominal' fee was charged.[11]

Trains continued to begin and end their journeys at Newport, where sheds were erected to accommodate the engines and rail motor. The motor was used regularly on an early morning working to Freshwater carrying the mail and newspapers. It operated off-peak services when one of the steam engines was stopped for attention, special runs to Yarmouth for the ferry to Lymington and was available for hire by groups in much the same way as the IWCR's saloon carriage. In 1914 the steam engines ran a total of 61,586 miles and the rail motor an impressive 10,486, roughly one seventh of the total. The need to make economies because of the war caught up with the railway in 1915, when the train service was cut back, reductions that remained in place until 1923.[50]

The FYNR could not afford to pay for a fitter, so one of the IWCR fitters was persuaded to work on a Sunday on a 'cash in hand' basis. No. 1 had a habit of losing a coupling rod at the most inconvenient times and both engines suffered from problems caused by poor-quality water at Freshwater. On one occasion a boilersmith and two mates from the GCR at Manchester were sent to patch the boiler on No. 1, only for the problem to reoccur after one of the crew's 'repairs' failed. This apart, engines were usually sent to Ryde Works for heavy repairs, the IWCR charging £3 in each direction for the passage of its lines. They worked bunker-first towards Freshwater but that was unpopular with crews in winter so in January 1916 the pair were dispatched from Newport to Sandown and back to Newport via Ryde St John's Road. For this, the IWCR charged £4 13s 8d.[12]

Both engines received full or partial repaints when in FYNR ownership, although when and how many times the work was done is uncertain. By 1919 No. 1 was still in green but had been given new lining in black outlined in white. The tank side was lettered 'F. Y. N.' in gilt shaded black, a matching

The FYNR's railcar seen at Freshwater, probably soon after purchase, illustrates its primitive nature. *IWSR Archive*

numeral '1' was on the bunker side and the maker's plate on the cab side. Its companion remained in LSWR livery for a considerable time, possibly until February 1917.[33] Following a repaint in 1919, it emerged 'in bright light green, almost like the 1947 LNER green, lined out with black and white, with red side rods, lettered F. Y. N.' and the number '2' on the bunker side.[41] Unusually, the LSWR Drummond-style dark green borders to the lining seem to have been retained. The brake hangers had been adapted to carry iron brake shoes, the steam-heating equipment disappeared but the LBSCR copper-capped chimney was retained.

Absorption of the FYNR by the Southern Railway did not go smoothly. The directors refused to accept £50,000 for their railway and insisted on £70,000 in the expectation that a Solent tunnel would be built. On 20 June 1923 a Railway Amalgamation Tribunal decided that the original offer was adequate and the SR took control of the line on 27 August. Newport FYNR station closed to passengers at the start of the summer timetable on 9 July, when all trains began running into the IWCR station. It remained open for parcels, etc. until 1 September. Taken into stock on 27 August, the engines were moved to the former IWCR Newport shed. Allocated Nos W1–2, they were repainted in SR lined green livery.[10]

No.	Olive green	Dark green
W1	5.1924	* 2.1929
W2	4.1924	* 1.1927
* Known overhaul dates, they may have been painted in this livery previously.		

In May 1924 W1 visited the former IWCR Newport workshop for the removal of the vacuum brake fittings and a repaint. It was then employed on Medina Jetty but with occasional trips to Shide and Cement Mills when rostered for the chalk train. In both cases weight restrictions precluded the use of engines heavier than W1 or the LBSCR 0-6-0Ts. It acquired the nickname *Papyrus* after the 1924 Grand National steeplechase winner, an indication of how the crews valued its haulage abilities. A study of operating practices in 1925 found that the engine on the Medina Wharf goods (duty 10) had to be away from shed for twenty-six hours at a time, resulting in the allocation of two engines to this one duty. Evidently there was so little siding space that wagons had to be moved immediately loading was completed. Duties were rearranged but that did nothing to assist management in their attempts to reduce the numbers in steam.

W1 underwent an overhaul in 1928, during which the boiler was retubed. The cab and bunker side sheets were replaced, the Westinghouse compressor was repositioned and the handbrake transferred to the fireman's side of the cab. Coal rails and front footsteps were added and three-link loose couplings replaced the more usual screw-link type. The nameplates *Medina* were bolted to the tank sides, while the maker's plates remained on the cab sides, the last Island engine to carry such plates. It was repainted in the passenger livery of lined dark green, a top-class finish that included lining to the prominent toolbox and sandboxes on the running plate and the Westinghouse compressor. W1 *Medina* left Ryde Works in February 1929 and returned to Newport for more goods work. In April

By 1919, the FYNR livery had become more elaborate although the company initials had been shortened, as displayed by No. 1. *K. Nunn*

FYNR No. 1 as repaired and repainted at Ryde early in 1929 and showing the features detailed in the main text. The pride the Ryde Works' painter took is very evident. Also of note is the 'S.R' embellishment to the headcode lamps. *A. B. MacLeod/IWSR Archive*

1932 the Westinghouse brake, name, number and maker's plates were removed but it remained in service until withdrawn in July. The next year was spent stored in the open behind Ryde shed with W13 *Ryde*. W1 departed from Medina Wharf on 23 June 1933 and was recorded as broken up at Eastleigh Works on 29 July.[25]

W2 visited Newport Works for a repaint in April 1924. The opportunity was taken to extend the coal bunker and fit the Westinghouse brake in place of the vacuum system. Some records suggest W2 was one of two members of the class equipped with pull-push equipment that year. If this was the case, one would have expected the engine to be used on the Merstone to Ventnor West trains. In reality, a return was made to the Freshwater line, usually in partnership with W9, or later with W10, with some occasional shunting at Newport and Medina Jetty. During the next overhaul in January 1927 LBSCR-pattern brake hangers and shoes were fitted, along with steam-heating equipment. In October 1928 *Freshwater* nameplates were attached high up on the side tanks between the 'SOUTHERN' lettering and numerals; the 'W' prefix was tiny. This arrangement looked too cramped, so in November 1929 the nameplates were lowered and the numerals and prefix moved on the bunker. Although returned to service on the Freshwater line, the stay was short-lived as in 1930 the Ventnor West branch beckoned.[53]

The LSWR Drummond boiler carried by W2 remained in use until January 1932, when the firebox was condemned. Surprisingly, a brand new A1X-pattern boiler was constructed at Brighton Works and dispatched to Ryde Works. The combined splashers and sandboxes were left in place, but other changes included the fitting of new cylinders, a hooter and LSWR Drummond-pattern chimney. After leaving Ryde Works in March, problems with hot axleboxes and leaking tubes restricted movements for a few weeks. On 8 April there was a change of identity to W8 *Freshwater*, freeing a block of numbers for class E1 0-6-0Ts.[54] Normally rostered for the Merstone to Ventnor West services, appearances were also

made on the Freshwater line and in August 1934 at Medina Wharf. During the next overhaul, probably in December 1937 when the boiler was changed, vertical handrails were attached to the tank front along with footsteps over the front driving wheels. Apart from a repaint in unlined green in 1941, W8 received little attention until May 1945, when it emerged from an overhaul in unlined black lettered 'SOUTHERN' in yellow with green shading. Following the next overhaul in 1948, 'BRITISH RAILWAYS' lettering was applied.[54]

W8 *Freshwater* returned to the mainland in May 1949 and visited Eastleigh Works for minor attention. The 'BRITISH RAILWAYS' lettering was left untouched but the bunker acquired the running number 32646 in plain yellow numerals. Based at Fratton shed for the Hayling Island branch services, apart from two short spells at Newhaven, visits were made to Brighton Works in December 1951 and February 1958 for overhauls, both of which included a change of boiler and a repaint. No. 32646 was withdrawn when the Hayling Island line closed on 4 November 1963 and was stored in Eastleigh running shed until purchased by the Sadler Rail Coach Co. for £600 in November 1964 and moved to Droxford on the closed Meon Valley line. The engine was sold in 1966 to the Portsmouth brewers Brickwoods, painted in LBSCR Stroudley livery as LBSCR 46 *Newington,* and moved to Hayling Island for display outside the Hayling Billy public house. After another change of ownership in 1978 it was returned to the Isle of Wight.

The rail motor continued to run approximately 8,000 miles a year until 1921 and 1922, when there was a decline to 4,356 and 24 miles respectively; clearly it was worn out.[50] After the SR took charge, the rail motor was allocated number 2462, that of a third-class carriage, but is unlikely to have carried any fare-paying passengers before withdrawal on 31 December 1924. It lingered on as inspection car 437S until broken up in October 1927 still carrying the FYNR livery. Although that was the end of the rail motor, the SR later purchased a larger Drewry four-wheel 'branch line coach' for the mainland and two similar vehicles for the Ryde Tramway.[52]

A1 0-6-0T W2 at Newport in March 1929 showing the cramped style of lettering on the tank side arranged to accommodate the new *Freshwater* nameplate. The very small 'W' prefix is barely visible above the nameplate. Pull-push piping and hoses are evident. *H. F. Wheeller/A. Blackburn collection*

Former FYNR No. 2 was renumbered W8 in 1932 to release the number for an E1. Here it is seen departing Merstone on Duty 22, the Ventnor West branch turn, soon after the Second World War and carrying unlined black with sunshine lettering. The pull-push fittings are clearly visible complete with legends on the buffer beam. Of note is that both headcode and tail lamp are being carried together, a common practice on the Ventnor West branch. *IWSR Archive*

W8 again seen at Merstone on the Ventnor West train in 1948, this time in the siding to the north of the station where the branch train would lay over to clear the Down loop. The engine still carries the unlined black livery, now patch repainted with 'British Railways' lettering. *IWSR Archive*

6

Ryde Pier Tramway

The history of the Ryde Pier Company and the various piers at Ryde is complicated.[4] Fortunately, we need concern ourselves only with the pier tramway and its extension through the town to the railway terminus at St John's Road. George Young became a director of the Company in 1854 and was elected Chairman in 1861. A wealthy London corn merchant, he was also a director of the IWR and Chairman of the RNR. He virtually bankrupted himself trying to fund the latter but, more than any other person, was the prime mover in the construction and extension of the Ryde Pier tramway.

A tramway to connect the pier head with the shore was first mooted in 1856, when a consultant recommended the provision of a second pier alongside the existing structure and a single-track tramway worked by horse or steam power. In September 1861 a contract was let for its construction, albeit with double track. The wooden pier was largely complete by April 1863 but lacked rails. Although steam traction on a pier was largely unknown, the directors felt that they should at least investigate whether it was possible.[55]

On 7 November 1863 Manning, Wardle & Co. of Leeds were asked to supply a small tank engine for a three-month trial period with the option to purchase, if satisfactory. According to the maker's records, the potential buyers of order number 1410 were the 'Ryde Pier Commissioners, Isle of Wight'. The firm supplied one of their outside cylinder class B 0-4-0 tank engines (maker's No. 111), of which fourteen were built between July 1863 and February 1872 mainly for export. Capable of hauling 86 tons at 7mph, it had a smoke consumer and condenser that fed steam back into the tank; the fuel space was no larger than a big coal scuttle. What livery was carried is not recorded. (Known dimensions are in Appendix 2.)[20]

Dispatched by Manning, Wardle on 10 March 1864, the engine arrived at Ryde two days later and was accommodated in a short-lived 'engine house' at Pier Gates. Named *Vectis*, trial running began on Monday 14 March in the presence of Charles Wardle, the directors and representatives of the Ryde Improvement Commissioners (the local authority). The *Isle of Wight Observer* predicted that a service would begin the following Monday but that did not happen. *Vectis* caused excessive vibration to the pier structure, even after track strengthening, and on 4 June the directors resolved to abandon steam traction in favour of horses. The engine was returned to the maker and a cheque sent for £153 in respect of the hire and transport charges. The maker sold *Vectis* to the Northfleet Coal & Ballast Co. in Kent, where it remained until sent for scrap in 1920. Two carriages had been purchased but were too heavy for horse power, so a delay ensued while a suitable lightweight carriage was obtained. The pier tramway opened to the public on 29 August 1864 six days after the Isle of Wight Railway commenced operations between Ryde and Shanklin.[55]

The tramway had made it easier to reach the shore but there remained a 'middle way' between the pier gates and railway terminus that promoters vied to fill with a railway or tramway. Eventually a tramway extension was constructed through the town to St John's Road and opened on 7 August 1871. It passed over private land except when crossing public roads and was laid to railway standards. By then there were three small four-wheel tramway carriages for the pier, six larger double-deck carriages for the extension and numerous horses. Steam traction would have been a decided advantage but there were complaints that year when an IWR engine, probably the first *Brading*, worked down to the Esplanade with stone from Ventnor quarry. The RNR obtained powers in 1872 to run passenger trains beyond the railway terminus to a stopping place near Simeon Street but local residents were still lodging complaints in 1878 after a Joint Committee engine and chalk wagons ventured onto the tramway.

A branch from the tramway to nearby docks opened in 1873 and generated a considerable amount of goods traffic. It has been suggested that George Young purchased the 0-4-0T *Bee* for this work, a task for which it would have been well suited. The voluminous minute books fail to mention this possibility and the traffic was worked using horses until the railway opened in 1880.

An 1870 Tramways Act authorised the operation of steam tram engines on the public highway under certain conditions. This prompted the directors to approach Merryweather & Sons Ltd of Greenwich Road, London, and on 24 June 1876 the two parties reached agreement for the hire of a suitable example. Merryweather supplied one with a horizontal boiler, controls at one end enclosed in an overall cab with glazing all around and doors at each corner. The motion was completely hidden from view by side skirts. The body was painted and lined in a two-tone livery, possibly the red and cream used on the tramway carriages, the waist panels being lettered with the name of the Tramway Traction Co. and an address in London. Although smaller than later examples built for street tramways in Britain and abroad, it was allegedly capable of hauling six fully laden tram vehicles at 6mph. The engine had reached the Isle of Wight by 9 September, when trials commenced over the tramway. Unfortunately, when demonstrated to members of Ryde Corporation they refused permission for its use between Pier Gates and Simeon Street, the most critical section. On 2 December the directors agreed to return the engine to the maker, citing the local authority's attitude, and added that its operating costs exceeded horse traction. Returned to the mainland later that month, the engine underwent a trial on the North Metropolitan Tramway at Leytonstone in March 1877 but then disappeared from sight.

Prompted by complaints about the horse tramway, the RPC made plans to construct a replacement single-track railway through a covered way under the Esplanade. At this point the LSWR and LBSCR came on the scene with their own proposals for a double-track railway. The local authority, RPC and IWR were placated by various agreements before Parliament gave approval for the line in July 1877. Although only 1 mile 16 chains in length, construction presented considerable difficulties for it entailed the provision of the covered way below the Esplanade and East Street, a short sea wall and three road overbridges. Preliminary borings were completed in February 1878 but it was the end of the year before work was in progress on the pier and along the length of the line. A Board of Trade inspector made a first visit on 20 February 1880, when a train of four first-class IWR carriages was headed by *Ryde* and *Ventnor.* Permission to open the railway from St John's Road to Esplanade was granted after a second inspection in April but bad weather then delayed opening to Pier Head until July; the station was finally completed in October. The tramway between the Pier Gates and St John's Road closed in January 1880.

Anxious to find an alternative to horse traction, during 1878 the RPC Secretary was in correspondence with Henry Hughes, Loughborough, and Stephen Lewin, Poole, concerning engines for use on the pier. None was suitable as in July 1879 the directors discussed wire rope haulage and gas propulsion. Joseph Bourne, the IWR Manager, was party

The only known photograph of the Merryweather steam tram locomotive at Ryde in 1876. It is standing with two of the small tramway carriages, either Nos. 1 or 2, and No.3. *A B MacLeod collection/IWSR Archive*

to a decision on 5 June 1880 to order two gas-fired steam tram engines from Frederic Bradley of Clensmore Ironworks, Kidderminster, a supplier of castings to the IWR but with no apparent experience of steam engines. Mr Bourne monitored their construction but was hardly impartial as he and Frederic Bradley later jointly purchased a Liverpool firm of crane and winch makers.[56] The mechanical parts were constructed by the firm but the wooden bodies were contracted out. When tested at the maker's works, 3,000cu ft of gas was consumed instead of the intended 1,000cu ft, so they were converted to burn coke at the rate of 5cwt a day. A gas holder erected at the Pier Gates was never used. A committee of enquiry later censured the directors for having wasted upwards of £1,500 on these 'experimental and costly' gas engines and hoped that some 'will retire and make room for some younger and more active men'. This was followed by the resignation of George Young as both Chairman and a director.[55]

The two tram engines arrived at St John's Road early in January 1881 for inspection and testing prior to entry into service in mid-February. Each had a vertical boiler powering an engine connected by a central jackshaft and side rods to four small driving wheels. The enclosed wooden body had double doors on each side, louvres above waist level, two short chimneys through the roof and open platforms at each end on which was a driving wheel. Photographs suggest they were painted in the existing red livery. Soon afterwards a shuttle service began operating along the west track using one or two trailers converted from the double-deck tramway carriages; the remainder were sold or scrapped. At the Pier Gates there was a spur to a covered area with coaling and watering facilities.

The tram engines were far from satisfactory as they were infernally hot and there was a constant fire risk from cinders falling on the then wooden pier. The weight of between 9 and 10 tons put a strain on the axles and after breakages in November 1881 and October 1882 alterations were made to reduce them to 7¾ tons.[17] Even then a writer to the *Isle of Wight Observer* in December 1882 complained of being 'smothered in a cloud from the Pier

One of the Bradley steam tram carriages at Ryde St John's. The less than pristine condition would indicate that this depicts it following withdrawal. Points to note are the two chimneys, the control wheel, handle and brake standard on the end platform and the quite elaborate lining to all panels. Not too much detail of the actual engine is visible, although the control and connecting rods may be seen. Note the carriage-style droplights to the doors.
Mark Brinton collection

The Starbuck conversion to an electric motor car. This is the only image that could be found and depicts the car running on the east track and hauling the 'Grapes' trailer. Date unrecorded. *IWSR Archive*

The west motor car was created from one half of the six-wheel Lancaster carriage. It is seen here at Newport in 1928 after withdrawal and removal of the traction equipment. The five windows and toplights, the round-topped door giving access to the saloon and the wrought iron railings are typical of Lancaster vehicles. *H. C. Casserley/IWSR Archive*

Company's own tram engine, which as it went by made the pier tremble like a jelly, and must sooner or later do the fabric serious injury'.[7]

The demanding conditions on the pier so badly affected performance that by February 1884 the engines were in a poor condition. Enquiries were made about electric traction, then in its infancy, and in May an agreement was made with Blanch, Brain Brothers, Chancery Lane, London, to equip a carriage with electric batteries. Trials proved disappointing and were abandoned in August after modifications failed to increase the tractive power. This left the Company in serious trouble as one engine was unserviceable and the other little better. A decision to order a new boiler for no more than £120 was quickly rescinded and on 24 October the directors agreed to revert to using horses. By then Mr Bourne had resigned from the IWR and left the Island. On 2 January 1885 a decision was made to place an advertisement in *The Engineer* offering to sell the engines, a carriage and luggage van. After a lengthy time in store at St John's Road, for which the IWR charged rent, in October 1886 the tram engines were sold to the Ryde Gas Co. for £42. Apparently dismantled before the end of the year, a single serviceable one was reassembled for hire to William Jackson, who was constructing the FYNR; it was then probably broken up.

Reliant once again on horse traction, several reputable firms were asked to quote for converting the tramway to electric traction. On 14 May 1885 a contract was signed with

Siemens Brothers of Charlton for the supply of gas-powered generating equipment, the installation of a current rail on the west track and the conversion of two trailers to motor cars. Work began on 4 October and was completed on 14 March 1886, although a full service was not possible before 4 April. The motor cars took turns to operate a shuttle service with one of the trailers. The changes were so successful that in November 1889 a decision was made to reinstate and electrify the east track, the work being completed the following summer. A more powerful generator was provided so that the motor cars, each with a trailer, could be used concurrently. One motor car and trailer were replaced in 1892 by a new six-wheel car but it proved too long and in 1907 was cut in two to create a matching pair. In 1911 the running gear from the older motor car was reused in a replacement constructed by Pollard & Sons of Ryde.[17]

By the time the SR assumed responsibility for the tramway in 1924, the electrical equipment was so obsolescent that its operation depended solely on the ingenuity of the fitters. An alternative source of electricity was sought but the Isle of Wight

RIGHT The east motor car had a locally built body mounted on a former Starbuck underframe. It is seen here jacked up to effect transfer to the 'main line' and movement to Ryde St John's in September 1927 following replacement by a new Drewry motor car. *IWSR Archive*

An official portrait of one of the new Drewry motor cars, possibly at the builders before delivery. The ornate Southern Railway livery shows well.
Terry Hastings collection

The interior of the new motor cars was somewhat spartan, with slatted wooden seats and minimal furnishings. This view is looking towards the engine and driving end.
IWSR Archive

Electric Light & Power Co. was unable to supply enough power at peak periods. Consequently, electric traction was abandoned.

On 26 March 1927 an order was placed with the Drewry Car Co. (order 2783) for two four-wheel rail motor cars. Construction was sub-contracted to Baguley (Engineers) Ltd, Burton-on-Trent, who allocated maker's numbers (1646 and 1647) and prepared a drawing (1525/27). The underframes were constructed in steel but the bodies, supplied by Craven Carriage & Wagon Co., were wood with metal cladding. The driving position was at one end of a saloon with bare wood seating along the sides for a nominal twenty-two passengers and standing room for eighteen, not that these limits were adhered to. There were hinged doors behind the driving position and a sliding door at the opposite end leading to a vestibule open at the sides and end. As previously, the cars were lit by electricity but unheated. Intended for the east track, in car No. 1 the driving position was on the east side of the car, whereas in No. 2 the driving position was on the opposite side. Motive power was in the form of a Baguley four-cylinder 25hp petrol engine connected by a chain drive to one axle. The engine and transmission was below floor level apart from the upper part of the engine, which projected through the floor in the driving position. The cars were painted in 'Company' green with black underframes.[17] Delivery was requested by 30 June but that date was not met and the existing cars remained in service for another summer season. During a brief period of closure, the electric motor cars were replaced by the new arrivals. According to the *Isle of Wight County Press*, they were in position by 5 November ready for a resumption of services the following week. The old motor cars were taken to Newport, from where the bodies were sold and that from the Pollard car has since been rescued for preservation.[7]

The motor cars were fitted with wooden buffers and tram-style couplings for use with the trailers and luggage trolley. The SR opted not to buy matching trailers, known locally as 'push-cars', and decided to overhaul and repaint the existing ones. A combination of more powerful motor cars and the absence of continuous brakes (the tramway was exempt from the necessary legislation) resulted in numerous mishaps when running backwards to the Pier Head. The most serious took place on 6 September 1935 when No. 2 wrecked a trailer by pushing it over the stop blocks at Pier Head. Known as the 'Grapes Car' because of its elaborate decoration, the remains were purchased privately, restored and presented to Hull Museum, where it remains. Eastleigh Works constructed two new trailers in 1936 and 1937. Management was still concerned about the risk of more mishaps as drawings show that a second driving position was considered for the trailer cars. In 1939 a further sketch was prepared of possible six-wheel replacements for all four cars with driving positions at the outer ends.[39]

Another petrol engine had to be purchased for No. 1 in 1933 and those from both cars were returned to the makers for overhaul in 1937 and 1938. Bedford petrol engines were fitted during the 1940s and Perkins P6 six-cylinder 30hp diesel engines were purchased for No. 2 in 1959 and No. 1 in 1960. Apart from occasional mishaps and repaints in SR green, BR red and back to green, there were no further changes before services ended in January 1969. The stock was broken up at Ryde Esplanade a year later with the exception of motor car No. 2; it was purchased for preservation.[17]

A 1953 view of Drewry motor car No. 1 with trailer No. 8 on the east track passing Ryde Pier Head signal box. Note the telltale wheel below the driving position, which engaged with a ramp to warn the driver when he was approaching the pier head station. *J. T. Fraser/IWSR Archive*

7
Southern Railway

The Southern Railway came into being on 1 January 1923 but six months elapsed before an organisational structure had been created and the principal managerial posts filled. The Company was divided into three sections for administrative and operational purposes, roughly corresponding with the lines previously owned by the LSWR, LBSCR and SECR. The Island railways came under the Western Section, giving Eastleigh Works effective control over the workshops at Ryde and Newport. The whole was presided over by Robert Urie, the LSWR Chief Mechanical Engineer, soon to be ousted when Richard Maunsell was appointed SR Chief Mechanical Engineer.

Prior to the formation of the Company, LSWR Managers visited the Isle of Wight on several occasions to ascertain what improvements were necessary to bring the railways up to the same standard as the mainland branch lines. Additional and more powerful engines featured high on the list of priorities. In the autumn of 1922 Eastleigh Works prepared a drawing of *Bonchurch* to show the type used on the IWR for comparison with the nearest LSWR equivalent, class O2. The Ryde to Ventnor line was laid with chaired track and could accommodate the class after the strengthening of a bridge and the removal of a small turntable at Ventnor. Before they could run elsewhere a programme of bridge and permanent way improvements had to be implemented.[27]

Designed by William Adams, sixty LSWR class O2 0-4-4 tank engines were constructed at Nine Elms Works between 1889 and 1895 for secondary and branch line services. There were also thirty-four class G6 0-6-0 tank engines for shunting and local goods duties that shared boilers, cylinders, driving wheels and other parts. The O2s were described as compact, business-like machines with neat side tanks, inside cylinders, exterior coal bunkers and roomy cabs, finished off with brass edging to the spectacle plates and splashers. The boilers had a centrally placed dome and separate enclosed safety valves on a saddle immediately in front of the whistle and cab. Originally fitted with Adams stovepipe chimneys, those sent to the Island carried a later Drummond-pattern.

Mr Bradley claimed that LSWR class 0415 4-4-2Ts were considered.[12] These suburban tank engines were older, heavier and in most respects inferior to the O2s. The majority of the seventy-one members of the class had been made redundant by electrification and lay derelict at Eastleigh awaiting disposal. Many of the O2s would have suffered the same fate had they not been selected for service in the Isle of Wight.

In March 1923 Nos 206 and 211, undergoing overhauls at Eastleigh Works, were earmarked for transfer to the Isle of Wight. The vacuum brake was replaced by the Westinghouse system, the most visible evidence of this being a compressor mounted on the left-hand side of the smokebox and a cylindrical reservoir on top of the left-hand side tank. No decision had been made which, if any, of the existing liveries from the constituent companies would be adopted, so they were turned out in the LSWR passenger engine colour: olive green with black lining edged in white. Gilt lettering spelled out 'L S W R' on the tank sides with a matching running number on the bunker sides.[15]

Mr Urie reported to the SR Locomotive & Carriage Committee on 3 May 1923:[28]

The engines taken over from the Isle of Wight and Isle of Wight Central and Plymouth, Devonport & South Western Junction Railways, which number 19, are in fairly good condition except the locomotive 'Sandown', belonging to the Isle of Wight Railway, which it is recommended be sold as scrap or broken up. Arrangements have been made to send two LSW tank engines of 177 (0-4-4) tank class to the Island and for these to be equipped with the Westinghouse brake.

The next day an Admiralty floating crane unloaded the O2s at Ryde Pier Head station and collected *Sandown* for return to the mainland. Allocated to Ryde shed for the Ryde to Ventnor services, the new arrivals proved most satisfactory, burnt less coal than the Beyer, Peacock 2-4-0Ts and were liked by the crews.

By August 1923 the SR management had decided that engines would retain their existing numbers but with prefixes: 'A' (Ashford), 'B' (Brighton), 'E' (Eastleigh) and 'W' (Isle of Wight). The mainland prefixes were abolished in July 1931, when most Eastleigh engines retained their existing numbers, 1000 was added to Ashford engines and 2000 to Brighton's motive power. The FYNR engines were allocated W1–2, the IWCR contributed W4–12, six from the IWR became W13–18 while the O2s took the numbers W19–32. In 1932 three A1X 'Terriers', W2, 3 and 4, were renumbered W8, 13 and 14 to create blocks of numbers according to class: W1–4 (class E1), W8–14 (class A1X) and W17–32 (class O2). The A1X 0-6-0Ts were later replaced by additional O2s W14–16 and W33–36.

Sir Herbert Walker, the General Manager, had a liking for inspection visits to all parts of the organisation. They were an opportunity to see progress on improvements, assess what expenditure was required and judge the performance of junior staff. The first three-day visit to the Isle of Wight began on 30 August 1923, a few days after the FYNR had joined the fold. Those present included the Chief Mechanical Engineer, who 'was asked to make arrangements to transfer two good tank engines – of a uniform type – to the Island each year for the next six years'. The existing ones were to be broken up 'unless it is considered necessary to retain one or two for dealing with extra traffic'. As a consequence of this decision, a few of the Island companies' engines were kept in service longer than might otherwise have been the case.[57]

During the inspection the managers decided that the Westinghouse brake would be used for braking trains. This was an acceptance of the existing situation as most engines and stock were so equipped and the opposite to the mainland, where the vacuum brake prevailed. In operation, the Westinghouse system used positive pressure and the vacuum system negative pressure to hold the brakes off. A Westinghouse-equipped engine could always be identified by the characteristic sound of the compressor as it maintained pressure when standing in the station. Mr Maunsell was asked to consider fitting steam-heating apparatus to those engines and stock not already equipped.[57]

In November 1923 Eastleigh Works began turning out passenger engines in a newly adopted livery, olive green, that Alistair MacLeod described in the following terms:[41]

The original Southern locomotive livery was always, for some reason, described as Sage Green, which for anyone acquainted with a sage bush, it certainly was not. In fact the colour was a true olive green, exactly the colour of a good green olive.

A specification, issued by Ashford Works, contained the following instructions for repainting passenger engines in the new livery (Presto green and Stewart's red are thought to have been the suppliers' names for the colours):[51]

- Scale and rust to be removed and cleaned off with turps substitute.
- Primer. One coat of lead colour.
- Stopping as required. This was a filler made from white lead and gold size, a type of thin varnish, that was allowed to dry before rubbing down with pumice bricks and water.
- Filling. Four coats to be applied and rubbed down. This liquid hid small cracks and depressions.
- One coat of lead undercoating, gently rubbed down when dry.
- One coat of Presto green.
- One coat of varnish colour and after drying apply lining as required.

LSWR O2 No. 211 at Eastleigh as prepared for service on the Isle of Wight. The Westinghouse brake pump and cylindrical air reservoir are prominent. Note also that the safety valves have no cover and the coal rails are open. This locomotive and sister No. 206 ran so numbered and in LSWR livery on the Island until 1925. *IWSR Archive*

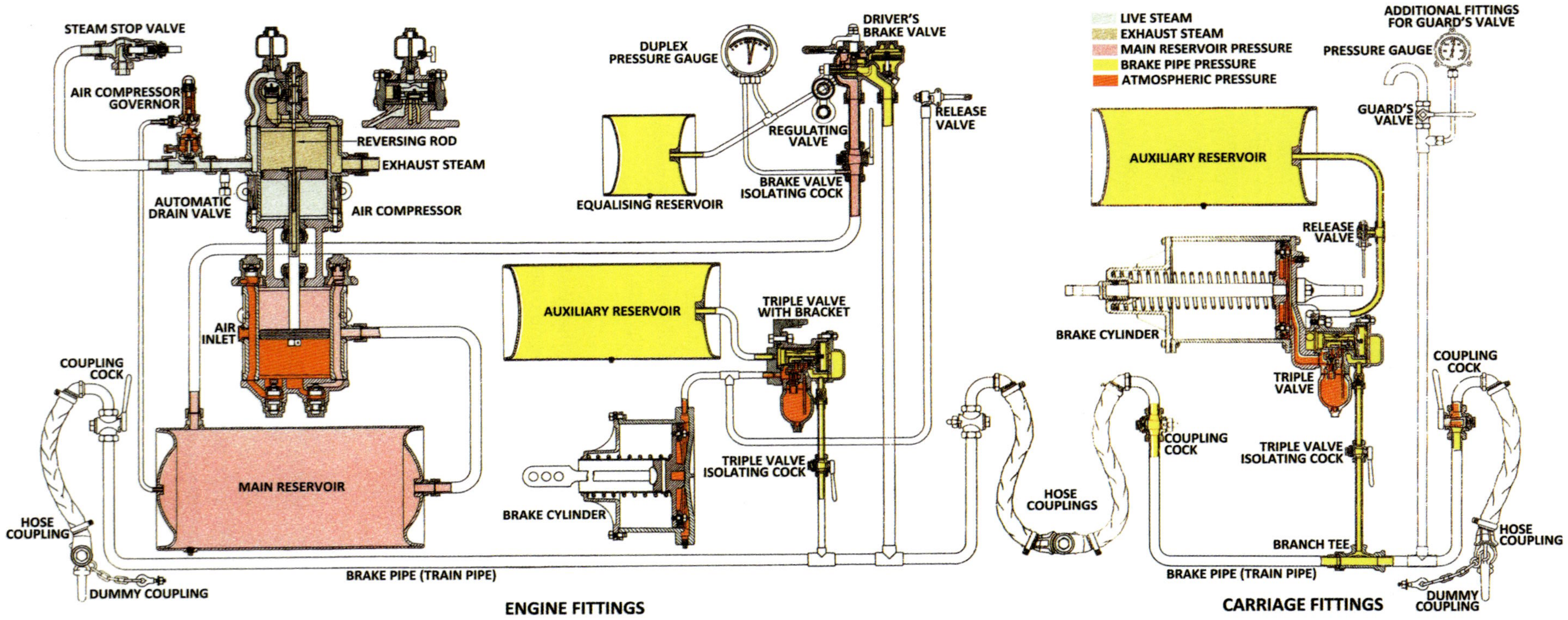

Diagram Labels

Colour key:
- LIVE STEAM
- EXHAUST STEAM
- MAIN RESERVOIR PRESSURE
- BRAKE PIPE PRESSURE
- ATMOSPHERIC PRESSURE

Carriage Fittings:
- ADDITIONAL FITTINGS FOR GUARD'S VALVE
- PRESSURE GAUGE
- GUARD'S VALVE
- RELEASE VALVE
- AUXILIARY RESERVOIR
- TRIPLE VALVE
- TRIPLE VALVE ISOLATING COCK
- BRAKE CYLINDER
- BRANCH TEE
- BRAKE PIPE (TRAIN PIPE)
- COUPLING COCK
- HOSE COUPLING
- DUMMY COUPLING
- HOSE COUPLINGS

CARRIAGE FITTINGS

Engine Fittings:
- RELEASE VALVE
- DRIVER'S BRAKE VALVE
- REGULATING VALVE
- BRAKE VALVE ISOLATING COCK
- DUPLEX PRESSURE GAUGE
- EQUALISING RESERVOIR
- TRIPLE VALVE WITH BRACKET
- TRIPLE VALVE ISOLATING COCK
- AUXILIARY RESERVOIR
- BRAKE CYLINDER
- REVERSING ROD
- EXHAUST STEAM
- AIR COMPRESSOR
- AIR INLET
- MAIN RESERVOIR
- BRAKE PIPE (TRAIN PIPE)
- STEAM STOP VALVE
- AIR COMPRESSOR GOVERNOR
- AUTOMATIC DRAIN VALVE
- COUPLING COCK
- DUMMY COUPLING
- HOSE COUPLING

ENGINE FITTINGS

WESTINGHOUSE BRAKE SYSTEM

Westinghouse Brake System

When the entire system is at atmospheric pressure the brakes are naturally off. When the compressor is activated, air is charged into the main reservoir, the equalising reservoir, the train pipe and the auxiliary reservoirs. The brakes are activated when the driver's valve releases air from the train pipe. When this happens, triple valves in each vehicle release air from the auxiliary reservoirs into the brake cylinders, the pressure depending on how much the driver allows the pressure into the brake cylinders to fall. The brakes are released by restoring the full train pipe pressure, causing the triple valves to recharge the auxiliary reservoirs whilst releasing the air from the brake cylinders to atmosphere. The equalising reservoir, in conjunction with the brake valve, ensures that the brake action is the same regardless of the length of the train and thus the volume of air in the system. The guard's valve, the passenger communication cord and an inadvertent train division will exhaust all the air from the train pipe and applies the brakes full on.

One of the second pair of O2s sent to the Island in June 1924, W21 is seen at Ryde St John's around June 1926. They were sent in a partly dismantled condition and the number '21' appears on part of the brake linkage and the rear guard iron, presumably to assist in the reconstruction. The sides of the coal rails have been plated in. *RP W5916*

- Two coats of varnish.
- Smokebox – one coat of drop black and one of Blundell-Spence Petrifying liquid (a brand of heat-resistant paint).
- Motion – two coats of Stewart's red.
- Buffer beams – one coat of priming, two of Stewart's red, two coats of varnish.
- Inside cab – two coats of yellow ochre and one of varnish.
- Numbering and lettering – as approved.

The layout of the lining was identical to that previously used by the LSWR but the colours changed to black edged in yellow. The tank sides were hand-lettered 'SOUTHERN' in primrose yellow using a type face described as 'expanded Egyptian' or 'expanded Clarendon' (after the Clarendon Press, Oxford). Laid out to fit the available space, it was positioned close to the top of the tanks above a prefix and running number; the number was repeated on the buffer beams. On a copy of the specification found at Ryde Works was a handwritten note stating that Isle of Wight engines were to be painted green. None received the goods livery: black with green lining.[51]

Oval number plates were affixed to the rear of coal bunkers. They measured 13⅝in by 7⅝in with ½in bolt holes at each end, surrounded by raised beading within which were the letters 'SOUTHERN RAILWAY' above the prefix with the running number underneath. The figures and beading were polished brass and the background colour was apparently green at this time. Those fitted to the Island engines were probably cast in the foundry at Eastleigh Works.[15]

In the light of experience with the first two O2s, in January 1924 Eastleigh Works prepared drawings that

added lifting links to the tanks, changed tyre sections and adjusted brake pull rods. In June Nos 205 and 215 were dispatched in a partly dismantled condition by barge to St Helens Quay. After being unloaded by the quay's 10-ton capacity crane, they were taken on flat trucks to Ryde Works and reassembled by fitters sent from Eastleigh as W21 and W22.[17]

The new arrivals had not been followed by any withdrawals of the Island companies' engines, apart from the IWR's *Sandown*, although most overhauls had ended. This changed after it was announced during an inspection in September 1924 the overall number would be set at twenty. However, local management felt that was insufficient as there had been a significant increase in services. This prompted a special visit to the Isle of Wight and a report dated 4 May 1925, part of which read:[10]

In view of the proposed summer service, we visited the Island on Monday and Tuesday last, the 27th and 28th ultimo, to discuss the workings and the Engine power available … after discussion it was proved that it would not be possible to reduce the number of Engines in steam daily. The services at present arranged, involve 17 Engines being lighted per diem. The total number of Engines on the Island is … Newport 13 … Ryde 8 … Of this number, two are always in shops undergoing a general repair and one is generally stopped for heavy running repairs. It will therefore be realised that the running repairs necessary to maintain these Engines in an efficient order have to be carried out during the night and the washing-out of Engines has also to be done in the very early hours of the morning … this is a practice which should at all costs be prevented, as the Engines go into the Depot, fires dropped, steam blown out, washed out with cold water, and lit up again in the space of a few hours with consequent serious effect and possible damage to the firebox. The Boiler Inspector also is emphatic upon the question of dirt being in those boilers due to the existing methods of washing-out.

The report concluded by recommending an increase in the allocation to at least twenty-four. During the next inspection in September 1925 Mr Maunsell announced the transfer of four O2s in the following year would be offset by the withdrawal of two engines, increasing the overall numbers to twenty-three: in reality, three were withdrawn. Despite these additions it was still necessary to wash out boilers overnight during the summer months. To be fair, this was not unique to the Island.[57]

During the winter of 1924–25 Ryde Works was re-equipped to maintain all the engines and rolling stock. The erecting shop contained the heavier equipment, including a metal cutter, two power hammers and blacksmith's forge. The machine shop, or turnery as it was usually called, was home to lathes, planing machines and radial drilling machines. The wheel lathe was capable of reprofiling the tyres on any wheels in use on the Island railways. The gas lighting had been replaced by electricity in 1917 but it was left to the SR to lay on a mains water supply before demolishing a windmill used to pump water from a bore hole, the redundant boiler house and its 66ft high chimney. For use with the O2s, in 1926 the existing hoist was replaced by a larger 25-ton capacity hoist dating from the 1880s that had previously seen service at Bournemouth shed. The hoist had been mounted on wheels but they were replaced by steel plates set in concrete. The existing pit under the hoist was later deepened and lengthened by 12ft. Erected just south of the old hoist, its position meant that engines had to face Ventnor before they could enter works. Six men were needed to lift the rear end of an O2 but four could manage the front (an electric motor was fitted during BR days).[17]

Unlike similar-sized workshops on the mainland, Ryde Works was capable of, and did indeed, perform all types of repair up to and including a general repair (the SR term for a general overhaul). The buildings were served by seven sidings:

Nos.	
1–3	led to the carriage and wagon workshops
4	gave access to the hoist and turnery
5	was used for carriage lifting (it had originally been the second engine shed road)
6	led to a corrugated iron carriage bogie shop
7	ran along the back of the site to the erecting shop

Engines entering the works would usually be stripped down in the yard on No. 4 road. The same road was used by those requiring light repairs or lifting for a hot axlebox. The chimney, Westinghouse compressor and reservoir, cab roof and side tanks were removed with assistance from a 2-ton mobile crane and set aside on flat wagons. The boiler was lifted out of the frames and placed on a trolley to await the removal of tubes, an internal inspection and light repairs. Those boilers in need of more extensive work were transferred on a boiler truck (converted from an IWR carriage truck) to St Helens Quay for shipment to the mainland. The frames were lifted off the wheels and moved on works trolleys over a pit for attention. They then entered the erecting shop or turnery, where the slow process of reassembly began.[17]

The last engine to receive an overhaul at Newport (W12) left the fitting shop in May 1925. Most of the machinery was moved to Ryde, although a wheel lathe and 20-ton wooden hoist in the yard remained available for use. The hoist was in an awkward position at the north-west end of the building, so a more convenient position was found south of the running shed when a replacement was erected in 1939. The fitting shop was used to strip spare parts from withdrawn engines and then lay empty until converted into a carriage paint shop in 1929.[58]

The running shed at Ryde supplied motive power for the Ryde to Ventnor line and Bembridge branch, while Newport took responsibility for the remaining lines. The sheds had their distinct allocations but often loaned engines to each other as cover for those undergoing repair. Owing to the prevailing gradients, Ryde-based engines faced Ventnor while those at Newport faced towards Ryde. At Ryde a new two-road shed with room for eight engines was brought into use on Sunday, 18 May 1930.[43] Constructed in concrete blocks with LBSCR overhead traction girders for the roof trusses and corrugated asbestos cladding, the generous inspection pits, washout points and staff facilities were a far cry from the shed's predecessor. Outside there was a new coal stage, ash pit and water cranes. At Newport there were frequent derailments on the flat bottom rails in the shed yard until they were relaid in February 1930. Plans to extend the shed were abandoned in favour of refurbishment with corrugated iron cladding; an additional £207 was spent on a new engine pit and ash dump. The redundant sheds at Ryde, Newport and Freshwater were removed.[21]

Returning to April 1925, after two years of service O2 No. 206 was in Ryde Works undergoing a 'general repair' and repaint as W19. Its companion later became W20. By then SR Floating Crane No. 1 had arrived for use within Southampton Docks. Able to lift up to 150 tons, the crane could be towed by tugs to Medina Jetty and became the preferred method for moving engines and stock to and from the Isle of Wight. The first journey on 26 April delivered W23 and 24 (previously LSWR 188 and 209), while a repeat visit on 25 June transferred W25 and 26 (LSWR 190 and 210).[59] W23 and 24 carried pull-push gear but were too valuable for such humble employment and the fittings were removed during overhauls in 1930 and 1931. The arrival of W23–26

The two O2s transferred in April 1925, Nos 23 & 24, carried the Urie olive green livery and were fitted for pull-push working, although the cocks and flexible hoses were left off, as seen here on No. 24 at Ventnor during 1925. The pipework identifier labels are in place, although the connecting hose for the steam heat has been removed. Other features are the LSWR lamp irons, with the three not required being painted white and the personalised clover leaf emblem on the smokebox door. *K. Nunn 4829*

O2 W28, transferred in March 1926, carries the revised dark green livery, although the positioning of the lettering remains as previously. The view shows the Drummond boiler and various details of the bunker, particularly the plating-in of the sides of the coal rails and the oval number plate. The lamp carries 'S.R' lettering; others have been noted as having the locomotive number instead. Newport c. 1930. *W. G. Boyden/IWSR Archive*

coincided with a relaxation of weight limits on the Sandown to Newport and Ryde to Cowes lines. W23 spent the 1925 summer season based at Newport shed, the first of what became a permanent allocation.[30]

W25 and 26 introduced a darker green livery to the Island.[10] Mr MacLeod wrote:[41]

In 1925 the locomotive colour had been changed to the coach green, a deeper mid-green shade similar to the old Great Central Railway locomotive colour.

In this book the colour has been described as dark green to avoid confusion with the earlier olive green and later malachite liveries. Evidently, the existing lining was not liked as it reverted to black edged in white! Some Island repaints in the olive green livery, including most of the 2-4-0Ts, had no visible lining to the front and back of the cab. W25, and presumably the other three O2s, perpetuated this arrangement but later arrivals were not only lined out on the cab but the tank fronts were also painted green and lined.[15]

O2s W19–26 carried Adams pattern boilers. It was LSWR practice to allocate the same numbers to boilers as those of the engines with which they were first paired (the O2s were numbered 177–236). The boilers of those sent to the Isle of Wight were renumbered temporarily in the LSWR boiler register as IW19–26, but in the succeeding SR Eastleigh register became Nos 369–373, 525, 720 and 861. These numbers had previously been carried by members of LSWR classes T7 and E10 withdrawn in 1926–27; the one exception, 861, was a blank number at the end of the list. Curiously, boilers belonging to the remaining Island companies' engines were allocated vacant numbers in the O2 series (see Appendix 3).[25]

The Adams boiler was carried by LSWR classes O2 and G6 but interchange was limited by there being only ninety-eight available for a total of ninety-four engines. Replacements were to the Adams design, apart from three to a Drummond-pattern with dome top lock-up safety valves built in 1907 and 1909 (Nos. 191, 223 and 278). Apparently, these boilers had long and trouble-free lives. To create a larger float of spares, Eastleigh Works constructed fifteen of the Drummond-pattern between 1925 and 1929 (Nos. 194, 202, 203, 204, 214, 862–866 and 932–936).[31] The dimensions differed from the Adams design in several respects. Of nine Drummond boilers allotted to class O2, six were carried by the next arrivals:[31]

No.	Mainland No.	Boiler No.	Date of transfer
W27	E184	862	3.1926
W28	E186	863	3.1926
W29	E202	864	4.1926
W30	E219	865	4.1926
W31	E180	866	5.1927
W32	E226	934	5.1928

These SR Drummond boilers suffered from erratic steaming and priming, so it was fortunate the O2s had been allocated to Newport shed where their duties were less exacting. Some of these problems could be put down to crews who were unfamiliar with the design as priming could occur if the boiler was over-filled. Those who mastered them claimed Drummond boilers steamed better and were more powerful than the Adams type. It was said that the larger steaming capacity of the Adams dome assisted in reducing priming, whereas on the Drummond pattern the dome-mounted safety valves tended to lift water into the dome when blowing off. Ryde Works swapped boilers around in an attempt to improve their performance but to no avail. Consequently, Eastleigh rebuilt more of the older Adams boilers and added another twenty to this design between 1927 and 1936 (Nos. 843–847, 944–948, 1002–1006 and 1042),[31] they differed from the original Adams boilers in having a heating surface of 830sq ft, the same as the Drummond pattern.[33]

The need for more boilers was caused, in part, by a decision that Ryde Works would not carry out heavy boiler repairs. That made it necessary to return them to the mainland and provide replacements. Although a few did make the journey more than once, it was pure chance whether the same boilers dispatched to Brighton or Eastleigh for reconditioning were sent back. Delays in shipment occasionally resulted in a boiler change weeks after completion of the overhaul.[25]

Early in 1928 management decided to allot names of local origin to the Island engines. In May Eastleigh Works prepared a drawing before casting a batch of nameplates. There were eventually twenty-seven pairs in three lengths:[18]

22in	Ashey, Chale, Cowes, Medina and Ryde
34in	Bembridge, Bonchurch, Brading, Calbourne, Godshill, Merstone, Newport, Ningwood, Osborne, Sandown, Seaview, Shanklin, Shorwell, Totland, Ventnor, Whitwell, Wroxall and Yarmouth
38in	Alverstone, Carisbrooke, Fishbourne and Freshwater

The nameplates were to the same design as those previously fitted by the SR to mainland engines. Irrespective of their length, each was 4¼in high with 3in high lettering and ¼in beading around the edge that was wider around the ½in-diameter bolt holes at each end. The lettering and beading were polished brass and the background red. The number plates and IWR nameplates carried by *Ryde* and *Wroxall* had their backgrounds painted red to match.[16]

The IWR 2-4-0Ts carried the 'SOUTHERN' lettering, nameplate, prefix and running number on the tank sides, so FYNR 0-6-0T W2 was turned out in this style when named *Freshwater* during October 1928. This coincided with the arrival of Alistair MacLeod, who was appointed to manage the locomotive, carriage and wagon departments. He evidently thought the tank sides were too crowded and ordered some changes. On the next to be named, W28 *Ashey*, the running number was reduced

A. B. MacLeod took this view of O2s W25 and W22 on 30 January 1929, entitling it 'Old and new styles of painting'. W25 was due for works, while W22 had just been released with lining on the cab and tank fronts and the wheels. Neither has had the coal rails plated in. *A. B. MacLeod/IWSR Archive*

in size and moved with the prefix to the bunker sides, leaving the 'SOUTHERN' lettering and nameplates on the tank sides. See the table below for the nameplates the O2s received.[10]

Those engines carrying olive green livery were repainted in the darker green before being named, a task that usually took place following an overhaul. On 27 April 1929 W10 and 24 were observed in olive green, W11 and 30 were in dark green but none was named. By April 1930 only W11, 24, 27 and 30 remained nameless.[29]

When repainted, the 'SOUTHERN' lettering on the O2s was lowered by a few inches, while the smaller engines were given lettering and numerals more suited to their size. Nameplates, number plates and wheels were lined out in

No.	Name	Fitted
W19	Osborne	1.1929
W20	Shanklin	3.1929
W21	Sandown	6.1929
W22	Brading	1.1929
W23	Totland	by 4.1930
W24	Calbourne	6.1930
W25	Godshill	5.1929
W26	Whitwell	8.1929
W27	Merstone	5.1930
W28	Ashey	10.1928
W29	Alverstone	9.1929
W30	Shorwell	6.1931
W31	Chale	3.1929
W32	Bonchurch	3.1929

an attempt to encourage crews to take pride in 'their' possessions.[41] Copying LBSCR practice, the top half of the Westinghouse compressor was painted green and lined on some engines.[15] The painter estimated that he and his assistant expended an extra £2 6s 9¼d per engine on this additional work, money well spent in Mr MacLeod's view. The compressor soon reverted to black but lined out nameplates, number plates and wheels remained a feature of the Island engines until the 1950s.[58]

In January 1930 Mr MacLeod's role was extended to include the traffic and commercial departments, becoming the first 'Assistant for the Isle of Wight'. In an effort to reduce overcrowding, train frequencies on the Ryde to Ventnor line had been increased on summer Saturdays in 1929 using turnover engines at Ryde Pier Head. Ready for a further enhancement of the service, O2s W17 *Seaview* and W18 *Ningwood* (previously E208 and E220) were sent from the mainland in May 1930 and allocated to Ryde shed. They received new Adams boilers and nameplates before transfer. Heavy traffic was not confined to the Ryde to Ventnor line but in most cases it was only during carnivals, regattas or other special events.[60] On 3 August 1931, a bank holiday Monday, traffic was so heavy that trains of ten four-wheel carriages were being worked in and out of Cowes station, necessitating the use of engines to top-and-tail each departure.[29]

It was the need for economies in operating the summer Saturday service on the Ryde to Ventnor line that prompted the provision of larger coal bunkers on the O2s. Some were running 200 miles a day and had to make repeated trips between Ryde Pier Head and St John's Road solely to replenish the bunkers. An increase in capacity was attempted by plating in the sides of the three coal rails with steel sheet, while in 1931 W27, 31, 32 (and

O2 W27 *Merstone* at Newport c1931 showing the four coal rails as an initial attempt to increase coal capacity. Other features are the Drummond boiler, a hooter, the lining applied also to the wheels and the lack of a 'W' prefix above the number. *A. B. MacLeod/IWSR Archive*

possibly another) gained a fourth rail. W27 had previously carried an additional handrail on the back of the cab just below the roof.

As the bunker capacity was inadequate, Mr MacLeod and Robert Sweetman, the works foreman, designed a bunker-top extension similar to those on many GWR tank engines with a capacity of 2½ tons. In March 1932 W19 *Osborne* entered service carrying the bunker but crews complained that the view through the rear cab spectacles was so restricted as to be dangerous. Within months a 3-ton version was devised in which the extension commenced at the buffer beam in the same manner as bunkers carried by SR classes W and Z, a design that had originated on a SECR class S tank engine rebuilt in 1917. On the O2s, the bunker sides were cut back and L-shaped extensions added that met up with the new backplate; joints between the old and new side panels were still visible. The rear buffers were packed out by an inch to provide sufficient clearance[58] and, naturally, the new bunker added to the weight in working order.[61]

No. 26 *Whitwell*, in works for an overhaul and boiler change, was the first to receive the larger bunker, followed quickly by W22 *Brading* and W23 *Totland*. Concentrating first on those based at Ryde, all the O2s had their bunkers rebuilt.(*See* table right)[10]

There were several incidents involving the O2s that caused some disruption to services. On 15 July 1931 W23 *Totland* was entering the crossing loop at Wroxall with the 10.14pm train from Ventnor when the right-hand gauge glass broke and the cab was enveloped in steam. The engine and train passed the starting signal at

No.	Name	Bunker Modified
W17	*Seaview*	not known
W18	*Ningwood*	after 10.1933
W19	*Osborne*	10.1933
W20	*Shanklin*	after 5.1933
W21	*Sandown*	by 2.1934
W22	*Brading*	9.1932
W23	*Totland*	9.1932
W24	*Calbourne*	1933
W25	*Godshill*	by 1934
W26	*Whitwell*	9.1932
W27	*Merstone*	6.1935
W28	*Ashey*	circa. 6.1935
W29	*Alverstone*	6.1935
W30	*Shorwell*	6.1935
W31	*Chale*	12.1935
W32	*Bonchurch*	2.1934

danger and split the points that had been set for the next arrival. The guard then wrongly authorised the driver to set back into the platform, with the result that the leading two close-coupled carriages derailed on the points and spreadeagled at right angles to the track. At the same time, W20 *Shanklin* was approaching under clear signals with a Ventnor-bound train and might easily have crashed into the wreckage if the fireman had been unable to place detonators on the line in time. None of

The modification made to the bunker of W19 *Osborne* involved a fully plated upward extension in place of coal rails but restricted the rearward view through the spectacle plates. Note that the LSWR lamp irons have been replaced by standard SR types, but still in all six positions. Ryde St John's 1932. *A. B. MacLeod/IWSR Archive*

The adopted design to increase the O2 bunker capacity was an outward extension from close above the buffer beam carried up to the level of the bottom of the rear spectacle plates, which increased the amount of coal that could be carried by 50%. W26 *Whitwell*, the first to be so modified, shows all the features in this view taken at Ventnor in 1933, including the packing out of the buffers by one inch to provide sufficient clearance and a standard four lamp iron arrangement. *A. B. MacLeod/IWSR Archive*

The first of the three A1X locomotive transferred by the SR was W3, seen here shortly after arrival in 1927; the pull-push fittings are prominent but the steam heating pipe, which can be seen running beneath the valance, lacks hoses. Note the blanking plate on the smokebox where the exhaust steam pipe has been removed; also the sandboxes beneath the running plate, replacing the combined splasher/sandbox as retained on the former Island companies' Terriers. *O. J. Morris/©Rail Archive Stephenson*

the passengers were injured but it took until 3.05am the next day to clear the line.

On 27 October, while working a Cowes to Sandown train, W29 *Alverstone* left the track on a curve near Alverstone after some boys piled stones on the track. Another train had hit some stones earlier that day without the same effect. On 11 December W32 *Bonchurch* was hauling a goods train from Ventnor to Newport but derailed at Shanklin on wrongly set points to the sidings. On 28 January 1932 a set of carriages being loose shunted into platform 3 at Ryde Pier Head collided with W18 *Ningwood*. Instructions were issued to cease the practice.[28]

Work to improve the bridges and permanent way on the branch lines had not kept pace with withdrawals of the Island companies' engines, so some replacement locomotives were not of Class O2, but lighter axle loading types suitable for those branches that had not yet been upgraded to accept higher axle loadings. LBSCR class A1 and A1X 0-6-0Ts had been inherited from the IWCR and FYNR, so it made sense to transfer more of the same class. The three concerned had been rebuilt with LBSCR Marsh-pattern A1X boilers, separate splashers, sandboxes below the footplate and steam sanding.[54]

W3 (ex B677) had been rebuilt in November 1911 but was stored at Brighton Works from September 1925 to December 1926. During an overhaul the boiler-feed pumps were replaced by injectors, the coal bunker extended and steam heating added. The copper-capped chimney, 12in diameter cylinders and pull-push fittings were retained. The 0-6-0T was turned out in the dark green colour and arrived at Medina Wharf in May 1927 as a replacement

for IWCR W9. *Carisbrooke* nameplates were attached in about August 1929.

W4 (ex B678) had also been rebuilt in November 1911 and stored at Brighton from September 1925 to February 1929. During an overhaul, it received a replacement boiler with an LBSCR Marsh chimney, new 14in cylinders and an extended coal bunker. The existing pull-push fittings were removed. Arriving in June 1929, W4 visited Ryde Works in September when the *Bembridge* nameplates intended for IWCR W8 were fitted along with steam-heating fittings.

W9 (ex B650) had been rebuilt in May 1920 and was active until sent to Brighton Works to receive an overhaul and extended bunker. The 12in cylinders and steam-heating were retained. W9 was transferred in May 1930 and ran for two months before being named *Fishbourne*.

An internal memo dated 6 November 1930 mentioned proposals to send a further member of the class although which one was not identified: there were a dozen possibilities. Mr MacLeod wrote that the three Island companies' engines FYNR W1 *Medina*, IWR W13 *Ryde* and W16 *Wroxall* were 'in sufficient good condition to work to end of 1931…It will not, therefore, be necessary for the fourth engine (Terrier class) to be sent to the Island for the summer of 1931.' This addition metamorphosed into an LBSCR class E1 0-6-0T when transferred the following year.[10]

The seven class A1 and A1X 0-6-0Ts were employed on goods work, including Cement Mills chalk trains, as well as passenger services on the Freshwater and Ventnor West lines. The Ventnor West branch needed suitably equipped engines for the pull-push trains. The SR inherited differing systems from its mainland predecessors and a decision which

W9, at Newport in 1930, does not show any evidence of pull-push pipework, but note the small bare area on the bunker side where the token holder has been removed since arrival on the Island. There are two different screw couplings on the front hook. *O.J. Morris ©Rail Archive Stephenson*

to adopt was not made until 1929. In the meantime those running in the Island were fitted with the LBSCR air-control system, a fortunate choice as this became the standard. Only W4 and the second W9 lacked pull-push gear, the former with its larger diameter cylinders being the first choice whenever FYNR W1 needed assistance on goods work.

Most of the pull-push gear was tucked away underneath the coal bunker, the only visual signs being three coloured hose connections and an electrical coupling on the buffer beam. They were identified by small lettering spelling out 'BRAKE', 'STORAGE' and 'CONTROL'. Pull-push fitted engines normally carried connecting hoses at both the leading and trailing ends but it was practice in the Island to remove and store any unused sets. There was a control cylinder that allowed the driver to work the regulator remotely from the leading carriage using compressed air, the position of the regulator being indicated electrically on a dial gauge. The driver used bell codes to communicate with the fireman who remained with the engine and could close the regulator in an emergency. The SR system was regarded as superior to those used previously but needed to be carefully maintained. It was not unknown for the fireman to be left in charge of opening and closing the regulator, despite instructions to the contrary.[62]

Following the withdrawal of IWCR 2-4-0T W8 at the end of 1929, one member of the class was loaned to Ryde shed to provide cover on the Bembridge branch while W13 *Ryde* and W16 *Wroxall* underwent overhauls. A second was then transferred to Ryde so the IWR 2-4-0Ts could be released for service on the Freshwater line. The allocations were matched to the cylinder sizes:[10]

Inevitably these arrangements became blurred when individual engines fell due for their overhauls. W3 followed W2 in receiving an overhaul early in 1932 when a reconditioned A1X-pattern boiler was fitted. It was renumbered W13 *Carisbrooke* before leaving works in May and W4 became W14 *Bembridge* in September or October. Mr MacLeod was anxious to improve the appearance of the Island's engines by adopting a standard chimney and discovered that a smaller Drummond design was carried by the LSWR class B4 0-4-0Ts. W8, 10–12 and 14 based at Newport were fitted with them during 1932 but W9 and W13 at Ryde kept their LBSCR Marsh and Stroudley chimneys respectively.[41]

Mishaps affecting the class were relatively minor. Services on the Freshwater line were disrupted on 27 February 1926 when an engine derailed with a broken rear axle near Yarmouth. A second derailment involving the IWCR W9 near Watchingwell on 19 October was attributed to excessive speed on the lightly laid track. W11 left the rails on points leading to the sidings at Shide on 3 October 1929 and a wagon derailed in the same place six days later, the accidents being blamed on the poor state of the track. On 6 November W3 was on the Bembridge turntable when the driver heard a passer-by shout 'right' and, believing it to be his fireman, drove off and promptly left the rails. The engine

12in cylinders	W3, 9	Bembridge branch
13in cylinders	W2, 11	Ventnor West branch
14in cylinders	W4, 10, 12	Freshwater line, goods and Cement Mills trains

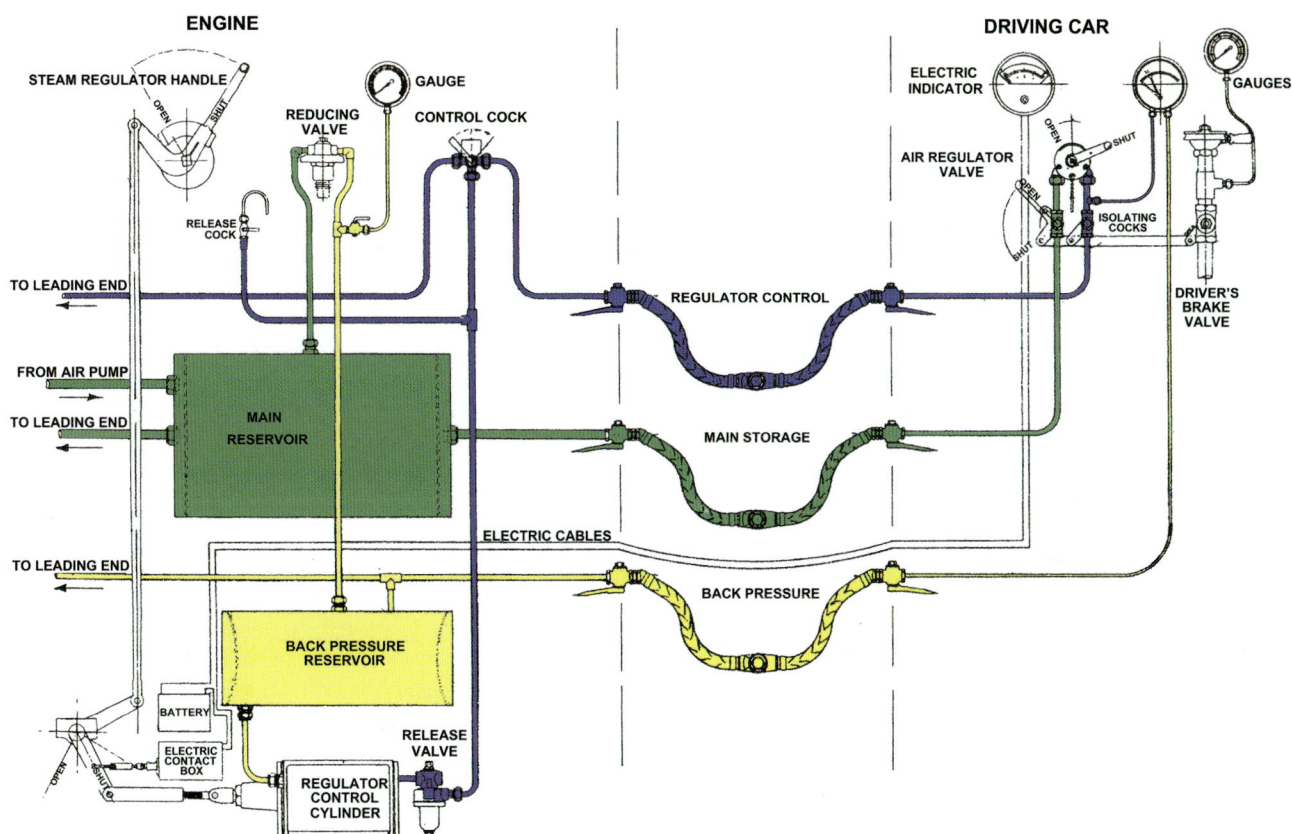

ENGINE

DRIVING CAR

STEAM REGULATOR HANDLE
OPEN SHUT
GAUGE
REDUCING VALVE
CONTROL COCK
RELEASE COCK
TO LEADING END
FROM AIR PUMP
TO LEADING END
MAIN RESERVOIR
REGULATOR CONTROL
ELECTRIC CABLES
TO LEADING END
BACK PRESSURE
BACK PRESSURE RESERVOIR
BATTERY
ELECTRIC CONTACT BOX
RELEASE VALVE
REGULATOR CONTROL CYLINDER
MAIN STORAGE
ELECTRIC INDICATOR
AIR REGULATOR VALVE
OPEN SHUT
ISOLATING COCKS
GAUGES
DRIVER'S BRAKE VALVE

The SR air-control push-pull gear as used form 1930 onwards

Compressed air for the system is supplied by the Westinghouse brake compressor. The reducing valve continuously supplies low pressure air to the back-pressure reservoir and one end of the regulator control cylinder to keep the regulator normally in the shut position. The driver, by means of the valve in the driving car, applies higher pressure air to the other end of the control cylinder to open the regulator. A transducer connected to the regulator linkage provides an electrical indication in the driving car of the regulator's position. The driver also has control of the air brake, but the reversing lever and all other controls are in the hands of the fireman who, in an emergency, can close the regulator by releasing the high-pressure air from the system.

derailed again at Bembridge on 2 August 1933 when part of a point blade broke off.[28]

Following a heavy snowfall early in 1929 brooms were fitted to the guard irons of IWR W16 *Wroxall*. A small snowplough was constructed and temporarily attached to the front buffer beam of O2 W18 *Ningwood*, but was never used in anger.

Mr MacLeod discovered that an engine had to be steamed specially whenever shunting was needed in Ryde Works yard; this led to the creation of *Midget*:[58] He described it thus:

A wooden chassis and a platform was made to suit the rail wheels and give enough space for two men to stand and turn handles that would be connected to a vertical shaft in a column by bevel cog wheels and thence to the gearbox. There would be a ratio of 1 to 1 for travelling light, and 4 to 1 for propelling the wagons, etc. The connection to the rail wheels would be made by chains with coupling rods on the wheels to stop slipping.

Midget measured 8ft 0in long over headstocks, 1ft 2in diameter wheels and had a 5ft 0in wheelbase; the weight was 1ton 15cwt. The body was painted wagon brown and black while the buffer beams, buffers and coupling rods were red. The nameplates were made of wood with some old gilt shaded black transfer letters on a red background. The letters 'SR' on either side of the nameplate were cut out of some IWR door transfers of the word 'FIRST' which were gilt shaded in red and white. The only self-propelled vehicle to be constructed at Ryde Works, *Midget* began work in January 1930 but was thoroughly disliked by the staff. It fell into disuse after Mr MacLeod left the Isle of Wight in 1934 and was broken up in 1938.[58]

By 1930 a system of power classification letters had been introduced. Being the most powerful at the time, the O2s were in power class 'A', W1, 4, 9, 10, 12 and 16 were class 'B' while W2, 3, 11 and 13 were 'C'. In 1924 most of the Island companies' engines had been equipped with LSWR-pattern lamp brackets, one at the base of the chimney and three at footplate level. The O2s arrived carrying additional brackets but they disappeared when replacement boilers were fitted.

MacLeod's innovative creation *Midget*, the hand-powered shunting trolley at Ryde St John's, probably when new. *A. B. MacLeod/IWSR Archive*

Ryde to Ventnor trains carried a headcode lamp with a white lens at chimney height and Ryde to Cowes trains had lamps over each buffer. Different combinations were used on the other lines. SR lamp irons were fitted to the engines and in February 1930 discs replaced the lamps.[30] The white 15in diameter headcode or route indication discs were painted black on the back with the engine number in white. The red-painted headcode lamps, retained for use at night, bore the white lettering 'S. R.' on one side.[29] Within a year duty boards made an appearance. Carried on a spare lamp iron, the rectangular boards were black with white numbers; Ryde duties were numbered 1–12 and Newport 13–24.[58]

On 19 October 1931 the early morning goods train ran through the crossing gates at Causeway Crossing, Freshwater. The engine involved was not identified but the driver received a reprimand and instructions were given that whistles must be sounded when approaching level crossings and tunnels. This led to complaints from residents principally about the shrill Beyer, Peacock whistles carried by the 2-4-0Ts. The O2s based at Ryde carried LSWR pattern whistles but several engines at Newport had Caledonian style organ-pipe hooters dating from IWCR days. In an effort to lessen the complaints the smaller engines were fitted with hooters. Following comments by crews about draughty cabs, engines were fitted with cab doors, painted green and lined out. Photographs suggest this change took place during 1932 and 1933. IWR W16 *Wroxall* never received cab doors while W31 *Chale* (and perhaps other O2s) ran with doors before receiving the large bunker. Other changes at this time included the fitting of double clack valves on the boiler feed and the repositioning of injectors and steam heat pipes.[58]

A new Medina Wharf with improved coal-handling facilities came into use in April 1931. This was followed by a decline in business handled at St Helens Quay and a corresponding increase in traffic over the lines from the wharf to Newport, Newport to Sandown and Newport to Ryde. Mr MacLeod convinced his superiors that none of the existing engines could cope with longer goods trains, some of which were divided or double-headed during the winter months. The obvious solution was the transfer of a more powerful version of class A1X, the LBSCR class E1 0-6-0T.

Designed by William Stroudley, Brighton Works turned out 78 LBSCR class E (later E1) 0-6-0 tank engines between 1874 and 1883 for short-distance goods and shunting work. There were also 125 class D 0-4-2 passenger tank engines that shared boilers and other components. The E1s had the characteristic Stroudley cab, round-topped tanks, inside cylinders, lever reverse and an exterior coal bunker with open rails. The first withdrawal in May 1908 was of LBSCR No. 93 (originally named *Calbourne*) but more than forty remained when four were selected for transfer to the Isle of Wight.

On 18 March 1932 Eastleigh Works was instructed to prepare three members of class E1 for dispatch to the Island. Those selected became W1 *Medina*, W2 *Yarmouth* and W3 *Ryde* (previously B136, B152 and B154). Previously painted in goods black, the three were turned out in lined green with name and number plates. Loaded at Southampton on 1 July, the floating crane carried the engines and some carriages across to Medina Wharf three days later. On 11 March 1933 authorisation was given to send a fourth E1; W4 *Wroxall* (ex B131) arrived on 16 June.[63]

The E1s had LBSCR Marsh-pattern boilers made in two rings with a large dome, modified Ramsbottom safety valves over the firebox and LSWR Drummond chimneys. The Stroudley whistles mounted above the cab gave off a much softer and muffled note quite different from the O2s. W1–3 had the sides of their coal rails plated in soon after arrival but W4 was transferred with the work already done. Ryde Works also fitted a second step to the front footstep. Although quickly fitted with cab doors, the large cab opening still made for a draughty existence when shunting on Medina Wharf. On 10 February 1934 Thomas Smeaton recorded in his diary that W2 and W4 had been

On 4 July 1932 three Class E1 0-6-0Ts were transferred to the Island. Nos W2 and 3 are seen loaded onto the Southampton Docks floating crane with W1 being positioned. A number of LCDR bogie carriages were also carried. *Southampton City Museums/IWSR Archive*

Two for the price of one! W3 *Ryde* and W4 *Wroxall* at Newport, the latter unusually facing the Cowes direction, allow details of both front and rear to be compared in one image. The coal rails have been plated in. *A. B. MacLeod/IWSR Archive*

fitted with black-painted folding screens on the right-hand side of the cab, 'the effect is odd and not very pleasing'. The screens took up too much room and were soon removed.[58] The arrival of the E1s prompted a revision of the Island's power classification system, making them power class 'A', the O2s became 'B' while the A1X 0-6-0Ts were 'C'. The letter was painted on the running plate valance just behind the front buffer beam.[30]

Based at Newport shed, the E1s took charge of the shunting duties at Medina Wharf and most goods workings.

Given a good head of steam, one could walk away with a loaded forty-wagon coal train up Fairlee bank when leaving Newport for Ryde. They rarely ran to Freshwater as their fixed wheelbase did not agree with the many curves but were only officially banned from the Bembridge branch. A few sidings remained with light flat bottom rails, including those to the chalk pit at Shide and Cement Mills, hence the continuing need for the smaller 0-6-0Ts on some goods work. When employed on passenger trains the E1s compared favourably with the O2s as the lower maximum speed was offset by better acceleration. However, complaints about surging and bumping had resulted in their restriction to goods work on the mainland. Beginning with W4 in October 1933, the wheels were rebalanced by Ryde Works but the work cannot have been very successful as the surging sensation was still evident years later. Duties were so arranged that one might be used on a passenger train to balance a goods working. They also assisted on passenger work on summer Saturdays when every available engine was in steam.

The 1931 summer timetable, which began on 5 July, featured a train that ran non-stop on Saturdays from Brading to Ryde Pier Head. This was developed in subsequent summers when short workings from Ryde to Sandown or Shanklin were matched by others that missed out some stations. Engines working these trains carried a second disc at footplate level on the centre lamp iron.

During the 1932 summer season beginning 18 June there was a weekday 'East & West Through Train' from Shanklin to Freshwater and back calling at Sandown, Merstone, Newport, Carisbrooke and Yarmouth (on Saturdays it started at Sandown). The six-carriage train proved very popular and often ran full to capacity. The timetable was so arranged that an O2 worked an early morning Newport to Ventnor goods train before returning with the through train to Newport, where an A1X 0-6-0T took over for the journey to Freshwater. The small engines struggled with the bogie carriages on these trains, as one visitor later observed: 'The almost exhausted beat of the engine as it breasted the Watchingwell bank, and the sudden burst of speed in descending towards Carisbrooke, with the ancient castle coming into view on the right, had a fascination not found elsewhere.' The return from Newport to Shanklin was hauled by an O2, which, after berthing the carriages at Sandown, ran on to Ryde. Within weeks the E1s had replaced the O2s on the through train but the A1X 0-6-0Ts had to manage until the following year when the O2s were cleared to run to Freshwater (and Ventnor West).[31]

Additional trains appeared in the 1933 summer timetable beginning on 3 June. The through train was renamed 'The Tourist' and ran on weekdays from Ventnor to Freshwater and back calling at Shanklin, Sandown, Newport and Yarmouth. An E1 worked an early morning goods train to Ventnor and returned to Newport with the through train before spending the rest of its duty shunting on Medina Wharf. An O2 hauled the train to Freshwater and then worked a round trip to Newport before returning to Newport with 'The Tourist'. A second E1 took over for the run to Ventnor before returning to Newport later in the evening with a goods train; a third E1 was employed solely on goods work. On summer Saturdays engines and their crews from both sheds interworked on trips from Ryde to Ventnor, Cowes and Freshwater. This avoided having to increase the number of crews based at Ryde.

On 22 April 1933 a fireman was fatally injured in Ryde shed when he was crushed between the buffers of W19 *Osborne* and W13 *Carisbrooke* while the latter was being pushed back to make room for W18 *Ningwood*. On Sunday, 21 May W26 *Whitwell* hauled W27 *Merstone* to St Helens Quay for weighing on the 50-ton weighbridge but upon returning to Brading W26's coupled wheels left the track on some worn points. The derailment blocked the branch and the Down main lines, so Ventnor trains had to use the Up line while Bembridge branch passengers made do with a bus until the engine could be recovered.[28]

After Mr MacLeod left the Isle of Wight in 1934, his successor John E. Bell continued to press for more improvements. During an inspection in October 1935, Mr Bell reminded senior management that even though weight restrictions had been relaxed, the Freshwater, Ventnor West and Bembridge lines were still worked by class A1X 0-6-0Ts. A second member of the class had to be kept in steam at Ryde shed in case of an emergency solely because the Bembridge turntable was too small for the O2s. This was taken to heart and the turntable was rebuilt during April 1936. While the work was in progress, W10 and W13 took turns to operate a pull-push train, the only occasion when the branch was so worked. In what became the norm, it displayed a single white route indication disc; previously two had been carried. On one trip W19 was attached to the rear of the train before being used to test the turntable. Soon afterwards the O2s took charge of services on the Bembridge and Freshwater lines.[57]

In May 1936 class O2 0-4-4T W14 *Fishbourne*, W15 *Cowes*, W16 *Ventnor* and W33 *Bembridge* (previously 178, 195, 217 and 218) were landed from the floating crane at Medina Wharf. During overhauls at Eastleigh Works they had received Adams boilers, extended bunkers, cab doors and hooters. This was the first occasion that Eastleigh had fitted the larger bunker, so new works drawings were prepared. W15 was unique among the Island O2s in having no brass beading on the splashers over the front driving wheels, an economy also seen on some members of class G6. W33 differed from the other Island O2s in having a cab roof made from three panels instead of the usual two. The most visible evidence of this was that the panels were joined with two T-section butt straps across the top of the roof instead of the usual single one placed centrally. They received nameplates taken from four of the Island's class A1X 0-6-0Ts and new brass number plates, even though they were disappearing from engines on the mainland. The O2s were sent in exchange for W12 *Ventnor*, laid aside in October 1935, W9 *Fishbourne*, W10 *Cowes* and W14 *Bembridge*. Having been deprived of their nameplates a few weeks beforehand, they were taken back to the mainland and towed to Eastleigh Works. W10 and W12, the former IWCR engines,

O2 Nos W15 *Cowes* and W33 *Bembridge* being loaded onto the floating crane at Southampton on 19 May 1936. Both locos had unique features among IW O2s; W15 has no brass beading on the splashers and W33 had a cab roof made from three panels instead of the usual two, connected by a pair of T-section joiners instead of a single one across the centre. *IWSR Archive*

were stripped of spare parts and left dumped in the open until scrapped in 1949.

A1X W9 was stored at Eastleigh until April 1937 when, following repairs, it was transferred to the service stock as 515S and employed at Lancing Carriage Works. In February 1952 an overhaul and boiler change was followed by a repaint as DS515, but the engine was in such good condition that in November 1953 it became 32650 and was sent to Fratton shed for the Hayling Island services. Further overhauls and a change of boiler took place in February 1957 and March 1963, not long before withdrawal in November.[12] Purchased by the Borough of Sutton & Cheam for display in the new town centre, 32650 instead went to the Kent & East Sussex Railway and ran for a time in SR livery as No. 10 *Sutton*. Laid aside in need of an overhaul, the engine was moved to the Spa Valley Railway in 2004.

A1X W14 was condemned in December 1936 but after a boiler change returned to traffic as 2678 in July 1937. Sent initially to Fratton, between April 1941 and June 1958 the engine was used on the Kent & East Sussex Railway before returning to Fratton for Hayling Island services. Painted in BR lined black as 32678 during an overhaul in September 1949, further overhauls and a change of boiler took place in July 1953 and September 1959. A transfer to Brighton in May 1963 for shunting on the West Quay at Newhaven was short-lived as withdrawal took place in October. No. 32678 was purchased by Butlin's in May 1964, painted at Eastleigh Works in an approximation of the LBSCR Stroudley livery and put on display at Minehead holiday camp. The 0-6-0T then went through several changes of ownership before being moved to the Kent & East Sussex Railway in 1988 and returned to service.

The exchange of engines in 1936 left the Isle of Wight with four class E1 0-6-0Ts, three class A1X 0-6-0Ts and twenty class O2 0-4-4Ts. The E1s monopolised Medina Wharf and worked goods trains to Sandown and Ventnor, to Ryde and to Cowes. The three A1X 0-6-0Ts had charge of the Merstone to Ventnor West branch and Cement Mills chalk trains. Beginning in 1935, additional footsteps and grab handles were fitted to the tank fronts to help crews when working the chalk trains. In 1938 the nameplates were removed for a few weeks but a proposed return to the mainland was abandoned. Of the O2s, eleven were based at Ryde while the other nine at Newport included W27–32 with Drummond boilers. Since Newport's engines took turns working on the Ryde to Ventnor line on summer Saturdays, they were given Adams boilers when overhauled between December 1935 and September 1938 (see Appendix 3). The disliked Drummond boilers were re-employed on the mainland. In addition to passenger duties, the O2s were rostered for the daily goods train from Ryde to Sandown, as well as those on the Bembridge and Freshwater lines.[31]

Only one accident involving the E1 0-6-0Ts appears in the official records, and that was a derailment of W4 *Wroxall* when shunting at Sandown on the evening of 29 February 1936. The same could not be said for the O2s.

W27 *Merstone* destroyed a permanent way trolley between Whippingham and Newport on 22 April, while W18 *Ningwood* derailed on points at Havenstreet on 21 September when shunting a ballast train; the points were declared overdue for replacement. W31 *Chale* derailed at Freshwater on 23 July 1935 and 2 August 1936. The first incident was blamed on a sudden change in the super-elevation on the sharp curve aggravated by the stiffness of the engine after having just left Ryde Works after an overhaul, while on the second occasion the porter-signalman moved the points too soon. *Chale* was involved in a serious accident on 25 January 1939 when the mail and passenger train derailed on the Freshwater line near Watchingwell after an embankment slipped because of heavy rain. Recovery was a most difficult task as the engine was lying on its side and could only be righted by jacking and packing.[28]

On 25 June 1939 a group of members from the Railway Correspondence & Travel Society made a visit to the Isle of Wight and travelled on the railways. During a conducted tour of Ryde Works they found W14 *Fishbourne* in the erecting shop 'freshly painted and beautifully lined out and ready to be hauled out the next day.' W11 *Newport* was in for 'general repairs and reboiling'.[31]

The outbreak of war in September 1939 coincided with the end of the summer season and the change to a winter timetable. By November several engines were being stored: W2, 11 and 29 at Ventnor (probably Ventnor West), W4, 18, 21 and 32 at Ryde with W24 and W26 at Newport.[12] However, the imposition of fuel rationing decimated the bus services and forced the local residents to make greater use of the railways. The timetable was changed to focus on Cowes, where there was a large increase in naval shipbuilding and aircraft production. Hopes that a 1940 summer service might operate were dashed on 9 July when the government issued an order prohibiting all but essential travel along much of the south coast. The Island became virtually an armed camp with large numbers of military personnel that needed transport, often at short notice.[60] Engines had to work a greater variety of services during the day, hence the appearance of members of class E1 on Cowes and Freshwater line passenger services in between their goods duties. Those in service in October 1942 included W14, 17, 18 and 20 on the Ryde to Ventnor line, W22–24 and 29 shared the Cowes–Newport–Ryde services, W31 was on the Bembridge branch and W11 on the Ventnor West branch. W13 was in steam at Newport, while W2 and W4 were in charge of the goods trains and shunting at Medina Wharf. After D-Day on 6 June 1944 travel restrictions were eased and business began to return to some normality.[12] The first summer service since 1939 began on 7 May 1945, the day Germany surrendered. On 12 June W11 *Newport* was in charge of the Ventnor West branch train, while W19 *Osborne* was on the Bembridge branch. The engines were said to be in a clean condition and well maintained, the majority being in steam by August.[31]

Considering the Isle of Wight's location, there were surprisingly few mishaps. On 7 April 1940 W16 *Ventnor* was signalled into Ryde St John's Road Down loop road during

One of the wartime repaints in unlined livery was W28 *Ashey*, reputedly malachite green although it is difficult to be certain in this view taken at Newport shortly after the Second World War. The power classification letter 'B' is just visible on the valance, behind the front buffer beam. *RP23031*

the blackout and collided violently with a brake carriage at the rear of an empty train. On 5 December a bomb exploded on the line about 40 yards north of St John's Road station immediately in front of the 6.35pm four-carriage Ventnor train and derailed W18 *Ningwood* on the damaged track. A similar incident on 24 May 1941 derailed W27 *Merstone* and two carriages near Medina Wharf.

The appointment of Oliver Bulleid as Chief Mechanical Engineer in 1937 coincided with experiments that culminated in the adoption of malachite green 'as bright a mid-green as there is', lined out in black edged in yellow.[41] This colour was accompanied by transfers with lettering adapted from a typeface used on advertising material.[15] The Bulleid lettering was in gilt with an internal black or green line to match the body colour. The gilt numerals on the bunker side and buffer beam had black shading but lacked the internal line. Inevitably, the introduction of this livery was badly disrupted by the onset of war.[15]

The changes in livery first manifested themselves at Ryde in October 1939, when W4 and 24 were turned out in unlined dark green and lettered in the Maunsell pre-war style.[10] The next repaints were apparently in malachite green. George Gardener, acting Assistant for the Isle of Wight, wrote an article that was published in the November–December 1941 issue of the *Southern Railway Magazine*. He stated that the new standard 'light green colour' had only recently been introduced to the Island.

'So far, fourteen engines (twelve O2 and two A1X) have been dealt with after passing through Shops for general repair.'[31] W18, which provided the motive power for an inspection in July 1944, was one of at least four O2s in unlined green with Maunsell lettering; perhaps all twelve O2s were in this style. (They were certainly not all in dark green with Bulleid gilt lettering, as claimed by Mr Bradley.[33]) W18 was also the first O2 to be photographed following the replacement of frame-mounted rear guard irons by bogie-mounted versions. The other O2s each had the guard irons changed, including new arrivals.

By the end of 1941 orders had been issued that the Island's engines be painted in unlined black. They were probably turned out with Maunsell lettering prior to the adoption of a cheaper 'Sunshine' lettering in Old Gold yellow with a black interior line, green shading and highlights picked out in yellow. As previously, the numerals lacked the internal line. O2 W15 was observed carrying Sunshine lettering and numerals on top of patches covering an earlier style. This sombre livery was still being applied at Ryde during the first half of 1945 when W8 and W23 received overhauls.[15]

Engines that underwent overhauls later in 1945 benefited from a change to malachite green with black lining edged in yellow. It was accompanied by a variation of the 'Sunshine' lettering and numerals with black shading. The livery was first carried by W13 when returned to service in November followed by W26 and W31 ex-works

Class O2 W34 *Newport* was repainted in a distinctively lighter shade than malachite when overhauled at Eastleigh in 1947 and is seen here at Newport soon after transfer. *IWSR Archive*

in February–March 1946.[33] P. C. Allen visited the Isle of Wight in April and noted the following liveries:[10]

Lined dark green	W11
Unlined dark green (first wartime colouring)	W4, 24
Unlined malachite green (second wartime colouring)	W18, 22, 28, 29
Unlined black (third wartime colouring)	W2, 3, 8, 14–16, 19, 20, 23, 25, 30, 32, 33
Lined malachite green	W1, 13, 17, 26, 31
Undergoing overhaul or repair	W21, 27

By then all departments were working hard to make up for the arrears of maintenance caused by the war. Mill Hill tunnel at Cowes was closed from 2 to 16 February 1946 so that the drains, ballast and track could be renewed. During that time passenger trains working to Mill Hill had to be 'top and tailed' by engines.[39]

The 1946 summer service was adversely affected by a lack of serviceable engines and stock. So many engines required attention that Eastleigh Works agreed to overhaul W18 and W29. However, the floating crane's first post-war visit to the Island was delayed until 22 February 1947, by which time Ryde Works had begun work on W18. W11 and W29 were collected from Medina Wharf and taken to Southampton, from where they were towed to Eastleigh on 26 February. A1X W11 *Newport* had become surplus to requirements following the cessation of cement production at Cement Mills on 30 June 1944.[48] This former IWCR engine was returned to service as SR 2640, later became BR 32640 and lasted until withdrawal in November 1963.

Following an overhaul and a repaint in lined malachite green, W29 *Alverstone* was taken back to the Island on 20 May 1947 accompanied by a spare boiler and an additional O2. W34 *Newport* (previously 201) carried an extended coal bunker and a SR whistle. Evidently, there was a shortage of malachite green paint as it was turned out in a lighter green colour, albeit lined out in the same manner as those engines in malachite green.[15] The manufacture of number plates had been discontinued, so a smaller version of the bunker side numerals were applied where a plate would have been located. These two Eastleigh repaints featured a deeper black border at the base of the splasher than those done at Ryde and had a 'W' prefix on the front buffer beam.[31]

The winter of 1946–47 was marked by a period of very cold weather with gales, heavy snow and ice that crippled Britain's transport system for weeks. Difficulties in working the goods trains highlighted shortcomings with the sanding arrangements on the E1 0-6-0Ts. By August 1947 three had been fitted with additional sandboxes to the front of the frames, the existing sandboxes in the splashers being left unused; W2 was dealt with later.[31] The painters had been hard at work and by November only three colours remained:[10]

Unlined black	W2, 3, 8, 14–16, 20, 23, 33
Lined malachite green	W1, 4, 13, 17–19, 21, 22, 24, 26–32
Lined light green	W34

In 1946-47, during overhaul that included repainting, some green O2s also acquired yellow and black lining to the front buffer beam. Just to be different, W16 *Ventnor* had

A1X W13 *Carisbrooke* was the first locomotive to be overhauled and repainted after hostilities ended and is seen at Ryde St John's in October 1945 in full post-war finery; she is stated 'to have demolished austerity single-handedly'! *A B MacLeod IWSR Archive, colour by John Faulkner*

Although primarily goods engines, on the Isle of Wight the Class E1 were painted in full passenger livery during SR days. W4 *Wroxall* is seen at Newport during the summer of 1947 following overhaul and repaint in malachite green. *IWSR Archive*

Class E4 2510 at Newport on 9 July 47 in a distinctly worn unlined black livery, on an unrecorded working. *IWSR Archive*

red coupling rods and the two A1X 0-6-0Ts carried copper-capped chimneys. In January 1948 W25 *Godshill* emerged following an overhaul, during which a Drummond-pattern boiler was fitted. Finished in lined malachite green, *Godshill* was the last Island engine to be turned out by Ryde Works lettered 'SOUTHERN'.[64]

The transition from Southern Railway to British Railways ownership was marked by a failed experiment involving a more powerful engine and a longer carriage. Mainland members of class O2 were usually loaded to a maximum of 100 tons but those working on the Island railways were expected to haul 150 tons during the summer, giving them

Although not of the highest quality, colour images of W34 *Newport* are rare. This view shows it shunting stock at Ryde Pier Head on 17 May 1948 and also shows that it had numerals on the bunker back instead of a brass number plate. In the background the paddle steamer *Ryde* is moored at Berth 2. *Howard Sprenger collection*

little reserve of power in emergencies. Six-coupled wheels and a sizeable bunker were essential but the SR had no modern classes with such features, so an LBSCR class E4 0-6-2T was selected.

Designed by Robert J. Billinton, seventy-five LBSCR class E4 0-6-2 tank engines were built at Brighton Works between 1897 and 1903 for secondary passenger and goods services. Compared with their Stroudley predecessors, they were much larger machines with a generous cab giving a more modern appearance. Most had received new or previously used Marsh boilers and the whole class was intact when plans were made to send one to the Isle of Wight.[65]

Preparations began in 1944, when clearances were checked using a template carriage.[60] Unfortunately, the SR was unable to use the 150-ton floating crane to transfer engines and stock as it had been hired to the Ministry of War Transport and could not be released from the Clyde before mid-1946. There was a 60-ton floating crane (MoWT No. 11) at Southampton but it lacked sufficient deck area to carry rolling stock and its use with a barge or Mark 3 LCT (Landing Craft Tank) was rejected on cost grounds. The larger floating crane finally arrived back at Southampton on 9 July 1946 but the need for an overhaul delayed its return to service until 18 January 1947.[59]

On 29 October 1946 class E4 0-6-2T 2510 entered Ashford Works for repairs. A shorter chimney is said to have been fitted sometime earlier but the footsteps also had to be modified to clear the loading gauge. Able to work with both Westinghouse and vacuum brake-fitted stock, it carried the wartime unlined black livery. The engine arrived at Eastleigh Works on 6 December for inspection and weighing but then had to be stored until the floating crane became available. Leaving the works on 17 January 1947, 2510 and a SECR 60ft-long carriage finally arrived at Medina Wharf on 22 February.[59]

After clearances were again checked, a decision was made not to run 2510 into Ventnor station as apparently the track could not be slewed without increasing an already wide gap between the platform and footboards of the carriage. Similar problems existed at Cowes. On 17 April 1947 Mr Gardener, by then the permanent Assistant for the Isle of Wight, was asked to employ the engine on normal passenger services for one week so that any effect on the bridges and permanent way could be observed, but it is unclear whether this was done precisely as requested. The longer carriage proved to be unsuitable and was returned to the mainland on 20 May. Further test runs with 2510 included a special working from Ryde St John's Road to Wroxall on 8 June.[59]

Although the transfer of a dozen of the class for the Ryde to Ventnor services had been envisaged, money to pay for the necessary alterations was not forthcoming, so the experiment had to be abandoned. The E4 was then sent to Newport as a spare. On 13 September 1948, 2510 was seen working a passenger train on the Freshwater line owing to the failure of W26 *Whitwell* but that was a rarity and latterly the engine was steamed only in dire emergency, usually for an occasional ballast train along the Sandown line. It returned to the mainland on 5 April 1949 still carrying the 'SOUTHERN' lettering, and this was followed by a visit to Eastleigh Works during which the BR number 32510 was applied during a repaint. The engine rejoined its companions in relative obscurity until 1962, when a derailment at Southampton docks was followed by withdrawal.[31]

8
British Railways

On 1 January 1948 Britain's four regional railway companies passed into public ownership. The creation of a fresh identity was a priority and instructions were given to letter engines 'BRITISH RAILWAYS'. In June the mainland workshops were told to begin using the Gill Sans alphabet and in September a lined black livery was introduced for certain classes. This was followed at the end of the year by the adoption of an emblem.[15]

Nationalisation was welcomed by the Island railwaymen who, under the direction of R. Meggett, the Ryde shed foreman, were quick to make some changes. Those engines that underwent overhauls were turned out in lined malachite green and lettered 'BRITISH RAILWAYS' in yellow shaded black. W15 *Cowes* and W33 *Bembridge* emerged from Ryde Works in April 1948, W20 in May and W31 in September. The majority were given new lettering when stopped for washout, etc. The work was done in easy stages, so there were occasions when one could be seen running in a partially finished condition. On green engines, the 'SOUTHERN' lettering was painted over using grey undercoat and, once dry, made good with a covering of malachite green; the patch was still visible in certain lights.

O2 W33 *Bembridge* at Freshwater c. 1948 following overhaul and the fitting of a Drummond boiler, repainted malachite green, lettered 'British Railways' and with numerals of the same size. *IWSR Archive*

E1 W4 *Wroxall* was recorded in traffic at Ventnor in 1948 with the 'Southern' painted over with grey undercoat, shunting LSWR Full Brake No. 1018. *Henry Meyer*

The application of 'BRITISH RAILWAYS' lettering was followed by a coat of varnish.[15] The first of these partial repaints was probably W17 *Seaview* seen on 24 April. Progress was swift and by 25 September only W25 and W34 remained 'un-nationalised'. On 13 September W34 appeared with grey patches but a week later both tank sides were in malachite green. The rest of the engine retained the light green received at Eastleigh Works in 1947. W2, 3, 8, 14, 16, 23 and 2510 were in wartime unlined black and never ran in lined malachite green. They were partially repainted but with 'BRITISH RAILWAYS' lettering in yellow shaded green. The sole exception, 2510, kept its 'SOUTHERN' lettering until returned to the mainland the following year.[31]

In the absence of transfers for the 'BRITISH RAILWAYS' lettering, the work had to be done by hand. Eastleigh Works prepared full-size drawings for the paint shops and from them created pounces out of thin card. The outline of the lettering was transferred from the drawing by pricking or piercing with a sharp point to produce a series of small holes. It was common practice to use pounces whenever transfers were unobtainable. One of the pounces was sent to Ryde Works. At the beginning of the painting process, the pounce was attached to the tank side and the whole area dabbed with a bag of chalk to

create an outline of the lettering for the painter. The basic colour in yellow paint was done first, then black or green shading, followed by a coat of varnish. Ryde omitted the Sunshine livery's highlights and internal lines, presumably to save time. The existing numerals with black or green shading were retained except on W33, which was turned out in April 1948 with smaller bunker side numerals to match the lettering. W15 had the bunker side numerals reduced in size sometime between April and October.[15]

In December 1948 the first of four O2s was seen in service painted black with red, yellow and grey lining. The lining was applied only to the boiler bands, running plate valance, tank and bunker side. The lining on the bunker extended no higher than on the tank sides and was a straight line to the ends of the valance. On W14 the 'BRITISH RAILWAYS' yellow lettering (the standard cream-coloured paint was as yet unavailable) was painted on by hand in the Gill Sans style accompanied by a matching running number and the SR power classification letter on the bunker side; the shaded numerals on the front buffer beam were unchanged.[15] It was ex-works at Ryde shed on 14 December, when Charles Woodnutt noted in his diary: 'W14 *Fishbourne* is painted black and lined as per LNWR. The result is not pleasing at first sight as lining does not

W31 *Chale* in full malachite livery with British Railways lettering stands at Wroxall on 20 March 1949. This is a working from Newport as evidenced by the barely visible, single disc over the locomotive's left-hand buffer and the SECR Brake Third at the Ventnor end of the train set. *IWSR Archive*

W29 *Alverstone* had been overhauled at Eastleigh in 1947; seen here at Newport on 15 September 1948 it has been hand-relettered 'British Railways' locally but still retains the broader black base to the splasher and a 'W' prefix on the front buffer beam from the Eastleigh repaint. *Pamlin*

W16 *Ventnor* stands at Ryde St John's in April 1949, newly repainted in lined black but without lettering or crest on the tank side. Note the low-level lining on the bunker side and the straight lining along the valance, also the lack of lining on the sandbox/splasher; the power classification appears beneath the number. *R. R. Bowler/IWSR Archive*

follow the bunker shape.' The other three were lined out but ran without any lettering for several months, pending the expected delivery of BR emblems. W21 was ex-works in January 1949, W16 in February and W17 in April.

A1X W13 *Carisbrooke* remained in lined malachite green and W8 *Freshwater* in unlined black. For several weeks W13 was alone in handling services on the Ventnor West branch as W8 was in Ryde Works undergoing an overhaul. Whenever possible *Carisbrooke* was stopped for a washout at weekends as the line had no Sunday service but on 17 and 24 September 1948, O2 W27 *Merstone* deputised. There were plans to take it into Ryde Works for attention during the following winter but instead the decision was made to send two further O2s as replacements. W13 worked the branch for the final time on Saturday, 23 April 1949 before being laid aside with W8 at Newport. The nameplates were removed before the pair left the Island on 4 May. After residing at the rear of Eastleigh shed, in August they visited the works for minor attention, removal of the pull-push gear and renumbering as 32646 (W8) and 32677 (W13) using Gill Sans yellow numerals.[15] The 'BRITISH RAILWAYS' shaded lettering was kept until their next repaints in 1951 and 1952. Residing at Fratton shed, both were employed regularly on the Hayling Island branch. No. 32677 was overhauled at Brighton Works in September 1952 but was withdrawn in September 1959 and broken up in April 1960. No. 32646, the former FYNR engine, was withdrawn in November 1963.[31]

Eastleigh Works fitted two O2s (ex 181 and 198) with extended coal bunkers and pull-push equipment recovered from previously equipped mainland O2s. The larger components were mounted on the left-hand running plate and to the front of the tank. Unlike W34, Eastleigh did not fit bogie-mounted guard irons. The smokebox doors retained additional lamp irons at the three and nine o'clock positions but they disappeared when the boilers were changed during the next overhauls; the guard irons were also changed at an unknown date. Becoming W35 and W36, the pair were towed by class Q1 0-6-0 No. C20 to Southampton on 7 April 1949 to await shipment to Medina Wharf on 13 April. W36 entered service on the Ventnor West branch on Monday, 25 April while its companion spent the day out of use at Newport shed with W8 and W13.

W35 *Freshwater* and W36 *Carisbrooke* were the first Island engines to carry the standard black livery with red, cream and grey lining. The lining followed the curved bottom edge of the running plate valance at each end and was taken up to the top of the bunker sides. The combined splashers and sandboxes were lined without regard to the black-painted brass beading. Cream running numbers and the SR power classification letter were carried on the bunker sides. The front buffer beam had a matching cream number in addition to small lettering that identified the pull-push connections. The tank sides were left blank ready for the emblem and nameplates, the latter being fitted at Ryde a few weeks after arrival. Beginning with W18 *Ningwood* and W28 *Ashey* in December 1949, the O2s were repainted in the standard black livery with cream lining, as carried by W35 and W36. The only difference was in the use of small, shaded numerals on the front buffer beam. Classed by BR as

Delivered in 1949, W35 and W36 were fitted with pull-push equipment, specifically for working the Ventnor West branch. This photo of W36 *Carisbrooke* at Merstone on branch duty soon after delivery provides a good depiction of the pull-push gear as applied to the pair of locos. A less tidy installation than on the A1X class, the control cylinder was fitted ahead of the tank and the back-pressure reservoir was situated beneath the Westinghouse pump, which supplied the compressed air for the system. Also of note are the modified front footsteps to clear the piping, lamp irons mounted on the smokebox door, no BR crest and a side tank patched from end to end as early as 1949. ©*anistr.com*

freight engines, the E1s were painted in unlined black.[15] See the table (right) for what the repainting dates are believed to have been.

By the end of 1949 the Island had received supplies of the emblem. Designed by Cecil Thomas FRBS, it was unkindly called an 'emaciated lion balancing on a bicycle wheel'; 'Lion over a Wheel' would be a better description. The lion was in chrome yellow, lined in red, the wheel red and white while the 'BRITISH RAILWAYS' lettering was in white on a black background. Left- and right-facing transfers were produced, so the lion always faced forwards, and there were two sizes. It was said W18 and W28 briefly carried the smaller version but it was rejected as unsuitable for the Island engines. That made it necessary to lower nameplates

No.	Date	No.	Date	No.	Date
W1	*8.1951	W19	1.1951	W28	12.1949
W2	*8.1949	W20	5.1951	W29	2.1950
W3	*11.1953	W21	12.1952	W30	4.1951
W4	*10.1951	W22	3.1950	W31	1.1952
W14	9.1954	W23	6.1951	W32	6.1953
W15	10.1950	W24	4.1950	W33	4.1953
W16	11.1951	W25	11.1951	W34	1.1953
W17	2.1952	W26	10.1950	W35	4.1949
W18	12.1949	W27	5.1952	W36	4.1949
*Unlined					

The application of the BR crest required the lowering of the nameplates; W17 *Seaview*, seen at Ryde St John's on 26 June 1950, has had the nameplate repositioned but the former area has not yet been made good. *Pamlin*

Of the four O2s painted in the first style of BR lined black, only W14 *Fishbourne* was lettered with 'British Railways', as depicted in this view of a Bembridge branch train at Brading in 1949. The lettering and numbering were in Southern yellow because the preferred BR cream was not yet available. The tanks of the other three locos, W16, W17 and W21, were left blank, pending delivery of BR crests. © *The Transport Treasury, colour by John Faulkner*

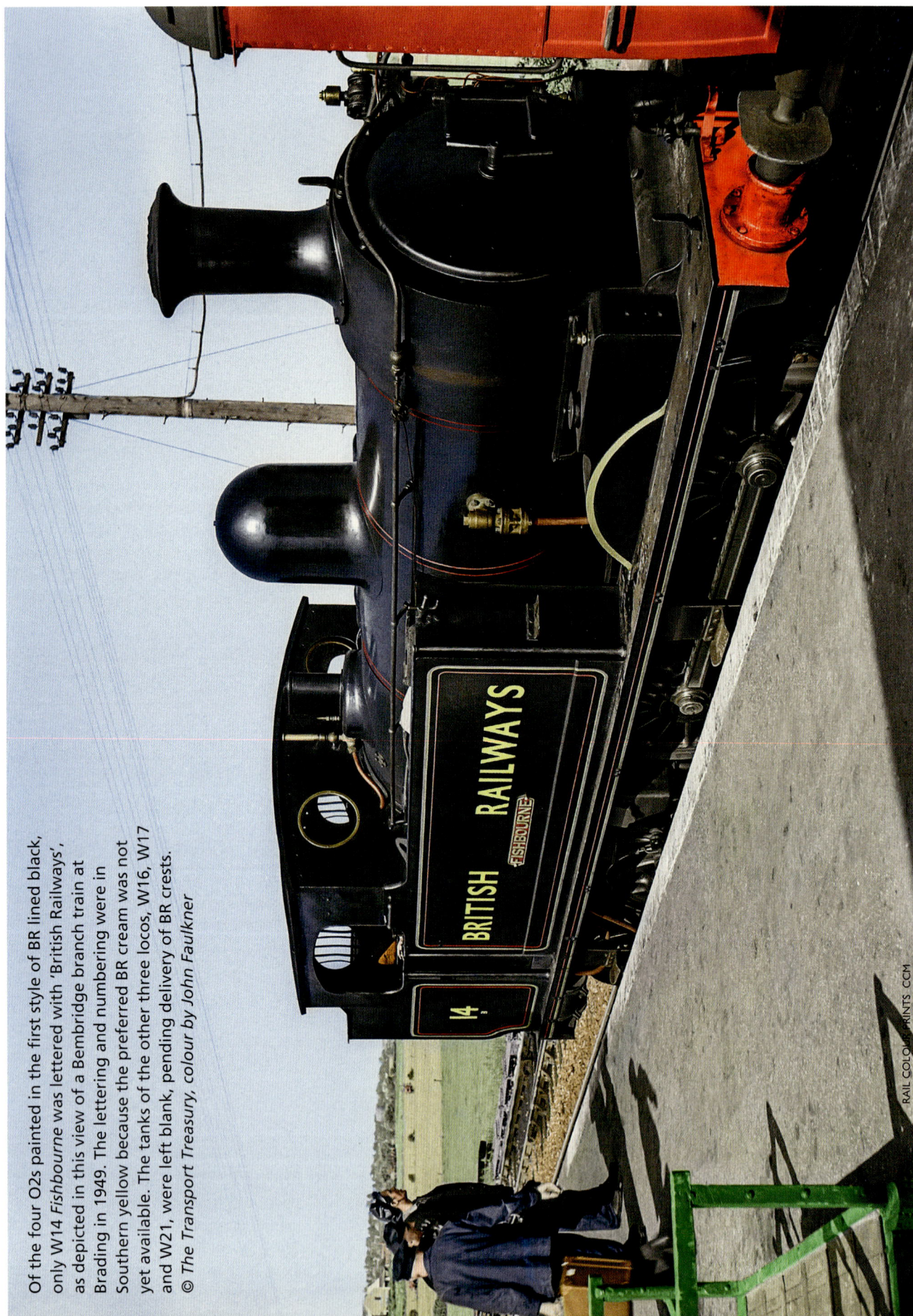

RAIL COLOUR PRINTS CCM

Early in BR days roof ventilators were fitted to the O2s apart from Nos. W33/5/6. This view of W24 *Calbourne* was taken at Wroxall during the summer of 1953 and shows the ventilator in the open position. W33 *Bembridge* was unique in having the cab roof in three panels rather than the usual two as seen here. Note also the bunker number plate with the 'Southern Railway' lettering chiselled off. Lining has been applied to the sandbox/splasher. *J. T. Francis*

CHARLES WOODNUTT'S APRIL 1950 OBSERVATIONS	
Lined malachite green lettered 'BRITISH RAILWAYS'	W1, 4, 19, 20, 25–27, 30–33
Non-standard lined black with emblem, lining on the splashers	W14, 17, 21
Non-standard lined black with emblem, no lining on the splashers	W16
Lined black with emblem	W18, 22, 28, 29, 35
Lined black with no emblem	W36
Unlined black lettered 'BRITISH RAILWAYS'	W3, 23
Unlined black with no emblem	W2
In works	W24, 34
Not seen	W15

on the O2s by approximately 4in in order to accommodate the standard size; it measured 15in by 15½in high. None of the green engines received the emblem and of those that were black, W2 *Yarmouth* and W36 *Carisbrooke* managed without until overhauled in 1952. W3 *Ryde* kept the 'BRITISH RAILWAYS' shaded lettering until November 1953.[15] Since the repaints only took place following overhauls, it was several years before the black livery and emblem predominated. Charles Woodnutt recorded the situation in April 1950 (*See* table above).

The last green engine to be painted black was W32 *Bonchurch* in June 1953. Ryde Works eventually got around

to repainting the four O2s that had been given yellow lining and numerals. On W14 *Fishbourne*, the emblem had replaced the 'BRITISH RAILWAYS' lettering by April 1950 but a full repaint with cream lining did not take place until the next overhaul in 1954. W36 was left unlined between July 1952 and December 1954 after its overhaul overran.[31]

In August 1950 it was reported that 'the Island O2 0-4-4Ts with BR emblems have had sliding roof ventilators fitted at Ryde Works. One or two engines in malachite green have also had this alteration carried out.'[31] Three did not receive ventilators: W33, W35 and W36.

W36 *Carisbrooke* ran in unlined black for over two years in 1952–54, as detailed in the text. It is seen at Newport heading a Sandown line train in 1953. By now the two lamp irons on the smokebox door and pull-push hoses have been removed, but the remainder of the redundant pull-push equipment is extant, as evidenced by the presence of the back-pressure reservoir on the left-hand side running plate. *J. H. Aston/IWSR Archive*

Although the SR number plates were retained, the Company's title was chiselled off, leaving only the prefix and running number. On W34–36, in lieu of number plates, the running number was repeated in small numerals on the rear buffer beam. BR number plates were never fitted to smokebox doors but in 1951 the engines did acquire small oval shed plates: 71F for Ryde and 71E for Newport, changed to 70H and 70G from 1 July 1954. After the closure of Newport shed in 1957, former Newport engines ran without any plates, an exception being W27 that carried a 70G plate until withdrawal, an oversight as by then 70G belonged to Weymouth. W2 had a brass star embellishment to the smokebox door handle, a feature carried by other engines during SR days and later by W22. Whistles and hooters on the O2s were swapped around seemingly at random. In 1953 those carrying a whistle were W14, 16, 18, 20, 24–27, 31, 35 and 36, while the remainder had hooters. During 1954 BR power classification letters ('0P' on O2s or '2F' on E1s) were applied to the bunker side above the running number, initially in addition to the SR letters 'A' or 'B'. Engines continued to display the route indication discs, albeit somewhat grubby at times. Also noted during BR days was a code for the handful of short workings between Cowes and Newport. Occasionally, a train might display a wrong or unlisted code but they were rare events. To accompany the black livery, headcode lamps for use at night were repainted more prominently in white.[64] Despite the imposition of the black livery, the engines were in a much cleaner condition than was usual on the mainland.[31]

Several mishaps reached the ears of officialdom, although the engines concerned were rarely recorded. In July 1948 W14 *Fishbourne* derailed while running round at Bembridge after the guard failed to reset the points and came to rest at a distinct angle. On 31 August W3 *Ryde* demolished a stalled van on a farm crossing near Alverstone when working a Newport-bound goods train. Accidents during the 1950s included two minor collisions at Ryde Pier Head, one with stop blocks at Newport, and two fatalities when staff were run down by trains in Ryde tunnel.[28]

The Isle of Wight railways were busier than ever during the summer season, with record numbers of visitors. Most engines were in steam on summer Saturdays but that contrasted with the winter months when many were stored for short periods, often before or immediately following an overhaul at Ryde Works. Easter 1950 was enlivened by a rail tour on 12 April operated for the Ian Allan Locospotters Club. More well-known was a tour on 18 May 1952 for members of the Railway Correspondence & Travel Society. W3 *Ryde* was rostered to haul a special train from Ryde Pier Head to Cowes before returning to Newport, where malachite green W32 *Bonchurch* was attached for the rest of the tour. Visits were made to Freshwater and Ventnor West before the train travelled from Merstone to Sandown and Brading. The only section not traversed was Sandown to Ventnor. From Brading the branch train, hauled by W14 *Fishbourne*, made two trips

with members to Bembridge and back before the special train continued to Ryde. A visit was made to Ryde Works, where W35 *Freshwater* was receiving the first general overhaul since its transfer to the Island and W29 *Alverstone* was in for attention to wheels and tyres. W32 then took the train to Ryde Pier Head, from where the group returned to the mainland.

Within months the first of several line closures took place. The Ventnor West branch had been worked by W35 and W36, although an E1 was used on a couple of summer Saturdays when there was a shortage of O2s. W14 monopolised the Bembridge branch, while latterly W28, 30 and 31 were regulars on the Freshwater line. However, on all three lines the final trains were hauled by other engines. On Saturday, 13 September 1952 W27 *Merstone* was working on the Ventnor West branch, on Saturday, 20 September 1953 W29 *Alverstone* was in charge of services on the Freshwater line, while W28 *Ashey*, which needed to be turned prior to a visit to Ryde Works, was on the Bembridge branch.[66]

Correspondence dated May to August 1954 between the Mechanical & Electrical Engineer at Brighton and the Chief Regional Officer disclosed that there were three members of class O2 for which no work was available. However, a commitment not to remove the permanent way on the closed lines for a year applied also to the disposal of surplus motive power. Three were in store but that was not an indication of their general condition as only one required heavy boiler repairs and replacement cylinders. Another two in service were possible candidates as they needed boiler repairs and one had fractures in the main frames. Once the engines had accumulated the maximum possible mileage they were to be exchanged for the two in store that were in better condition. Orders were subsequently issued to withdraw three from service during 1955 and a fourth after the Sandown to Newport line closed a year later. A fifth was reprieved because light-engine mileage was expected to increase following the closure of Newport shed.[66]

Although the O2s concerned were not identified, W23 *Totland* was last seen by Charles Woodnutt running in service on 1 December 1953 but by 21 February 1954 it was lying disused in the stores siding alongside Ryde shed. *Totland* was an unpopular spare with no regular crew, needed boiler repairs and had a cracked cylinder. W19 and W28 were in use until June 1954, when they joined W23 in store; both required boiler repairs and W19 had cracked frames.[67]

W34 *Newport* had not been earmarked for early withdrawal. The investment in conversion for Isle of Wight service and shipment across the Solent as late as 1947 would have given it a high 'book' value that would gradually depreciate over time and this would have had a bearing on writing off the loco. A free-steaming loco and well-liked by the regular crew, W34 remained in service until 19 March 1955, two days before entering the works for a general repair. However, it was wheeled out again on 3 April and the works return for 9 April noted W34 'Found to be beyond

The E1s, being now considered solely goods engines, were also painted unlined black. W2 *Yarmouth* displays this sombre livery at Newport on 14 September 1953. Note also the 'A' power classification below the number and the 71E shed plate. *IWSR Archive*

Laid-aside locomotives awaiting their fate in the stores siding beside Ryde Shed on 3 September 1954. Barely visible, nearest the buffer stop and facing chimney towards the pier, is W23 *Totland*, which had been languishing on this spot since February or earlier. Next is W19 *Osborne* and in the foreground is W28 *Ashey*, both having been stored in the siding since June. W28 was reprieved in April 1955 when W34 *Newport* was found to be beyond repair during a scheduled general overhaul. *RCTS Image Archive*

repair'. There is no record of the specific fault (or faults) that condemned the loco, but it is known that it had the oldest cylinders in the O2 fleet and, like a number of other O2s, the frames were fractured. Worn cylinders alone would not have been a terminal fault, but possibly the frames were more seriously fractured than those on other locos. Clearly, W28 *Ashey* would be less expensive to repair and so was reprieved, entering the works on 25 April for a general repair and then remaining in service until the last day of steam. W23 and 34 were formally withdrawn on 13 August. According to official records, W34 was scrapped by 8 October but many components would have been salvaged. The driving wheels replaced those on W24. W23 was photographed in an intact state in the stores road alongside Ryde shed on 17 September. By 23 October, a now dismembered W23 was photographed at roughly the same spot. Resting on works trolleys and comprising only the frames, buffers, draw gear, bunker, footplate, parts of the running plate and horn guides, the lush and undisturbed weeds growing alongside the loco suggest that stripping for reusable parts had taken place elsewhere. W23 was recorded as scrapped on 5 November. The driving wheels went to W20.[68]

The third withdrawal was W19 *Osborne* on 5 November 1955. The cylinders were worn out, the frames fractured

and, according to a former Ryde Works foreman, the drawbar gusset was buckled. This was a thick vertical plate between the frames through which the entire drawbar load was transmitted when hauling a train chimney first. Said to be one of the more powerful O2s, the buckled draw gear may be evidence that this was true. Sadly, these afflictions were overwhelming and this engine was dismantled early in the following year.

W15 *Cowes* visited Ryde Works in June 1955, when the wheels were removed for fitting to W16 *Ventnor* and a worn set substituted from W28 *Ashey*. Returned to service for the summer season, no recorded observations have been found of W15 *Cowes* in use after 19 September, the first day of the winter timetable. The O2 had been laid aside in the stores siding at Ryde by 25 November facing the Pier Head and was still in the same situation on 29 December. No final decision to withdraw the engine had been made as it was subsequently photographed facing the other way after having been taken around the Sandown–Newport–Ryde triangle shortly before the Sandown line closed. Officially withdrawn on 12 May 1956, as late as 7 August W15 was largely intact, carrying nameplates but without the forward drawbar. W16 entered Ryde Works for a general overhaul on 30 July and it has

E1 W2 *Yarmouth* was undergoing a General Overhaul at Ryde on 28 June 1949; the buffer beam has probably been removed to facilitate cylinder reboring and port facing. The O2 on the right is W30 *Shorwell*. *A.E. West/ Mike King collection*

been suggested that a hybrid was created using the best parts from the two. Whatever the truth of this, cutting up of W15 was completed on 29 September, another engine with fractured frames and worn cylinders.[67]

The line closures and declining coal traffic took away most of the work done by the class E1 0-6-0Ts. They ran far fewer miles than the O2s, cost more to maintain and spare parts were not readily available. W3 carried cylinders dating from 1923 and a boiler fitted in December 1944. The E1s had been rostered for 'The Tourist' through train between Ventnor and Newport during the summer months but that work ended with the closure of the Freshwater line.[63] The last remaining passenger duty seems to have been a schools train between Cowes and Sandown but that too ceased running when the Sandown to Newport line closed. A rearrangement of rosters left them with just one weekday goods duty. The E1s were thus disposed of in preference for more O2s.[67]

E1 W2 *Yarmouth* was last recorded in service by Charles Woodnutt on 20 October 1955 and W1 *Medina* on 6 October 1956. After a general overhaul lasting almost six months, the return to service of W4 *Wroxall* in September 1956 was quickly followed by the withdrawal of W2 *Yarmouth* and six months later by W1 *Medina*. The two remaining E1s were transferred to Ryde, where W3 *Ryde* was last seen in service on 25 October 1958, although not officially withdrawn until June 1959. By then an O2 was deputising on goods work whenever an E1 was unavailable. Ryde-based crews were used to working on mixed passenger and goods duties during the course of a day but it was different at Newport, where the E1s had been a decided asset. It was fortunate that

lengthy goods trains were now a rarity. W4 *Wroxall* remained active until 10 September 1960, the last day of the summer timetable.[64] Withdrawn the following month, breaking up took place in the upper coaling road beside Ryde shed but was rather protracted as it depended on the available manpower. The boiler was sold on 19 December 1961 for heating glass houses in the Arreton Valley but scrapped when the site was redeveloped.[66]

Towards the end of each summer season Mr Gardener, the Assistant for the Isle of Wight, would hold a meeting with the foremen to agree a programme of repairs during the winter months, a mixture of general overhauls interspersed with light and intermediate repairs. Between 1954 and 1962 a Ryde Works general overhaul took an average three months, ranging in duration from six weeks to six months, an expensive operation for a cash-strapped BR. The first mainland O2s had been withdrawn in February 1933 and that was followed by a decision on 6 January 1936 to cease manufacturing most major components for the class. Consequently, the workshops had for years been recovering boilers and other spare parts from withdrawn engines. Classes O2 and G6 were whittled down until December 1962, when the last mainland survivors were taken out of service. Transferring spare parts to the Isle of Wight became more difficult following the closure of the Bembridge branch and St Helens Quay. A lack of suitable cranes at Medina Wharf meant that heavy items such as boilers had to be shipped by British Road Services barge to Thetis Wharf, Cowes, and taken by lorry to Newport or Ryde.[67]

The long-term survival of the O2s depended mainly on the condition of the boiler, firebox, cylinders and frames. The inability to return boilers to the mainland for refurbishment soon had repercussions at Ryde. The boilersmith was able to give some a fresh lease of life by replacing boiler tubes and firebox stays but any in need of more extensive repairs had to go for scrap. Withdrawals on the mainland helped maintain a flow of replacements but they were a rather mixed bag, usually about thirty years old, but a goodly number were rebuilds of much older boilers. Inevitably the Drummond pattern made a reappearance:

No.	Name	Boiler No.	Fitted	Removed	
W18	*Ningwood*	194	5.1958	3.1962	
W22	*Brading*	932	3.1963	1967	Withdrawn
W25	*Godshill*	223	1.1948	11.1951	LSWR boiler
W27	*Merstone*		2.1956	7.1961	
W29	*Alverstone*		2.1950	9.1952	
W30	*Shorwell*	862	5.1954	1.1957	
W31	*Chale*	194	1.1963	1967	Withdrawn
W33	*Bembridge*		4.1948	12.1950	

The age and condition of cylinders varied considerably. W34 had carried a pair fitted in 1926 but that was exceptional, the remainder having been installed between 1933 and 1956. Cylinder wear was inevitable and sometimes hastened by poor lubrication and excessive priming. Reboring and port refacing was required several times during a cylinder block's life. This was achieved by removing the front buffer beam and machining the cylinders in situ. A corrosive mix of cinders and ash building up on top of cylinders would also shorten their lives and eventually the walls became so thin that they could, and sometimes did, crack, requiring complete replacement. Cylinder blocks were cast in one piece in the foundry at Eastleigh and machined to size before delivery. The procedure for installing a cylinder block was to clamp it in position, drill and ream fastener holes in the block's flanges through the existing holes in the frames and then install fitted bolts, which were made to suit. Engines rarely received used cylinder blocks because the holes in the frames were not jig drilled and were unlikely to align with those in the cylinder block. The cylinders in the E1s comprised steam passages on each side that protruded into cut-outs in the frames and could only be taken off by removing the front buffer beam and jacking the frames apart.[51]

Three of the four O2s withdrawn in 1955 and 1956 had cracked frames. On 14 May 1957 R. J. Menzies, the locomotive foreman, wrote to Mr Gardener reporting that cracks had been welded in the frames of W16, 18, 25, 29, 30, 31, 35 and 36, while W22 was awaiting the same treatment. In most cases the frame holes for the horn bolts were so badly worn that bushes had to be welded in.[10] Worn brake blocks could be replaced in the running shed but attention to axleboxes and wheels necessitated a visit to the locomotive hoists at Ryde or Newport. There was a continuing need to attend to bearings in the axleboxes and reprofile wheels on the wheel lathe. Wheels that required new tyres or coupling rod crank pins had to be returned to Eastleigh for attention. Clearly the many station stops, gradients and curves did the engines no favours. Problems had existed with the class A1X 0-6-0Ts on the Bembridge branch, where the fixed wheelbase aggravated gauge widening and knocked out curves, especially when they were driven imprudently. The E1s rarely ventured onto the Freshwater line for the same reason. Closure of the branch lines lessened but never cured the problem.[66]

Mention has been made of the cab roof ventilators, whistles and hooters but there were many more differences among the O2s. W15, 27 and 28 carried plain coupling rods rather than the original fluted variety: W34 had arrived from the mainland carrying such a set. Those from W15 passed to W24 and then to W16. W28 ran for years with a prominent repair to the right-hand running plate, W36 arrived with tanks that had been patched from end to end, while those on others had lesser repairs, a confusing picture as tanks were changed whenever one began leaking. A variety of countersunk and button-headed rivet patterns could be seen on smokeboxes and buffer beams, while latterly W30 had a smaller, plumper dome cover quite unlike those carried by its companions. The redundant pull-push gear on W35 and W36 was removed during overhauls in March 1955 and December 1954 respectively.[31] Whatever physical differences existed, their age and condition meant that seemingly identical engines had to be driven and fired differently – each was an individual. Performance could vary considerably,

W16 *Ventnor* was recorded at Ryde St John's on 25 June 1957 still bearing the first style of lined black livery with early crest, the only addition being the new '0P' power classification above the number. The board carrying the number '7' was the duty number, but the old 'B' classification remains. *R. C. Riley/IWSR Archive*

although most crews had their regular steed that inevitably became a favourite; only spare engines had no friends.

The line closures were followed by a temporary redistribution of engines between the two running sheds, or 'Motive Power Depots' as BR liked to call them. On Sunday, 22 May 1955 Charles Woodnutt noted their disposition:

In service	Ryde to Ventnor	W15, 18, 36
	Cowes to Ryde	W16, 31
	Cowes to Sandown	W29
On shed at	Ryde	W17, 20, 22, 24, 27
	Newport	W1-4, 25, 30, 32, 33, 35
Stored at	Ryde	W14, 19, 23, 34
	Newport	W26
Under repair	Ryde Works	W21, 28

At least one Ryde duty had involved going 'around the houses', as the Ryde–Sandown–Newport–Ryde triangle was called. The engine concerned then ran facing the opposite direction until the next round trip. The duty was also used to turn round a Newport engine before and after a visit to Ryde Works. Closure of the Sandown to Newport line removed the ability to turn them, so the engines were run around the triangle so they all faced the same direction. The last to leave Ryde bunker first was W17 on 5 February 1956 with the 3.30pm departure for Cowes before hauling the final Up train on the Newport to Sandown line, the 7.36 pm from Cowes to Ventnor. At Merstone, the train crossed with W33 *Bembridge* hauling the final service in the opposite direction, the 7.30 pm from Ventnor to Cowes.

During the winter months between 1958 and 1963, spare locomotives were stored in Brickfields Siding at Sandown. Over 1962–63 it was the turn of W14 *Fishbourne*, W18 *Ningwood* and W17 *Seaview*. W14 had undergone a light intermediate repair between 15 October and 14 December 1962 before being moved to Sandown. All three carry the short-lived metal shields around the Westinghouse pumps. W14 lacks cab-side covers, although it would be more than two months before the loco was taken back to Ryde. A. E. Bennett ©*The Transport Treasury*

W25 *Godshill* in the process of demolition in Ryde Works yard during 1963. The boiler tubes have been carefully removed by collapsing the ends, as would be the case during tube replacement, which is a mystery. Perhaps it was initially intended to retain the boiler. The smokebox, steampipe and regulator head have also been removed rather than cut off. Many components from W25 were observed in Ryde Works as late as 1965. *A. W. Blackburn/IWSR Archive*

The abandonment of the branch lines mainly affected Newport shed. The run-down had begun in 1951 when the shed ceased to have its own foreman. There then followed a gradual reduction in the number of duties matched by the disappearance of jobs for drivers, firemen, guards and depot staff. In March 1957 a committee reported on the work necessary to effect the shed's closure. Transfer to Ryde would make it unnecessary to spend £700 on improved drainage to the ash disposal pit and correct subsidence in the shed roads. Duties were to be recast to begin and end at Ryde, even though this increased light-engine mileage at a cost of £2,823. This was quite acceptable given that staff economies would total £10,680 per annum. When Newport shed closed in November 1957, Ryde had to accommodate an allocation of nineteen O2s and two E1s.[66]

A significant number of engines were being stored in the winter months. By February 1956 five were in store: W15 at Ryde and W28, 29, 32 and 35 at Newport. During the following winter it was the turn of W14 and W16 at Ryde and W29 at Newport, prior to a visit to Ryde Works for an overhaul. Newport shed was used for the 1957–58 winter to store W25, 30, 31 and 33 but the building was then declared unsafe, so in subsequent years engines had to be kept in the open at Brickfields siding, Sandown. Important parts of the motion received a coating of grease, the chimneys were covered over and boards affixed to the cab sides to keep out the rain. Those known to have been stored in this fashion were W27, 16, 32, 18 (1958–59), W22, 20, 30, 29 (1959–60), W21 (1960–61), W17, 33 and 28 (1961–62), W14, 18, and 17 (1962–63). A couple of engines spent exceptionally long periods out of use. W32 accumulated a total of 3½ years in store between 1953 and 1964, while W29 was not used at all between October 1959 and May 1961.

In the spring of 1957 transfers for a different emblem were introduced, described by P. C. Allen as 'The half lion emerging from the crown holding a crumpet'.[10] The background to the emblem was transparent, the lion red,

the wheel silver and the crown, lettering and surround were gold, the latter two being edged in black. The smaller of two sizes was used in the Island and measured 30¼in by 14¾in high.[44] Rapid progress was made in its application as by April 1958 the old emblem was carried only by W3, 4, 16 and 29. The two E1s were destined never to carry the second emblem. It was a copy of a Grant of Arms awarded by the College of Heralds and initially there were left- and right-facing versions. However, the College complained that they had authorised only one version, so the right-hand emblem ceased to be applied once stocks became exhausted. The first repaint solely with left-facing emblems emerged in December 1960. By then the SR power classification letter had disappeared from the bunker side, leaving only the BR version.[15]

The number of duties during the summer season had fallen to fifteen, while in winter seven sufficed. See the table (below) for the position on 11 February 1961.[31]

Shortly after undergoing a general overhaul, W25 *Godshill* derailed on trap points at the south end of St John's Road station on 22 August 1957, undoing previous frame repairs and cracking the driving wheel spokes. However, it was patched up and sent back to work. The O2 was stored for several months early in 1961 prior to a visit to Ryde Works for repairs and a repaint; another brief visit to the works occurred on 1 December 1962. Later that month heavy snow badly disrupted road and rail services. On 28 December W25 was seen in service leaking steam and, although used the following

In service	W17, 20, 24, 26, 31, 35, 36
Ryde shed	W14, 18, 22, 25, 27, 28, 29, 32, 33
Stored at Sandown	W21
In Ryde Works	W16 stripped for overhaul
	W30 ready for painting
Awaiting scrapping	W4 intact but minus nameplates

day, was withdrawn on 30 December. Dumped in the stores road next to Ryde shed minus the nameplates, a move to the works yard had taken place by 4 April 1963 but the removal of various parts did not begin until August; they included the rear buffers, part of the bunker and the chimney. The tanks and coupling rods went to W28 *Ashey*. Work on cutting up the remains began the following month.[67]

Other mishaps had less serious consequences. On 18 March 1959 W29 *Alverstone* stalled on Apse Bank with a fractured piston head while hauling a Ryde to Ventnor train and causing some disruption before a rescue could be mounted. The oldest of the O2s, W14 *Fishbourne*, had for years been a poor steamer, hence its use on the Bembridge branch. However, in 1960 there was such a transformation following a general overhaul and change of boiler that it could be rostered for the most exacting duties. All good things come to an end and in *Fishbourne's* case this was during snow on 28 December 1962 when heading the early morning mail train to Ventnor. Before the driver became aware of their existence, the train collided with a herd of steers that had escaped onto the line and were sheltering from the cold under Truckell's Bridge between Smallbrook and Brading. Despite killing six animals, only a side rod was bent and the leading steps knocked off, although the engine thereafter suffered from hot axleboxes. The same crew, but on W24 *Calbourne*, repeated the incident a year later.[67]

For most engines, general overhauls ended after W18 left works in June 1962 but W22 and W31 received heavy repairs and Drummond-pattern boilers early the following year. Both accrued high mileages, especially W22 that by the end of 1964 had amassed more than 215,000 miles since its general overhaul in 1955. Thereafter the O2s visited works only for intermediate overhauls or running repairs. W14, 17, 18, 22, 27, 33 and 35 were fitted with metal shields to prevent the Westinghouse compressor from splashing adjacent vehicles and passengers with oily water but they made it difficult to access the compressor so were soon removed.[67]

Enthusiasts began to take more interest in the Isle of Wight's railways and crews frequently encountered photographers in the most unlikely of locations. On Saturday, 18 May 1963 a large group from the Gainsborough Model Railway Society visited the Island on an 'Isle of Wight Special' rail tour. They landed at Cowes but the five-carriage train hauled by W16 *Ventnor* was quite inadequate and many lost out on non-stop runs to Ryde Pier Head and then behind W31 *Chale* to Ventnor and back. As with other rail tours, a headboard was carried to mark the occasion. That summer, eleven engines were needed to operate the Monday to Friday service, fourteen plus one spare on Saturdays and nine on Sundays. The one remaining weekday duty on goods work was often allocated to an engine fresh from works. On Friday, 26 July eleven were at work: W31, 32 and 33 were out of steam outside Ryde shed, W22 was inside standing alongside W17, which was undergoing a boiler washout. W29 was under repair in the works, while W25 had been withdrawn.[67]

During the winter of 1963–64, the railway pier was closed for rebuilding, so passenger services terminated at Ryde Esplanade. There was no means of running round trains at Esplanade, so a second engine was attached to the rear of Up trains at Ryde St John's Road before becoming the train engine on the next Down departure. The contractors working on the pier brought two Grafton, self-propelled steam cranes across from the mainland. Latterly only one was fit for use and both were broken up for scrap when the contract was completed in 1967.[67]

That winter, W20 and W26 lay out of service in the Chalk Siding at Brading but with none of the protective coverings used in previous years. This was the last occasion when serviceable engines were stored away from Ryde shed. W20 was seen being towed back to Ryde on 15 May 1964 and both re-entered service.[31] W36 *Carisbrooke* was last noted in service on Easter Sunday, 29 March 1964 shortly before a start was made on ultrasonically testing the thickness of cylinder walls and other components. On 27 June the *Isle of Wight County Press* disclosed that the O2 had failed a 'fitness test' and after others were examined three more had to be laid aside; W27 and W31 were two of the victims. The chargehand was said to have broken one set of cylinders when checking the thickness using his usual method, viz. hitting with a hammer and listening to the ring. A high-temperature epoxy was used to make temporary repairs but an attempt to repair a cracked cylinder failed when the patch blew off as soon as the engine moved under its own power. New cylinders were unavailable because the foundry at Eastleigh Works had closed but the *Railway Observer* reported that two unused sets had been found at Eastleigh and Exmouth Junction. One set was fitted to W31 but the second was a raw casting that needed machining before despatch to the Island. Cylinder blocks were also recovered from withdrawn mainland members of classes O2 and G6, but how many were fitted to the Island O2s is open to debate. Problems with the cylinders had been foreseen four years earlier when the transfer of some replacement motive power was considered (see Chapter 9).

With only eleven engines fit for service, the summer Saturday timetable on 4 July 1964 was replaced by the weekday frequency. Saturday duty rosters were hurriedly rearranged to suit a maximum of eleven by cutting out light running to Ryde shed and creating a coaling point at Ventnor with a road crane hired (at a cost of £43 10s 6d) for the purpose. This temporary arrangement began the following weekend. A full Saturday service resumed on 25 July after the return to traffic of W16, 22 and 31. Saturday, 4 July was marked by the first of several breakdowns involving trains in service. W21 *Sandown* failed at Ashey with a burst tube when working the 11.30am Ryde to Cowes train. That resulted in several cancellations and delays to the Ryde to Ventnor service. There were more problems on Saturday, 1 August when W32 *Bonchurch* failed when working a Cowes line train, so W14 *Fishbourne* was taken off a booked working to Shanklin and sent on a rescue mission. Some normality had returned by Monday, 10 August, when W14, 16, 17, 20, 21, 22,

W27 *Merstone* undergoing cylinder replacement in Ryde Works, road 4, on 2 September 1964 after the cylinders were condemned as 'dangerously thin' during ultrasonic measurement. The long duration of this visit, forty-six working days as opposed to twenty days for W31, which underwent cylinder replacement immediately beforehand, suggests that W27 was the recipient of cylinders from a scrapped locomotive, thus making the installation much more complicated. The bores of the redrilled fastener holes glisten in the sunlight, while the two rear, lower left holes appear to be still filled with weld, ready for redrilling. *Mark Brinton collection*

26, 28, 30, and 31 were in steam while W18, 29 and 35 were having a shed day. The next day W26 *Whitwell* had to be rescued after failing at Havenstreet with a fractured coupling rod.[67]

It was fortunate that the summer timetable had ended when on Sunday, 4 October 1964 W22 *Brading* disgraced itself about ½ mile south of Mill Hill when working the 4.31pm train from Cowes to Ryde. A crank pin on the right-hand side sheared off and the flailing coupling rod punctured the side tank, smashed a rail chair and slightly damaged the leading carriage. Services beyond Newport were suspended for the day and the train's passengers had to walk back to Mill Hill station to join a specially summoned bus. After the breakdown train arrived, W22 was parked out of the way at Medina Wharf, the damaged carriages were propelled to Cowes and then a replacement set followed, so that a normal service could begin the next morning. The mishap occurred on the same day as 'The Vectis Farewell Rail Tour', operated for members of the Locomotive Club of Great Britain. It ran to Ventnor and back behind W14 *Fishbourne* but a trip to Cowes behind W28 *Ashey* had to be cut short at Newport. Members had to use the tramway along Ryde Pier as the railway pier was again out of use for rebuilding.[31]

Ryde Works was overwhelmed with work. After W31 was discharged on 22 July 1964, W27 was taken in and the driving wheels and cylinders removed so that a replacement, probably second-hand, set of cylinders could be fitted. It was followed in quick succession by W26 and 22, both of which needed repairs following the crank pin failures.[68]

W32 *Bonchurch*, the youngest of the Island O2s, was last in service on 16 October 1964, two weeks before official withdrawal. Long overdue for an overhaul, its poor condition made it deeply unpopular with crews. Ivor Davies, the works foreman, described *Bonchurch* as utterly worn out and beyond repair, 'the only salvageable things on that engine are the spectacle glasses'. He had been overruled two years previously when trying to dispose of it instead of W25. Towards the end of a nine-and-a-half-month stay in the Chalk Siding at Brading, the local graffiti artists painted on the left-hand tank side 'This engine belongs to Steptoe and Son' (a popular television programme at the time). W32 was towed back to Ryde shed by W17 on 27 August 1965 and had the graffito concealed with grey paint before entering works for cutting up. Meanwhile, W36 had been residing in the erecting shop acting as a donor. When photographed on 10 April 1965 it consisted of the forward two-thirds of the

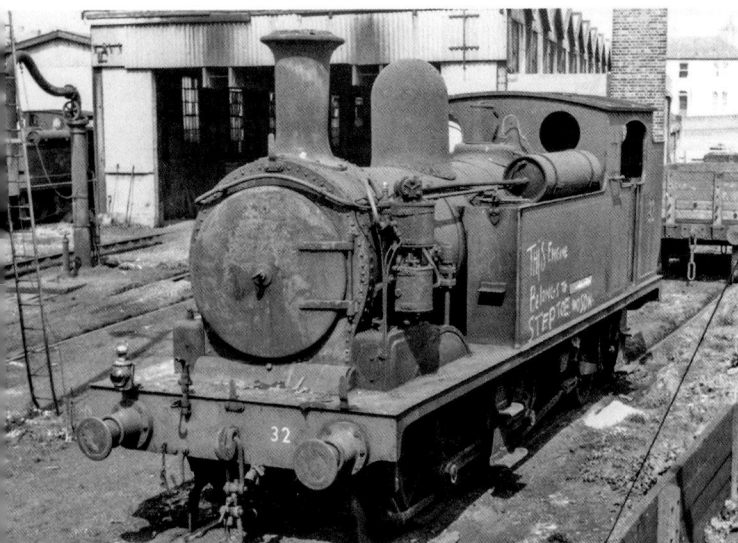

After nine months dumped in Chalk siding at Brading, W32 was hauled back to Ryde St John's yard for scrapping by W17 *Seaview* on 27 August 1965. Viewed shortly afterwards in the stores siding, the tail lamp from the tow is still in place, as is the graffito 'This engine belongs to Steptoe and Son', which was quickly obliterated with grey paint. *A. Blackburn/IWSR Archive*

frames, the boiler, cylinders, front buffer beam and a few smaller components. Completely dismantled during the autumn, the remains had gone by 8 November, apart from the boiler, which remained in store on the boiler truck until finally broken up in July 1966.[67]

The year 1965 began with another mishap when W31 *Chale* broke a crosshead near Wroxall on 26 January, wrecking the new cylinders. The overnight theft of one of the nameplates at Ryde St John's Road while it was awaiting repair prompted a decision to remove the name and number plates from all the remaining engines. That did nothing to improve appearances as standards of cleanliness had declined and many burnt smokeboxes were in evidence.[67]

W24 *Calbourne* was especially favoured when the O2 underwent a general overhaul between February and May 1965. The existing boiler was scrapped and replaced by Adams boiler 208 that had been constructed in 1889 but rebuilt in October 1926. Previously a mainland resident, the boiler had been carried by DS3152 (class G6 No. 272) before withdrawal in August 1960. After being refurbished, the boiler was sent to the Island in January 1965 and placed on the frames by 28 February. The frames were welded, the axleboxes re-metalled and two replacement hornblocks fitted. These probably came from W36, which was being cannibalised for spares while *Calbourne* was undergoing overhaul. During an overhaul in preservation it was noted that the right-hand tank had never been drilled for *Calbourne*-length nameplates in the BR black era. There were only welded up holes for short and long plates at that level, indicating that the tank had probably also been carried by W36 *Carisbrooke* previously. The driving wheels

were stamped 'W29', the right coupling rod with 184 and 35 and the left coupling rod with 212 and 35. The last engine to receive a full repaint at Ryde Works, the unlined black was relieved only by an emblem, running number and BR power classification lettering. The lack of lining was attributed to the urgent need to get the engine back into service. This stark appearance prompted staff to call *Calbourne* 'The Black Maria'. On 1 June W24 was given a run to Newport prior to entry into service at the start of the summer timetable.[51] W31 *Chale* was then taken into Ryde Works to receive a replacement set of cylinders. The cylinder block may have been intended for *Calbourne* but its cylinders were only ten years old, so W31 received a second new cylinder block within the space of one year! It was discharged back into service on 22 June.[64]

Management claimed that a regime of rigorous examinations and the ultrasonic testing of components meant that the engines were in a better condition than for many years. On Saturday, 19 June 1965 W22 *Brading* derailed the rear bogie wheels on Ryde Pier. Single-line working had to be operated until rerailing was effected several hours later. On Sunday, 3 October members of the Locomotive Club of Great Britain on 'The Vectis Farewell Rail Tour' rode in a packed train from Ryde Pier Head to Cowes behind W24 *Calbourne* and then to Ventnor and back double-headed with W14 *Fishbourne*. Both had been specially cleaned for the occasion but few of the other O2s showed signs of similar attention. Two days earlier the position was:[31]

In steam	W14, 16, 17, 20, 21, 26, 27, 28, 31
At Ryde out of steam	W18, 24, 29, 30, 33
Under repair in Ryde Works	W22, 35
In works for cutting up	W32, 36

The last locomotive to receive a General Overhaul at Ryde was W24 *Calbourne*, seen here on 10 April 1965 in the process of being reassembled. Just visible extreme left are the remains of W36 *Carisbrooke*, which was dismantled to provide spare parts. *R E Francis*

At the last overhaul, W24 was turned out in plain, unlined black and minus nameplate. She was recorded running round at Ventnor in summer 1965. *Eddy Keough Memorial collection, IWSR Archive*

On 4 October 1965 Ryde railway pier was again taken out of use for rebuilding but the planned closures of the Ryde to Cowes and Shanklin to Ventnor lines were postponed until 21 February and 18 April 1966 respectively. W14, 18, and 21 had boiler or firebox problems, while W26 and 30 had worn cylinders.[43] W30 *Shorwell* made a final run in service on 6 September shortly before withdrawal. The last to be dismantled in the works, it had been cut up by 26 November. W21 *Sandown* was employed intermittently until 30 November, W26 *Whitwell* was last seen working on 6 December and W29 *Alverstone* made a final outing on 16 April 1966. W21, 26 and 29 were withdrawn on 1 May and after sale to H. B. Jolliffe of Cowes were broken up between June and August in the goods yard at Ryde.[67]

Once the pride of Ryde shed, W18 *Ningwood* was not seen in use after 15 September 1965 but withdrawal was delayed until 5 December. There was evidently some reluctance to send it for scrap as the boiler from W36 was kept back, possibly so that *Ningwood* could be returned to service; instead W14 *Fishbourne* was reprieved and, being the oldest engine in the fleet, went on to haul the final passenger services from Cowes and Ventnor. After losing the driving wheels to another O2, W18 lay in the erecting shop until expelled when the works closed later in 1966. With one discarded driving wheelset reinstalled, W18 had become a unique 0-2-4T, then spent the autumn parked on the disused Down line in various locations between St John's Road and the north side of Rink Road Bridge.[67]

In April 1966 the Isle of Wight's Member of Parliament asked that the remaining engines be given back their nameplates. Rather than risk the valuable brass plates, Ryde Works made up and welded on some half-length steel replacements painted black with cream lettering. Eleven remained in working order, enough for a summer service between Ryde Pier Head and Shanklin that needed seven on weekdays, eight on Saturdays and four on Sundays. On Saturday, 25 June the position was:

In service	W14, 16, 17, 20, 24, 27, 33, 35
On shed ('day off')	W28, 31
Under repair in Ryde Works	W22
Withdrawn	W18, 21, 26, 29

On 30 July 1966 W27 *Merstone* left Ryde Works for the last time. Thereafter, any engines in need of attention had to be dealt with in the running shed. No longer would visitors to the works see one dismantled for overhaul or lifted for a wheel change. In over a century of service, Ryde Works and its craftsmen had so prolonged the lives of the engines and stock that the Island's railways had become a working museum.[69]

There were relatively few failures in service during the 1966 summer season. W14 *Fishbourne* had a near miss with a gangers' trolley near Havenstreet on 8 August, putting severe flats on the driving wheels. That may have contributed to a failure in traffic on 14 August, when W27 had to take its place. Undoubtedly the worst performer, *Fishbourne* was

used sparingly until the end of the summer season and then laid aside.[67]

The summer timetable came to an end on Saturday, 17 September 1966 and was replaced by an hourly weekday service between Ryde Esplanade and Shanklin worked by four engines. A fifth was steamed whenever a materials train was needed. Preparations for electrification began with deliveries of rail and flat wagons to Medina Wharf, from where a materials train ran to a permanent way yard at Sandown; a start was made on installing the conductor rail. On 19 October, W33 *Bembridge* took several wagons to Wroxall station, where rails and points were recovered for reuse. Two days later the loaded wagons were retrieved by W20 *Shanklin,* the last steam engine to venture far into the closed Shanklin to Ventnor section. The last train to leave Medina Wharf was probably on 24 October, a load of conductor rails hauled by W28 *Ashey.*[67]

W35 *Freshwater* had been used intensively during the summer and was in charge of the last train to pass Smallbrook Junction before the signal box closed on 17 September 1966. Seen in service on 30 September, firebox problems resulted in its withdrawal a few days later. W20 *Shanklin* was working a passenger train to Shanklin on 17 December when hot water was seen spewing from a burst boiler feed pipe as the train arrived at St John's Road station; it never ran again. W33 *Bembridge* was last noted in service on Sunday, 11 December and W16 *Ventnor* hauled its last passenger train on Friday, 30 December, when a steam-heating pipe failed at Smallbrook. W14 *Fishbourne* was steamed on 20 December for the first time in months and two days later took some withdrawn wagons to Newport for disposal. A second trip included W18, which was left in the Freshwater yard. Several requests had been made that *Fishbourne*, the oldest working passenger engine on BR, be rostered to haul the final passenger steam train.[67]

Despite poor weather, enthusiasts helped clean the engines ready for the last day on Saturday, 31 December 1966. W14 *Fishbourne*, W28 *Ashey*, W27 *Merstone* and W17 *Seaview* (duties 1–4) handled the service trains, while W24 *Calbourne* and W31 *Chale* (duties 6 and 7) took charge of a special five-carriage 'Isle of Wight Steam Farewell Rail Tour' for the Locomotive Club of Great Britain. W16 *Ventnor* (duty 5) and W22 *Brading* (duty 8) were also in steam but did not venture beyond Ryde.[64] Peter Harbour and Ray Knapp, the driver and fireman on W14 *Fishbourne*, later recounted their final trip to Shanklin and back. Peter had this to say about their return to the Ryde shed:[6]

The whole yard was dark and deserted and there was just one light on in the shed. While Ray dropped the fire and cleaned up, I removed the wreath which had been placed on 14's bunker. Quickly and quietly I placed this into my car boot as a memento of that last trip, and then returned to say my farewells. It was a peculiar, almost eerie atmosphere as Ray and I looked over Ryde yard across the condemned engines.

W22 Brading derailed on Ryde Pier on 19 June 1965. Even though standards of cleaning were at an all-time low by this time, it still manages to retain a semblance of dignity in disgrace. *M. Morant/IWSR Archive*

TRAIN SERVICES ON SATURDAY 31 DECEMBER 1966						
Down trains – Ryde Esplanade to Shanklin				**Up trains – Shanklin to Ryde Esplanade**		
Booked departure	**Train engine**	**Banker***		**Booked departure**	**Train engine**	**Banker***
Mail	W14	not known		6.50	W14	W27
6.45 ex Ryde St John's Road	W17	-		7.45	W17	W14
7.30	W27	W14		8.55	W27	W28
8.30	W14	W17		9.45	W14	W17
9.30	W28	W27		10.45	W28	W27
10.30	W17	W14		11.45	W17	W24, W31
11.30	W27	W28		Empty to Ryde Esplanade	W16 or W22	W14
12.15 LCGB special	W24, W31	W17		12.45	W27	W28
12.30	W14	W16 or W22		13.37 LCGB special	W24, W31	W22
13.30	W28	W27		13.45	W14	W17
Empty to Ryde St John's Road	W22	W31, W24		14.45	W28	W27
14.30	W17	W14		15.45	W17	W28
15.30	W27	W28		16.45	W27	W17
16.30	W28	W17		17.45	W28	W14
17.30	W17	W27		18.45	W17	W27
18.30	W14	W28		19.45	W14	W17
19.30	W27	W17		20.45	W27	W14
20.30	W17	W14		21.05 to Ryde St John's Road	W17	-
21.40	W14	W27		22.12 to Ryde St John's Road	W14	-
* = Between Esplanade and St John's Road.						

W14 *Fishbourne*, by then the oldest passenger steam locomotive on BR, had the tank, cab and bunker sides especially cleaned for duties on the last day of steam, 31 December 1966. Seen here at Shanklin having arrived with the 12.30 from Ryde Esplanade, it carries a 'Last Day' headboard and wreath as well as the replacement 'tin' nameplate. *G. S. Cocks*

The final steaming of a locomotive on the Island by British Railways occurred on 18 April 1967 when W27 *Merstone* was prepared and used to shunt its companions onto the former Freshwater line for cutting up. Suitably adorned for the occasion, W27 then suffered being the first to be scrapped. From the front are W27, W28, W17, W33, W14 and W22. Yet to be added to the melancholy line-up are W20, W16 and W35. *I. E. Whitlam*

Thus ended a period of steam working that had lasted more than 100 years. W14, 16, 17, 20, 22, 27, 28 and 33 were officially withdrawn on 2 January 1967. All members of classes A1X, O2 and E1 that survived into BR days clocked up well over a million miles (known final mileages are in Appendix 3) and it is doubtful their makers could ever have foreseen they would have such long and useful lives. W24 and W31 were retained to assist with the electrification works.[68]

Just as the line closures had thinned the ranks of the staff employed on the railways, so the end of steam was marked by the retirement of both the engines and many of those who worked with them; they included Mr Gardener, the last Assistant for the Isle of Wight. Others would have to learn new ways of working or pursue their careers on the mainland.

W22 had often been employed on materials trains during the autumn and continued to be used for that purpose on 1–3 January 1967 despite being listed as withdrawn. W24 was steamed on 3 January before delivering the remaining carriages to Newport, where A. King & Sons of Norwich were dismantling stock in the Freshwater yard. W18 was propelled to Cement Mills siding, where H. B. Jolliffe & Co. began cutting it up that week. This was the last time an engine ventured north of Newport. W24 made several more trips to Newport that month with redundant stock.[68] On 28 January 1967 W24 hauled nine O2s in three separate trains to Newport: W17, 28 and 22; 14, 33 and 27; 35, 20 and 16. Pairs of engines were not permitted to cross Newport drawbridge, so there was probably some to-ing and fro-ing using a couple of barrier

wagons to get them across in safety but the authors have been unable to confirm what actually took place. W17, 28, 22, 14, 33 and 27 were placed in the Up bay road with 35, 20 and 16 in the Up main platform. Sold for scrap, W27 was steamed on 18 April to haul its companions into a more accessible position on the remaining stub of the Freshwater line. H. B. Jolliffe began cutting up W27 as soon as the boiler had cooled, followed by W16, 20, 35, 28, 17, 33, 14 and 22; the work took until August to complete. The ferrous metal was taken to the breaker's yard on the outskirts of Cowes. When the yard was cleared several years later some Westinghouse compressors were salvaged and sold to the Isle of Wight Steam Railway for further use.[67]

W24 *Calbourne* was last noted in steam on 2 February 1967. When withdrawn on 14 March it had clocked up 1,639,478 miles, including 40,354 miles since the overhaul in 1965. The engine was offered for sale on 2 May and purchased by the Wight Locomotive Society.[51] After standing out of use since 31 December 1966, W31 *Chale* was observed shunting at Sandown on 7 February 1967 and in use on 28 February, a few days before the power supply was switched on. By the time withdrawal took place on 14 March, connections with the Cowes line at Smallbrook Junction had been severed. Consequently, W31 remained in the sidings at Ryde until sold for scrap to A. King & Sons. Cutting up began on 24 August but was halted after part of one tank had been removed while a Hampshire preservation group attempted to raise funds for its purchase and transport back to the mainland. Work resumed in September and this time there was no reprieve.[6]

9

British Rail, Network SouthEast and Island Line

The transfer of more modern motive power to the Isle of Wight had been under consideration for years. As long ago as April 1951 the Southern Region's motive power superintendent suggested that diesel electric or mechanical traction would reduce workshop costs. This was not pursued because the construction of a small number of diesel engines to suit the restricted loading gauge and axle loading was quite uneconomic. Instead, virtually every type of steam tank engine was considered but rejected because of unsuitability, age or condition. The matter remained in abeyance until 1958, when a Ventnor resident and the local council wrote complaining about the elderly rolling stock. The region's General Manager was told on 5 September that the existing motive power could be maintained for ten years but an 'appreciable saving in works repair costs would accrue from the transfer of modern LM class 2 2-6-2T locomotives (if suitable) which will be displaced by electrification in 1959'.[66]

Thirty standard BR class 2 2-6-2 tank engines were built in 1953 and 1957 as Nos 84000–84029, the final ten being allocated to the Southern Region. Despite being larger than anything previously seen on the Island railways, only they and the similar London, Midland & Scottish Railway (LMS) Ivatt 2-6-2Ts were remotely suitable. Early in 1960 Eastleigh Works prepared a series of drawings showing how they could be adapted to fit the loading gauge. This included a reduction in the chimney height by 6½in, the dome casing by 2 1/16in and the cab roof by 1in. The guttering over the side cab windows was also to be removed; fitting the Westinghouse brake was a minor matter. However, despite rumours that at least three were destined for the Isle of Wight, funding for their conversion was not forthcoming. The ten BR 2-6-2Ts were transferred to the London Midland Region on 10 October 1961.[39]

On 18 June 1960 the *Isle of Wight County Press* reported that a review was under way to establish the most economical way of operating the railways. Management wanted to use multiple units and diesel traction as it avoided the cost of a third rail and associated equipment.

Steam traction was expensive and the need to bring coal from Medina Wharf prevented closure of the Ryde–Newport–Cowes line. However, no existing diesel engines were suitable and the cost of new stock was prohibitive. The most practical solution proved to be electrification on the SR third-rail system at 700–750v DC and the use of second-hand London Transport (LT) tube stock.[66]

In January 1965 the Chief Mechanical Engineer, prompted by the failure of W31 *Chale*, expressed his concern about the condition of the O2s and asked for the General Manager's views on the transfer of 2-6-2Ts 'as a stopgap'. He warned that the remaining engines would otherwise have to be returned to the mainland at the end of 1966 for heavy repairs and new boilers each at a cost of £10,000. It was estimated that a 2-6-2T would cost £725 to modify and £6,000 to overhaul.[66] In May Eastleigh Works dusted off the drawings, added more, and requested the transfer of the ten remaining members of BR class 2 from the London Midland Region. On 24 October No. 84014 arrived at Basingstoke en route from Stockport to Eastleigh Works in advance of 84010, 84013, 84015–84017, 84019, 84025–84026 and 84028. Transport to the Island and their modification at Ryde Works had been costed at £110,000 but when 84014 was inspected it was realised they were very run down and required more extensive overhauls than envisaged. As electrification was being actively pursued, the project was abandoned and movement of the other nine 2-6-2Ts to Fratton, due to begin on 10 November, never took place. No. 84014 was withdrawn at Eastleigh in December and towed to Newport, South Wales, on 28 March 1966 for breaking up. The other nine were condemned in January 1966 and sent for scrap.[66]

A decision to spend £500,000 on electrification of the line from Ryde to Shanklin was made public in July 1966. A total of forty-six tube cars built between 1923 and 1934 were selected from a quantity of cars whose disposal for scrap had been delayed. Each was adapted and refurbished at LT's Acton Works before going to BR's Stewarts Lane

Unit	'A' DM	T	T	'D' DM	Unit	CT	T	'D' DM
041	S20S	S27S*	S41S	S13S	031	S26S	S47S	S1S
042	S22S	S29S*	S42S	S15S	032	S28S	S92S	S3S
043	S2S	S31S*	S43S	S19S	033	S30S	S93S	S5S
044	S4S	S33S*	S44S	S21S	034	S32S	S94S	S7S
045	S6S	S48S	S45S	S23S	035	S34S	S95S	S9S
046	S8S	S49S	S46S	S25S	036	S36S	S96S	S11S

Spare driving motor S10S. *Control trailer used as trailer. 'A' end cars were formed at the Ryde end and 'D' end cars at the Shanklin end. S21S, S22S and S26S had been originally been S17S, S12S and S38S respectively. (The numbers 51–62 and 71–86 were occupied by Waterloo & City underground stock.)

depot for a repaint. They were among the first rolling stock to appear in a new rail blue livery, offset by brown underframes, grey roofs, yellow driving ends and a 'double arrow' emblem in white with matching lettering. This livery change followed the adoption of a new corporate identity and the abbreviated title 'British Rail'. The cars were formed into four-car and three-car units designated 4-Vec and 3-Tis in recognition of Vectis, the Roman name for the Isle of Wight, running as seven-car trains during the summer and four in the winter. In September, with the project's costs threatening to overrun, three more cars were sent for scrap and a seventh three-car unit disbanded to leave just a spare driving motor. (Three cars that had been finished were renumbered before entering service.)[70]

These all-steel cars were described by LT as 'standard' or later as 'pre-1938 stock', they were built by three separate manufacturers and were standard only in having compatible equipment. Being just over 50ft long and at 9ft 6in high, the cars were shorter and lower than the stock they replaced. This had consequences as the Ministry of Transport insisted on step-free access that could only be achieved by adjusting platform heights. They had air-operated doors, giving access to a saloon compartment containing ample standing space and a mixture of side and longitudinal seating; BR installed a luggage rack in place of some seats. The forty-three cars consisted of:[70]

- Nineteen driving motors, of which thirteen (S1S–S11S, S13S and S15S) were built by Metropolitan Carriage & Wagon Co. in 1931 and 1934. At 51½ft, they were 2ft longer than the older cars. Four driving motors (S19S–S22S) were built by Union Construction and Finance Co. in 1928 and 1929 and two (S23S and S25S) by Metropolitan in 1927. They all had a large equipment compartment behind the driver's compartment, a feature that greatly reduced their seating capacity.
- Ten control trailers (S26–34S and S36S) were built by Metropolitan in 1925 and 1927. Apart from the provision of a driver's cab, they were similar to the trailers.
- Fourteen trailers (S41–49S and S92–96S) were built by Cammell Laird in 1923. The cars were selected in preference to newer, 1931-built trailers because

they were in better condition, had a greater seating capacity and lacked passenger end doors, whose use had been forbidden by the Ministry on the sharply curved platforms at Ryde Esplanade.

Prior to entry into service the cars were formed into their units (see table above).[70]

On 1 September 1966 control trailer S38S (later S26S) was taken on a low-loader via the Portsmouth to Fishbourne vehicle ferry from Fratton to Ryde St John's Road goods yard, where a temporary unloading ramp had been constructed. Trips to Shanklin took place on 4 and 25 September with O2 W24 *Calbourne* and a match truck to check clearances and platform heights.

The other forty-two cars were tested between Wimbledon and Woking before moving to Fratton, from where crew training trips were run to Haslemere. Their transfer to Ryde began in December and took until the following April to complete. The first train under electric power reached Shanklin on 1 March 1967. Then followed a series of almost

W24 *Calbourne* with an LBSCR covered van as match truck takes Control Trailer S38S on a gauging trip on 4 September 1966, seen from Foxes Bridge north of Sandown. W24 is in the plain black livery with replacement 'tin' nameplates. *J. Mackett/IWSR Archive*

As electric stock was transferred it was formed into sets and stored pending entering service. 'D' end Driving Motor car S21S in 4-Vec Set 044 stands in the works headshunt at Ryde St John's on 22 January 1967. *A. Blackburn/IWSR Archive*

daily test runs carrying 'interested spectators'. The first train reached Ryde Pier Head on 14 March, six days before passenger services recommenced on Monday, 20 March.[67]

Ryde Works was transformed into a depot for the tube stock. The sidings were reduced to four, the carriage and wagon workshop became a maintenance shop while the turnery continued to be a machine shop, the erecting shop was deprived of its roof and the carriage bogie shop was demolished. The running shed was used as a temporary workshop and then lay empty until the building and sidings on that side of the station were removed in 1969.

Up to five trains an hour could be operated at peak times but a fall in passenger numbers soon permitted some reductions. The cars were expected to have an operational life of five to ten years but repeated refurbishments doubled that period. Acton Works supplied a replacement driving motor for accident victim S15S in March 1971 but that was an exception and three cars withdrawn in 1973 were not replaced. The units were allocated class numbers 451 (three-car) and 452 (four-car) in 1969, a first repaint following arrival took place in 1971–72 and a second in 1976 when the passenger doors and shoe gear were painted light grey and the 'S' suffix to the running number omitted. In January 1982 one unit appeared in Inter-City blue and grey with yellow and black ends. The side panels were lettered in white 'Isle of Wight', while new class numbers 485 (four-car) and 486 (three-car) appeared in black on the ends of the driving motors. Seven cars were withdrawn at various dates between 1975 and 1985. That year, the remainder were reformed in five-car units 041–045 and two-car units 031–032.[70]

From 1976 the plain BR blue livery was enhanced by painting the doors grey. 'A' end DMS S2 arrives at Ryde St John's in September 1981 leading a seven-car formation. *IWSR Archive*

The next alteration to livery was the adoption of blue and grey in 1982, coupled with the cab window surrounds picked out in black and the positioning of the unit number beneath one window as well as the brand 'Isle of Wight' and the BR double arrow on the motor car sides. 'A' end DMS S22, now without the suffix letter, stands ex-works at Ryde on 24 July 1985 awaiting reuniting with its set companions. *R. A. Silsbury*

In a bid to reduce the draughts, 1985 saw the cab-front doors plated over and the adoption of a 'Ryde Rail' logo on cab ends and body sides. 'D' end DMS S5 was the first to be done and is seen at Ryde Works on 24 July 1985. *R. A. Silsbury*

A five-car set, nominally 032, is seen at Brading with a Down working on 28 August 1987. The blue/grey livery is shown to advantage, but the Ryde Rail logo is omitted from the doored-end of the driving car. *John Faulkner*

In 1987 the final livery change for the old 'Standard' stock was a repaint into Network SouthEast red, white and blue with modified 'Ryde Rail' logos and the omission of the 'S' prefix. Unit 485 041 forms an Up working approaching Rink Road bridge on 9 March 1990. *John Faulkner*

Between 1989 and 1992 nine two-car units, designated TOPS class 483 and made up of pairs of 1938 tube stock motor cars, replaced the 'Standard' stock. A number of driver training runs took place on the mainland between Fratton and Haslemere on the Portsmouth direct line. Unit 483 002 is seen arriving at Haslemere on 20 September 1989. *John Faulkner*

In 1987 the creation of Network SouthEast, a new sector of British Rail, was marked by the appearance of cars in a striking grey and blue livery enlivened with red and white stripes; this time the 'S' prefix was left off. Work was carried out to renew lighting, plate over the cab front doors to stop water ingress and draughts and refurbish control trailer 28 for use in a new three-car unit 031. This merely deferred the inevitable as more withdrawals, including the older driving motors, further depleted the fleet. By then the cars were in such poor condition that replacements had to be purchased. The stock ran in passenger service for the final time on 12 January 1991.[70]

Network SouthEast bought forty-four redundant LT '1938 stock' tube cars built by Metropolitan Carriage & Wagon Co. in 1939 and 1940. Eighteen driving motors were sent to Eastleigh Works and completely rebuilt. The bodies were stripped, the electrical equipment refurbished or replaced, underfloor control equipment waterproofed and the interiors refitted to modern fire safety standards. Becoming class 483, the nine two-car units were painted in the Network SouthEast livery of blue and grey with red and white stripes in a different arrangement from those cars they replaced; the individual cars were numbered 121–129 and 221–229. Between July 1989 and April 1992 they were taken via the Portsmouth to Fishbourne vehicle ferry to Sandown and unloaded by cranes; the return journey was made with old stock. The cars had a higher seating capacity than previously but needed to be semi-permanently coupled in pairs. The number of tracks in the depot building had been reduced from three to two in the mid-1980s and a roller shutter door gave access to road 1 (formerly 2). Prior to the arrival of the 1938 stock, two wider roller doors were fitted across the front of the building and No.1 road was realigned and raised to permit access to the underfloor equipment. Units 001–009 were ample for the peak service of three four-car trains an hour but a further decline in passenger numbers resulted in the withdrawal of six cars between 1994 and 1996.

As part of the privatisation of Britain's railways and the creation of franchises, operation of the renamed 'Island Line' was taken over by Stagecoach Group in October 1996. Five of the six surviving units were painted in a dinosaur-themed livery in 2000 but the sixth flood-damaged unit (007) was eventually returned to service in LT 1930s red with a grey roof and yellow ends. By 2008 all six units were red, including one that had been laid aside (002). The franchise was taken over by South Western Railway in August 2017 but there was little immediate change apart from the appearance of a white logo and 'Island Line' branding on units 006 and 008. Such was their unreliability that in 2019 and 2020 services had to be reduced to hourly or even suspended on occasions. By the end of 2019, only units 006 and 008 were operational, while unit 007 was undergoing an overhaul. On 25 November 2020 unit 006 failed and was laid aside, priority now being given to returning 007 to service. For the time being 008 soldiered on alone but this unit failed a routine exam on 4 December

For a time, the 'Standard' and 1938 stock could be seen running in tandem. In this view 485 044 crosses with 483 001 at Sandown on 23 February 1990. *John Faulkner*

A long refit on 483 007 began in the autumn of 2017, but with increasing breakdowns of the remaining serviceable units priority was given to completing the overhaul. A pristine 483 007, destined for preservation at the Isle of Wight Steam Railway, heads up Ryde Pier on 11 December 2020, its first day back in service. The London Transport red had been the standard livery on all remaining units since 2008, having replaced an earlier dinosaur-themed livery, chosen owing to the preponderance of dinosaur fossils found on the Island. *John Faulkner*

and was taken out of service permanently. 007 returned to service on 11 December, then 006 was repaired and resumed service on the 19th. One or the other of these two units operated a one-train service until the 483 era drew to a close on 3 January 2021, on which day 007 ran during the morning and 006 in the afternoon and evening. Several units were destined for preservation or alternative use.[71]

On 16 September 2019 it was announced that five refurbished two-car units of former LT 'D78' surface-line stock were to be sent as replacements for the tube stock.[43] Built by Metro-Cammell between 1979 and 1983, the 450 cars featured wide, single-leaf sliding doors rather than the traditional double doorways, but they proved to be a hindrance during rush hours; the cars last ran in LT service on 21 April 2017. As the aluminium bodies were in good condition, 226 cars were purchased by Vivarail for further use. The firm planned to refurbish the units for use in a variety of modes including diesel, electric, battery or diesel/battery hybrid. The original bodies and the bogie units, which had been fitted new from 2000, were retained, everything else being brand new. The driving motors destined for the Island are being configured to operate on the third-rail system with drive provided by AC induction motors sourced from Austria. Designated class 484, and with the unit numbers 001–005, the first pair of cars arrived for testing on 19 November 2020. With a length in excess of 60ft and a height of 11ft 10in, the cars were too large for the then existing infrastructure. In August 2020 the trackbed under two bridges was lowered but other work to adjust platform heights and add a crossing loop at Brading had to wait for a line closure during the first half of 2021.[71]

In the 1960s, the employment of re-geared diesel shunters had been rejected in favour of electrification but one diesel engine was sent to assist in the electrification works. D2554 was one of sixty-nine 0-6-0 diesel mechanical shunters supplied by Hunslet Engine Co. of Leeds between 1955 and 1961. The locomotive was powered by a Gardner 8L3 engine developing 204hp at 1,200rpm. The transmission was a troublesome Hunslet-patent clutch, pre-selective power-assisted gear change and four-speed gearbox linked to a jackshaft and coupling rod drive.[51]

Ex-works in May 1956, BR No. 11140 (maker's No. 4870) was one of a first batch (D2550–D2573) built with a low cab roof. The number was changed to D2554 during routine

With the class 483 more than eighty years old, dwindling in numbers and increasingly unserviceable the decision was made to replace them with retired London Underground D78 sub-surface stock. The first of five fully reconditioned two-car units arrived in November 2020 and a programme of intensive testing, carried out at night, was required before the trains were accepted into service. However, on 8 December 2020, with all 483 units unserviceable, testing was carried out by day. 484 001 approaches Ryde St John's Up Distant signal on the first day of testing at full line speed. *John Faulkner*

To work engineering trains during and after electrification a Class 05 0-6-0DM D2554 was transferred to the Island on 7 October 1966. In green livery it stands in the Up yard at Ryde St John's on 22 January 1967. *A. Blackburn/IWSR Archive*

maintenance at Stratford in January 1959. Employed at Harwich Parkeston Quay for some ten years, the engine was then selected for transfer to the Island. A few weeks were spent at Fratton training drivers before a low-loader carried it across to Ryde on 7 October 1966. D2554 carried the BR unlined green livery with yellow and black chevrons at each end and an emblem on the cab sides above the running number. Initially a resident in Ryde shed alongside the remaining steam engines, the diesel was unofficially christened 'Nuclear Fred' and occasionally carried a red-painted nameplate on the radiator grille. Extensively used over the next few months, trips were made onto the Newport line and beyond Shanklin to recover signalling equipment. On one occasion when taking a materials train to Shanklin, D2554 broke down and had to be rescued by O2 W31 *Chale*. On 10 March 1967 it reached Ryde Pier Head with six bolster wagons, a match truck and tube car. This was just a few days before the power supply over that section was switched on. Equipped only with vacuum brakes and conventional couplings, any shunting of the tube stock had to be carried out with the assistance of a match truck.[67]

After passenger services recommenced, D2554 took up residence in the engineers' sidings at Sandown. Classified under the newly introduced TOPS (Total Operations Processing System) as a member of class 05, by the end of 1968 its mainland companions had all been withdrawn from BR service. There was a proposal that it be replaced by a smaller class 02 diesel transferred from the London Midland Region, but that did not happen.[73] During a visit to Ryde depot in 1972 the engine was painted in rail blue

livery and numbered 2554. The running number was changed to 05 001 in 1974 and a final departmental number 97 803 was painted on in 1981. The low top speed proved a handicap when a trip was made to Ryde Pier Head with a cab full of stranded passengers after snow halted the passenger service. The gearbox was declared defective in April 1982 but could not be replaced as a spare was found to be incompatible. Although repaired in March 1983, there were problems with the battery and after a test run on 22 April it was declared a failure. The diesel was sold to the Isle of Wight Steam Railway and moved to Havenstreet on 23 August 1984.

In April 1984 03 079 was sent to the Isle of Wight as a replacement for D2554. A member of class 03, this diesel mechanical 0-6-0 had a generous cab looking out over the engine compartment and a stovepipe-shaped chimney at the front end. Under the bonnet was a Gardner 8L3 diesel engine rated at 204hp. It was controlled by a more amenable five-speed gearbox.[72] One of nine members of the class equipped with vacuum brakes, 03 079 was built at Doncaster Works as D2079 and allocated to Thornaby in December 1959. Later based at Gateshead, it was employed as station pilot at Newcastle Central when not out-stationed to Berwick-upon-Tweed; the change of number to 03 079 took place in January 1974.

The engine's move to the Island began in October 1983, when it was taken by rail via York and Salisbury to Eastleigh Works. The final part of the journey by low-loader and aboard the vehicle ferry *St Helen* was made on 7 April 1984. Two hired cranes lifted it onto the tracks at Ryde St John's Road the following day. A test run on the

The first Class 03 0-6-0DM shunter was transferred in April 1984 and required a reduction in the height of the cab roof to allow safe passage beneath two bridges in Ryde. It was usually to be found in the engineer's siding, formerly the Newport bay, at Sandown, as seen here on 7 April 1989 newly repainted in BR blue. *John Faulkner*

night of Monday, 9 July established that clearances under two of the bridges at Ryde were too tight, so 03 079 entered the workshop in September to have the height of the cab reduced. This was achieved by removing the roof vent and lowering the centre of the cab roof by 6in. Painted in plain blue with yellow ends, 03 079 was nicknamed *Woodlouse*. The engine spent most of its working life residing in the engineers' sidings at Sandown; a departmental number 97 805 was allocated in April 1984 but never applied before a change of policy resulted in a reversion to 03 079 in 1989.[73] Intended to be used as a source of spares for its replacement, in the event that did not happen. Instead, 03 079 acquired a fresh coat of BR blue paint before continuing to carry out the bulk of the permanent way maintenance until the work was let out to private contractors who brought over their own equipment. Thought to have been last used in July 1994, 03 079 was officially withdrawn in 1996, although a short run was made at Sandown early in November 1996. It was sold to the Derwent Valley Railway, near York, on 5 June 1998.[67]

A second class 03 diesel arrived on 30 June 1988 aboard the ferry *St Cecilia*. D2179, later 03 179, was built in 1962 at Swindon Works and had been employed at Hither Green Depot in South London, followed by Ipswich docks until withdrawn in 1987. Reinstated and sent to the Isle of Wight on 30 June 1988, the cab roof was cut down in August prior to a repaint in the Network SouthEast colours of blue and grey with red and white stripes. 03 179 differed from 03 079 mainly in having dual brakes.

Nicknamed *Slug*, a faulty fuel pump kept the new arrival out of action for some time and even then it saw only limited use. The engine was transferred to departmental stock in January 1989 and allocated (but never carried) the number 97807.[73] Within weeks the remaining mainland members of the class were taken out of service. Officially withdrawn in 1993, a lengthy period in store at Ryde was followed by a test run to Shanklin after the close of services on 31 May 1998 before the engine was put up for sale. Purchased by West Anglia Great Northern Railway, 03 179 was then employed as a depot shunter at the firm's depot at Hornsey, North London, where it was named *Clive* and repainted in their colours. A change of franchise was followed by a repaint in the First Capital Connect livery in about July 2006. The last member of class 03 in Network service, 03 179, failed during a visit to the Nene Valley Railway in February 2008 and then saw little use. After another change of franchise to Govia Thameslink, it was sold to the Rushden Historical Transport Society (Rushden, Higham & Wellingborough Railway) on 19 July 2016.[67]

Mention should be made of the line's other self-propelled vehicles, all of which passed into the hands of the Isle of Wight Steam Railway. Sent across during the autumn of 1966, DS72, a Matisa tamping machine, was delivered to the Southern Region on 22 September 1955. It became a mobile compressor in 1965 when the tamping machinery was isolated. Used mainly in Ryde tunnel, it was repainted from grey to olive green livery in 1972 but was declared redundant and sold in May 1975.

The second Class 03 0-6-0DM shunter, 03 179, arrived on the Island in 1988 and the cab roof was similarly lowered. It was repainted from BR blue to NSE red, white and blue while in works and is seen parked north of Ryde St John's Road bridge on 31 March 1989. *John Faulkner*

DS3320 was a type 27A gang trolley, one of a batch of sixteen built by D. Wickham & Co. of Ware, Herts, and delivered in 1953 as No. PWM3766. Later renumbered DS3320, it went to the Island during the winter of 1973–74 but was sold in 1976. The Wickham had much in common with the FYNR rail motor with its open sides and petrol engine. Permaquip personnel carriers 68809 and 68810 arrived in 1997 and 1995 respectively. These were more sophisticated diesels with hydraulic transmission and a fully enclosed single-ended body with an integral turntable so that the cab could be turned to face the direction of travel. Able to travel at speeds up to 40mph, each could carry nine members of staff and was equipped with full messing facilities. Both were sold in January 2005. In recent years a variety of road-rail maintenance vehicles and tamping machines have been employed by contractors for brief periods.[39]

Sadler-Vectrail, the proposed operators of the Ryde to Cowes line, planned to operate a service using light rail coaches. In 1967 a prototype was built for the Sadler Rail Coach Co. by Strachan's (Hamble) Ltd, a local firm of coach builders. Called the 'Pacerailer', the single-ended, four-wheel vehicle utilised an AEC 'Reliance' coach chassis adapted to run on rails. Painted in a blue-grey livery, the coach had fluorescent lighting, air conditioning, radio telephone, public address system, emergency window exits, an auto-ticket issuing machine, change-giver, air-operated doors and folding steps for use at halts without platforms. There were seats for fifty passengers or seventy-five at a closer spacing, plus room for prams and luggage. The prototype did not generate any orders and Strachan's ceased trading in 1968. Apart from a visit to the Island Industries Fair at Ryde Airport in June 1967, the coach resided at Droxford station on the Meon Valley railway until burnt out by vandals in 1970. A small diesel named *Spitfire* kept at Droxford was also earmarked for transfer to the Isle of Wight, an event that did happen in 1972 but under somewhat different circumstances.[43]

10
Isle of Wight Steam Railway

When the Wight Locomotive Society was founded in 1966 the prospects for saving one of the LSWR class O2 engines were not good as there were other groups that had similar objectives. Fortunately, the artist David Shepherd took an interest in the project and on 7 November met with members at Ryde to select a suitable candidate. W24 *Calbourne* was the first choice but it and W31 had already been reserved by potential buyers. BR staff hoped that W14 *Fishbourne*, the oldest, would be chosen and had set aside a spare set of driving wheels. Instead, the mechanically minded members of the party chose W22 *Brading*, despite the Drummond boiler, although W33 *Bembridge* was thought to be in a better condition and another possible contender. In the event, the Society was able to purchase W24 *Calbourne* and a quantity of spare parts for £900 on 22 May 1967. Then followed a move by low-loader to Newport on 15 August 1969 and a busy day on 24 January 1971 when *Calbourne* hauled the Society's small collection of rolling stock over the closed railway to a permanent home at Havenstreet, the first steps in the establishment of the Isle of Wight Steam Railway.[39]

Members encountered a situation even more difficult than the first Isle of Wight companies faced during the 1860s. Maintenance had to be done in the open as there was a lack of any suitable buildings until a workshop came into use in January 1981. *Calbourne* had been the preferred choice for preservation as the boiler was in fairly good condition. A final BR inspection on 23 February 1967 merely stated that it needed to be washed out and the tubes cleaned. However, it was in a run-down condition with numerous defects that soon became abundantly clear. Various components required re-metalling, part of the framing was corroded, cracked and distorted and the smokebox needed attention. The engine was dismantled late in 1972 but the repairs dragged on and would have taken even longer without the assistance of Bill Smith and Joe Snellgrove, who had retired from their jobs at Ryde Works as chargehand and boilersmith. Steamed again in August 1975, *Calbourne* re-entered service a year later.[39]

While *Calbourne* underwent its overhaul, a passenger service was maintained by an 0-4-0 saddle tank. *Invincible* was built by R. & W. Hawthorn, Leslie & Co. of Newcastle in 1915 (maker's No. 3135), one of twenty supplied to the Royal Arsenal, Woolwich. *Invincible* was withdrawn from service at Woolwich in 1956 but reinstated and given a replacement boiler (Hawthorn, Leslie No. 12195, new 31 July 1944) in 1959 before transfer to the Royal Aircraft Establishment (RAE), Farnborough. The engine was used to haul coal through the streets from the railway station but became redundant in April 1968 after the site was converted to oil heating. Purchased by Tom Jefferis and stored under cover at his yard in Southampton, a chance conversation resulted in its loan to the railway. The first steam engine to come to the Isle of Wight since 1949, *Invincible* was transferred by low-loader via the Portsmouth to Fishbourne ferry *Camber Queen* on 3 June 1971 and first steamed on 28 December. Painted green with yellow

W24 *Calbourne* following unloading in the former FYNR yard at Newport on 15 August 1969. *J. Mackett/IWSR Archive*

On 3 June 1971 this small Hawthorn Leslie 0-4-0ST was placed on loan to the IWSR. Painted in a Southern Railway style and given fleet number 37, *Invincible* is seen at Havenstreet on 24 August 1994. *R. A. Silsbury/IWSR Archive*

Ruston Hornsby 0-4-0DM *Spitfire* was loaned to the IWSR between 1972 and 1988. It is depicted here in June 1977. *IWSR Archive*

Ajax arrived at the IWSR on 30 November 1972 but was not restored to working order until 2004, when it was completed in a pseudo-IWCR lined black livery as No. 38. *John Faulkner*

lining and the number 37 on the front buffer beam, *Invincible* maintained the service for the next four summer seasons and, following completion of the overhaul of *Calbourne*, deputised on the lighter trains for many years. Purchased by the IWSR in 1979 and renamed *Vectis*, more recently a return was made to the original name and the maroon livery of the Royal Arsenal Railway. On 18 July 1993 members of the Railway Enthusiasts Club chartered a train hauled by *Invincible*, one of several visits by groups of enthusiasts over the years. This small shunting engine cannot cope with today's heavier passenger trains and has been out of use since the boiler ticket expired in 2009. However, the simple design makes it ideal as a means for apprentices and volunteer engineers to gain experience in carrying out repairs and maintenance.[39]

Although members had resolved to use steam traction on passenger trains, it was realised that an economical diesel engine was needed for shunting and permanent way trains. *Spitfire* was a 17-ton type 88DS 88hp 0-4-0 diesel mechanical shunter built in 1946 by Ruston & Hornsby, Lincoln (maker's No. 242868). The engine spent its life in the ownership of the Gas Light & Coke Co. at Southall Gas Works but was declared redundant in 1965. Purchased by Henry Frampton-Jones, in February 1966 *Spitfire* was moved to the closed Meon Valley line and kept first at Wickham and then Droxford. The diesel arrived at Havenstreet on 6 June 1972 on loan; the number W39 was allocated but never carried. *Spitfire* was

well worn but did see some use until a more reliable replacement arrived in 1980. Returned to the mainland in 1988 and later sold, the engine's latest owner has recently given it an overhaul and a new name, *Heather*.

The next arrival was the 0-6-0T *Ajax* on 30 November 1972. This Bahan-class shunting engine was built in 1918 by Andrew Barclay & Co. (maker's No. 1605) for the Sulphide Corporation Ltd of London but was requisitioned by the Ministry of Munitions for service in Persia, where it remained for several years, latterly in the ownership of Anglo-Persian Oil Co. *Ajax* was then employed at the firm's Llandarcy oil refinery in Wales before going to Stanton Iron Works, Ilkeston, and passing into the ownership of Stewart & Lloyds. Finally working at Harlaxton Ironstone Quarry in Lincolnshire, it was withdrawn and sold in 1968. Also owned by Henry Frampton-Jones, the 0-6-0T was unfit for use and remained in store until purchased by the IWSR in 2004. Asbestos lagging was removed prior to an overhaul and boiler repairs that included a new smokebox, steel inner firebox and a repaint in lined black livery. Carrying the number 38, *Ajax* entered service in 2005 and spent the next ten years in useful employment. However, it tended to pitch and yaw when in motion, which compromised passenger comfort and had an adverse effect on the permanent way.[51]

W11 *Newport* spent almost ten years on display at Butlin's holiday camp at Pwllheli before Sir Peter Allen was

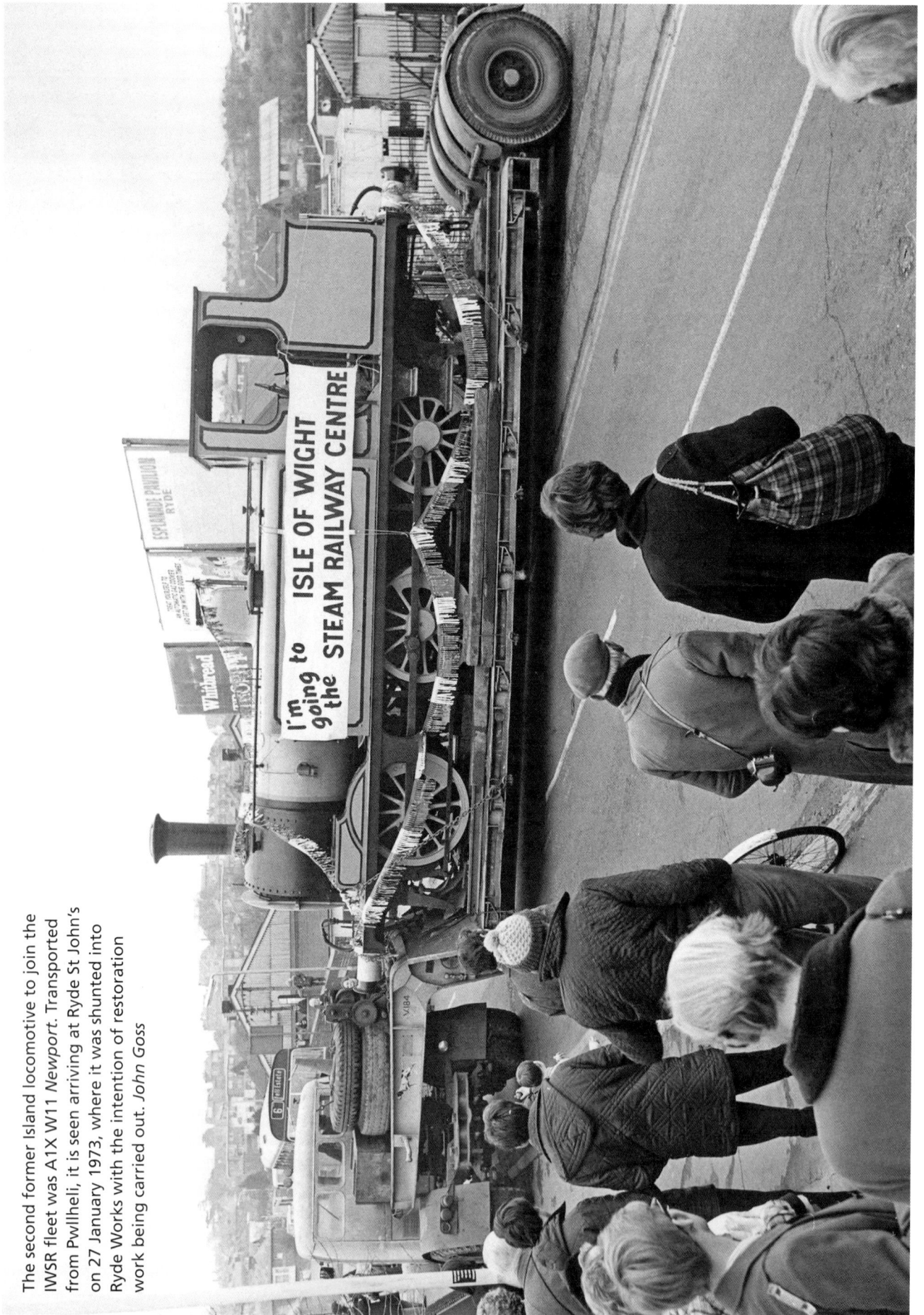

The second former Island locomotive to join the IWSR fleet was A1X W11 *Newport*. Transported from Pwllheli, it is seen arriving at Ryde St John's on 27 January 1973, where it was shunted into Ryde Works with the intention of restoration work being carried out. *John Goss*

Another Island Terrier joined the IWSR fleet in 1979, the former FYNR No. 2, which was restored as its later identity, W8 *Freshwater*. It is seen at Havenstreet on 22 August 1999 resplendent in SR dark green livery in company with sister W11, at that time bearing SR wartime unlined black livery with Sunshine lettering. The IWSR endeavours to present its historic locomotive in a range of authentic liveries *R. A. Silsbury/IWSR Archive*

able to secure its return to the Isle of Wight on loan. There were hopes that restoration could be carried out at Ryde Works, so the 0-6-0T was delivered there on 27 January 1973. Two years later, after being moved to Havenstreet, No. 11 was unveiled on 24 August 1975 in IWCR lined black livery complete with a replica Wheeler & Hurst chimney, all paid for by Sir Peter. Purchased for £3,500 on 4 July 1976, a return to operational condition was greatly handicapped by the need for specialist repairs to the cylinders. No. 11 finally entered service on 13 August 1989. It was later repainted in SR livery as W11.[39]

In 1978 Sir Peter Allen negotiated the purchase of W8 *Freshwater* for a nominal sum. Members gave the engine a repaint in SR dark green livery before its removal from Hayling Island on 18 June. W8 was in a better condition than No. 11 and entered service on 27 June 1981. To mark the centenary of the FYNR in 1988 the engine was repainted and lettered as FYNR No. 2 but later reverted to SR livery as W8 *Freshwater*.

An additional diesel shunter came to Havenstreet in 1980. Built by North British Locomotive Co., Glasgow (maker's No. 27415), the diesel was one of three built in 1954 for the English Steel Corporation Ltd. The power unit was a Paxman 6VRPHXL diesel developing 312hp at 1,250 rpm connecting with Voith/North British type L24V hydraulic transmission. Purchased by Esso for use at the Fawley oil

refinery, a lack of air brakes resulted in its sale to the IWSR for a nominal £1. Named *Tiger* after Esso's then well-known advertising feature, air brakes were fitted in 1984 so that it could substitute for a steam engine in an emergency. Unfortunately, nothing could be done about the worn hydraulic transmission so *Tiger* was sold in June 1991 to the Scottish Railway Preservation Society, operators of the Bo'ness & Kinneil Railway.[39]

Being of some historic merit, the class 05 diesel D2554 was purchased in April 1984 for static display. However, following an overhaul and repaint in BR green livery, the diesel has seen some use, albeit not on passenger trains because of the lack of air brakes. The troublesome gearbox still makes *Fred* particularly 'difficult to drive'.[51]

In November 1988 another diesel shunter was purchased as a more reliable standby should a steam engine fail in service. D2059 was ex-works from Doncaster on 29 May 1959. Later renumbered as 03 059, it was in working order and had both vacuum and air brake equipment. Arriving in BR green, the diesel reverted to its original number D2059, and acquired the name *Edward*. Later repainted in the earlier BR black livery, D2059's moment of fame came in March 2002 when hired with two wagons to help in ballasting the Ryde to Shanklin line. (The dimensions of D2059, D2079 and D2179 were identical when built.)[39]

The IWSR has also acquired several diesel shunting locomotives over the years. On the left in red livery is North British 0-4-0DH *Tiger* assisting with the unloading of Class 03 D2059 at Havenstreet on 4 November 1988. *Tiger* was sold in 1991, but D2059 remains a key part of the IWSR fleet. *R. A. Silsbury/IWSR Archive*

The IWSR has two Hunslet 'Austerity' 0-6-0ST, both ex-Army. No. 192 *Wagonner* bears the blue livery carried during her latter MoD-service days and is pictured running round at Smallbrook on 26 May 2013. *John Faulkner*

No. 235, a small 0-4-0DM shunter was obtained from the MoD with the two Austerities. Not being fitted with continuous brakes, it is used as the Havenstreet works shunter and is seen following overhaul and repaint on 29 September 2016. *John Faulkner*

The extension to Smallbrook Junction in 1991 created a need for more motive power. The Royal Corps of Transport Museum Trust offered on loan the first of two 'Austerity' 0-6-0 saddle tanks. A batch of fourteen shunting engines had been supplied in 1953 by Hunslet Engine Co. (maker's Nos 3790–3803) to the Army, where they became Nos 190–203. Based on a design dating from 1937, several hundred were built for the War Department, the National Coal Board and other industrial users. No. 198 *Royal Engineer* entered service in 1956 at a military stores depot at Steventon but after two years was moved to the Bicester Ordnance Depot and later to Long Marston. When overhauled in 1987–88 the engine received a repaint in the Army's deep bronze green with black below the footplate, red coupling rods and white tyres. No. 198 was the last Army-owned operational steam engine when withdrawn in 1991. Intended for display in a museum at Chatham, *Royal Engineer* arrived on a low-loader at Havenstreet on 12 February 1992.[74]

No. 192, later 92 *Waggoner* saw service on the Longmoor Military Railway before moving successively to Histon, Bicester and Long Marston. Stored at Shoeburyness from 1969 to 1974, the engine then went to Marchwood Military Port, opposite Southampton, where an internal passenger service was being operated. During an overhaul at Shoeburyness in 1979 it was painted in the Longmoor Military Railway Oxford Blue livery lined in red but without the large white LMR lettering. Having clocked up only 6,000 miles in military service and briefly displayed in the Museum of

Army Transport at Beverley, *Waggoner* was moved to Havenstreet in February 2005.[39]

The two Army engines proved to be a good choice as they were able to haul the heavier trains, were economical and easy to maintain. Unfortunately, the high centre of gravity has done the permanent way no favours. *Royal Engineer* ran 83,707 miles in IWSR service before undergoing a general overhaul, completed in 2017. *Waggoner* managed 48,000 miles before following *Royal Engineer* into the workshop for its overhaul. The 0-6-0STs (and *Ajax*) have received bronze slide valves in place of the original cast iron versions in an effort to reduce cylinder wear and prolong their lives.[74]

The Army also loaned a small 0-4-0 diesel mechanical shunting engine built by Andrew Barclay & Co. of Kilmarnock (maker's No. 371) and delivered on 20 September 1945 as No. 235. Having driving wheels of 3ft 3in diameter and weighing 22 tons, a new 195hp engine was fitted in July 1969. Painted in Army green with large chevrons on each end, 235 arrived at Havenstreet on 14 February 1992 for use as a yard shunter and rejoices in the unofficial name *Mavis*. The three Army engines passed into IWSR ownership in May 2008 but have retained the existing green and blue liveries as an acknowledgement of their previous service.[39]

The Isle of Wight Steam Railway came to the attention of Peter Clarke and Roy Miller, who were looking for a new home for their engines. The Ivatt Trust had two 2-6-2 tank engines 41298 and 41313, a 2-6-0 tender engine

46447 and an Austerity 0-6-0T *Juno*, all residing at the Buckinghamshire Railway Centre, Quainton Road, near Aylesbury. Moved to Havenstreet between 2006 and 2010, the four have since passed into IWSR ownership.

Designed by H. G. Ivatt, Chief Mechanical Engineer of the LMS, 130 2-6-2 tank engines and 128 of the tender version were constructed by the LMS and BR. The BR class 2 2-6-2Ts considered for service on the Isle of Wight railways in the 1960s were based on the design. Intended for light duties, labour-saving features included an inward-sloping coal bunker, hopper ash pans, rocking grates and a blowdown facility for flushing out the boiler.[51]

No. 41298 was built at Crewe in 1951 and allocated to Bricklayers Arms for empty stock workings in and out of Victoria station. In 1953 the engine was transferred to Devon for work on the branch lines around Barnstaple. Ten years later 41298 was at Weymouth for boat train and local passenger duties. Moved to Nine Elms in October 1966, the final few months were spent on empty stock workings. Withdrawn with a mileage of 367,288 when steam working ended in July 1967, the engine was purchased directly from BR and initially housed on the Longmoor Military Railway in Hampshire. Moved to Quainton Road on 12 December 1980, an overhaul was already well under way when 41298 was transferred to Havenstreet on 28 November 2008. The Westinghouse brake was fitted in accordance with drawings prepared for the proposed BR 2-6-2T modifications in the 1960s with the compressor on the right-hand side of the boiler and air reservoirs between the frames; the existing vacuum brake was retained. No. 41298 re-entered service in September 2015 painted lined black with the second BR emblem and other mainland features such as a smokebox door number plate. Above the driver's seat inside the cab is a small plate reading *Driver Peter Clarke*; similar plates were carried by the O2s. The 2-6-2T has been described as 'a fireman's dream' when compared with the older engines.[39]

No. 41313 was built at Crewe in 1952 and entered service at Brighton in May. After a month the 2-6-2T was reallocated to Exmouth Junction shed, displacing LSWR Drummond M7 0-4-4Ts on local passenger work in the Exeter area. In April 1953 41313 spent a few weeks at Three Bridges in West Sussex before moving to Faversham, Kent. An overhaul at Eastleigh Works in 1959 was followed by a transfer to Barnstaple and then to Brighton in 1963, where the work included passenger turns to Horsham and Guildford, shunting, parcels trains, and the 'Lancing Belle' workmen's train to and from Lancing Carriage Works. After a final transfer to Eastleigh in May 1964, 41313 was withdrawn in June 1965. Sold to Woodham Brothers scrap merchants in February 1966, the engine lay in their yard at Barry Docks, South Wales, until purchased by the Ivatt Trust in 1975 and taken to Quainton Road as a source of spare parts. It was then realised it was too good to break up but no work was done apart from the application of a protective coat of red oxide paint and some greasing. On 3 August 2006

41313 was the first of the Trust's engines to arrive, albeit temporarily carrying the boiler from 46447. Sent to the East Somerset Railway, Cranmore, for an overhaul, 41313 returned to Havenstreet on 24 October 2017 and entered service on 4 April 2018 in BR lined black livery with the name *Driver Roy Miller* in the cab. Fortunately, the 2-6-2Ts are able to operate over the existing line without the need for any of the loading gauge modifications envisaged in the 1960s.[39]

No. 46447 was built at Crewe in 1950 and employed in the London Midland Region until withdrawn in December 1966 and sold for scrap to Woodham Brothers, South Wales. The engine was purchased for preservation and moved to Quainton Road on 7 June 1972. Although restoration was by far the most advanced of the three engines, 46447 was in a dismantled state when moved to the Isle of Wight in several loads during October 2008. Intended to be a static exhibit, some work was carried out before 46447 went to the East Somerset Railway to be restored and remain on loan for ten years. The engine entered service at Cranmore two years later painted in BR lined black livery. In May 2018 46447 returned to Havenstreet for an 'Ivatt weekend' to claim the honour of being the first tender engine ever to run on the Island railways. As it lacked Westinghouse brakes a through pipe was fitted so it could double-head passenger trains with one of the 2-6-2Ts.[39]

Juno was built by Hunslet Engine Co. in 1958 (maker's No. 3850) to the same dimensions as the Army 0-6-0 saddle tanks, a member of a class that eventually totalled 484. Employed at Stewart & Lloyds ironstone quarry at Buckminster, the engine was declared redundant in 1968 and purchased for preservation in May 1969. When residing at Quainton Road, *Juno* regularly hauled passenger trains on one of the demonstration lines before being laid aside. The stay at Havenstreet was brief as in October 2010 *Juno* was loaned to the National Railway Museum. Still largely in its original condition, the engine has been put on display at Locomotion, Shildon.[39]

LBSCR class E1 0-6-0T 110 *Burgundy*, the 100th engine to be built at Brighton Works, entered service on 22 March 1877 having cost £2,800. No. 110 was withdrawn in February 1927 and sold to Messrs Cohens, scrap merchants on 5 April for £925. Later that year it was resold to the Cannock and Rugeley Colliery Co., becoming 9 *Cannock Wood*. In 1929 a larger boiler was made and fitted by W. G. Bagnall of Stafford (works No. 7496), resulting in an increase in boiler pressure from 140 to 175psi. Other alterations included new wheels, a tapered chimney and the provision of cab side windows. When taken out of use in August 1963, No. 9 was the last surviving member of class E1. Purchased by the Railway Preservation Society (West Midlands District) at Chasewater, in February 1975 a group of IWSR members got together to buy it but were put off by concerns about the condition of the boiler. The next owner moved the engine to the East Somerset Railway where, following expensive repairs, No. 110 was employed from 1993 until withdrawn with

Representing Isle of Wight 'might have beens', the IWSR owns two LMR design Ivatt 2MT 2-6-2T, Nos. 41298 and 41313, as well as a tender version No. 46447. All three are lined up at Havenstreet during an Ivatt Gala on 24 May 2018. *John Faulkner*

firebox problems in 1997. There then followed a further period in store until the IWSR received a legacy in 2010 that contained the wish that it recreate W2 *Yarmouth*, the first of the four Isle of Wight E1s withdrawn in the 1950s. With that in mind, the engine was bought and moved to Havenstreet on 30 October 2012. Fitted with a Drummond chimney previously carried by W31 *Chale*, a new boiler, firebox and other significant work is required before *Yarmouth* can return to service.[39]

At the time of writing, the IWSR is negotiating with the National Trust for the loan of *Haydock*, a Robert Stevenson & Co. 0-6-0T built in 1876 (maker's No. 2309). The engine is a member of the class that included *Freshwater*, the contractor's engine employed on building the FYNR; it differs principally in having 3ft 6in wheels. The first buyer of *Haydock* is unknown but in 1903 it was being employed by Naylor Bros, who had a contract to widen the North Eastern Railway between Copmanthorpe and Church Fenton. The engine was later sold to Richard Evans & Co., the owner of collieries and a private railway system north of Warrington that passed into the hands of the National Coal Board in 1947. During an overhaul in Haydock Workshops in 1955–56 the boiler was rebuilt with Ramsbottom safety valves in place of the original Salter's pattern, new square side tanks were fitted and the buffers changed. For many years *Haydock* was employed shunting at a timber wharf on the Manchester Ship Canal at Acton Grange. Made redundant when the wharf closed in February 1963, it was given to the National Trust in September 1966 and put on display at Penrhyn Castle, North Wales.[75]

A number of more humble machines have been acquired to help maintain the permanent way, including several that worked previously on the Ryde to Shanklin line. The Matisa tamping machine DS72 bought by a member in 1975 was soon scrapped. A more useful addition was Wickham trolley DS3320, purchased in 1976. It was joined by Permaquip personnel carriers 68809 and 68810 in 2005. Already out of use, 68810 was stripped for spares and then scrapped but *La-La* (68809) is still active and carries the colourful Network SouthEast livery. A third example, 68800, and a second type 27A Wickham, DS3327 (previously PWM3959 and B33W), were purchased from the mainland during 2017. As on the Island Line, there have been brief visits from various tamping machines.

The ability to transport engines to and from the Isle of Wight was greatly helped by the introduction of larger vehicle ferries on the Portsmouth to Fishbourne route. Visits have been made to Havenstreet by the Bluebell Railway's LBSCR class E4 0-6-2T 473 *Birch Grove*, followed by LBSCR Terrier 0-6-0Ts *Fenchurch* and *Stepney*; as *Fenchurch* was dual braked it could haul passenger trains. Other visitors have included LMS 0-6-0T 47298, masquerading as 'Thomas the tank engine' and LSWR Beattie 2-4-0 well tank 30585. The annual Diesel Galas have featured 03 197, 03 399 and the much larger 33 202 *Dennis G Robinson*. W8 *Freshwater*, W11 *Newport*, *Invincible* and W24 *Calbourne* have made reciprocal visits to railways on the mainland.[39]

Operating the relatively modern 0-6-0STs and 2-6-2Ts has helped to reduce wear and tear on the Railway's more historic possessions. They handle most services but *Freshwater*, *Newport* and *Calbourne* appear at busier times when there are additional passenger or demonstration goods trains. Loadings for the 'Terriers' are now restricted to 80 tons and the older engines clock up a much lower mileage between repairs than was common during BR days. This makes it easier to manage maintenance, 'little and often' is the best description, with work scheduled for the winter months just as in IWR days.[67]

LBSCR class A1X 0-6-0Ts W8 *Freshwater* and W11 *Newport* have been regular performers during the summer months. The boiler carried by W8 (No. 1012 built at Brighton in April 1913) fitted during an overhaul in February 1958 had so deteriorated that a new one was ordered at a cost of £35,000, one of a pair purchased jointly with the Kent & East Sussex Railway. Delivered in 1998, it returned to service later that year in the SR dark green livery as W8 *Freshwater*. The boiler carried by W11 (No. 967 built at Brighton in May 1912) and fitted in November 1958 was worn out but by the time a replacement was delivered on 15 September 2010 the cost had risen to £70,000. W11 returned to service in March 2014 finished in SR olive green livery without nameplates or steam heating. W8 carries the Drummond chimney from W11 and is apparently unique in having opening cab-front spectacles fitted during or shortly after the 1939–45 war. Both have the original combined splashers and sandboxes, 14in diameter cylinders and, for practical reasons, the front footsteps and handrails added during the 1930s.[51]

In 2002 O2 W24 *Calbourne* was taken out of service for an overhaul. The boiler (No. 208) dated from 1889 but had undergone numerous refurbishments over the years. With financial help from the Heritage Lottery Fund, the boiler barrel was replaced and the copper firebox given extensive repairs; the engine returned to service in August 2010. Despite this work, *Calbourne* remains very much a vintage engine with many original components including some previously carried by other O2s. The most recent overhaul begun in December 2019 was followed by a repaint in malachite green, the latest in a variety of liveries carried during preservation. In addition to the small number of spare parts purchased with the engine, a remarkable collection has been salvaged from its companions. They included a crank axle, a complete bogie, buffers, chimneys, Westinghouse compressors and regulator handles from many of the other twenty-two Isle of Wight O2s. 'Unfortunately it's the big pieces that are missing.'[67]

Following closure of the Ryde Pier Tramway in 1969, motor car No. 2 was purchased by the Isle of Wight Vintage Transport Group, an offshoot of the Wight Locomotive Society. In preparation for a move to Newport on 21 February 1971, the body was removed and stored; it was later broken up after useful fittings had been removed. The chassis assisted during the move to Havenstreet and was used briefly as an open railcar but was then laid aside. In 2011 a small group of members began work on a project

The only locomotive class from BR days on the Island not to have been preserved was the E1 0-6-0T. The IWSR was fortunate in being able to acquire the last example in existence and will be restoring it in the guise of scrapped sister W2 *Yarmouth*. Cosmetically restored to that identity, the former LBSCR 110 is displayed at Havenstreet on 13 May 2013. *John Faulkner*

to recreate the motor car and a replica trailer. Alan Keef Ltd of Ross-on-Wye were contracted to do the work of constructing a motor car incorporating the surviving components. The car has a more powerful Perkins 404D engine, a higher floor height to match current platform levels and a second driving position for use until the trailer car can be completed. This apart, every effort has been made to keep the appearance as close to the original as possible. The body from the Pollard motor car has survived and is on display at Havenstreet.[39]

When the last of pre-1938 tube stock was taken out of service in 1991, the acquisition of a representative car was not pursued due to the presence of asbestos and a lack of space for its display. Since then, construction of the Train Story building has made it possible to accept the gift of a 1938 stock unit from South Western Railway. The cars concerned are Nos. 127 and 227 (LT 10291 and 11291. As unit 483 007, they came to the Island on 12 March 1990, entered service on 18 May and were withdrawn from service on 3 January 2021.[39]

More than sixty steam engines worked on the Isle of Wight railways in the years up to 1966. Most have long since been broken up but many nameplates remain. IWR nameplates and maker's plates from *Ryde*, *Shanklin*, *Ventnor*, *Wroxall* and *Bonchurch* are on display in the museum at Havenstreet. A Manning, Wardle maker's plate for FYNR No. 1 also exists. Of the SR nameplates, some are in private ownership but examples from *Medina*, *Osborne*, *Totland* and *Wroxall* can been seen at the National Railway Museum, York with *Newport* and *Calbourne* at Havenstreet. Other survivors include SR number plates and the final BR nameplates.[16]

11

Industrial and Other Locomotives

When carrying out research for this book it became evident there were businesses that possessed railways and tramways but whose histories lay outside the development of the Island's railway system. However, information about these undertakings is sketchy and fragmented. The following are known to have used engines, but there may well have been more whose existence has not yet been traced.

During the 1920s and '30s contractors frequently made use of narrow-gauge war surplus railway material. Cheek Bros[76] are known to have employed a petrol engine[67] and tipper wagons while working on improvements to the Shorwell Road at Bowcombe, west of Carisbrooke. During the reconstruction of the Military Road at Compton Bay between 1932 and 1936 the contractors Northcott operated a 2ft gauge line using at least two Motor Rail[67] petrol engines. In more recent times, when the water supply through Ventnor tunnel was renewed in 1986 there was a 1ft 6in gauge railway and a Wingrove & Rogers 4-wheeled battery electric locomotive (fleet no. JM 100).[67] A sewage

improvement scheme at Ryde in 1989–90 necessitated the construction of a 1ft 6in gauge railway worked by two locos owned by the contractors Miller Construction Limited and were 4-wheeled battery electric vehicles. One was their L15 (Clayton Equipment B0109A of 1973) and the other remains unidentified.[67 & 75] None of these contractors' engines were permanent residents, unlike the following.

The West Medina Cement Mills had a network of narrow-gauge tracks, including a 1ft 7½in (50cm) gauge tramway to the clay pit. Motive power was provided by a Motor Rail petrol engine (maker's No. 4566) purchased in 1928. It was said to have been transferred to Frognall Clay Pits, Bapchild, Kent, in about 1939 but is more likely to have remained on site until 1944.[48] The locomotive survived in Kent until scrapped in September 1963.[67]

Saro Laminated Wood Products Ltd at Folly Works, Whippingham, operated a 1ft 11½in or 2ft gauge tramway between the works and a jetty. A Lister petrol engine (maker's No. 10500) was purchased in 1938. The tramway fell into disuse in about 1954 and the engine was sold for scrap two years later.[77]

Island Bricks Ltd opened extensive brickworks at Rookley in about 1950 and added a 2ft gauge tramway in 1954 to connect with clay pits about 400 yards to the west. The Company owned three engines:[75]

- Ruston & Hornsby 20hp diesel (maker's No. 223700) built in 1943 purchased in 1954. It was later rebuilt with the cab and works plates taken from the Hunslet engine.

- Ruston & Hornsby 16/20hp diesel (maker's No. 186318) built in 1937 purchased in about 1969.

- Hudson-Hunslet diesel (maker's No. 3109) built in 1943 arrived in about 1967 but was out of use by 1972.

A four-wheel Austro-Daimler petrol-mechanical engine employed by Cheek Bros on road works at Bowcombe, west of Carisbrooke, seen on 10 April 1934. *Collection John Maskell*

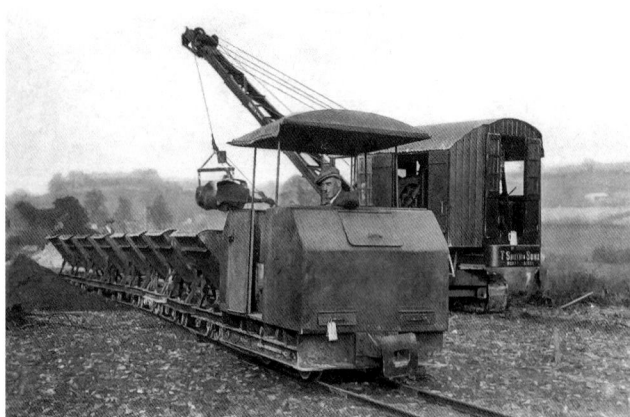

The Military Road reconstruction west of Compton Bay illustrates the scale of the undertaking. A small locomotive and tippler can be discerned upper left – unfortunately no better view of a locomotive could be sourced. *Collection John Maskell*

When the brickworks closed in 1973 the engines passed into the hands of a group based at the Albany Steam Museum, Newport. Work began on the construction of a railway and more engines were added from the mainland. They included *Peter Pan*, a Kerr, Stuart 'Wren'-class 0-4-0ST steam engine (maker's No. 4254) built in 1922. After the museum closed in 1977 everything went to various railways on the mainland.[78]

Several railways were constructed for carrying tourists. At Sandown, a miniature railway operated briefly during the summer of 1932 on the beach in front of Guadeloupe Terrace. Of 8¼in gauge, the motive power was a scale model of a London & North Eastern Railway tender engine made by Bassett Lowke Ltd of Northampton.[79] The Sandham Minature Railway, in Sandham Grounds, was a 100 yard long line which operated from 1949 until 1961. The 5in gauge track was carried on metal trestles, with the driver and passengers sitting astride the carriages and motive power was a freelance, red-painted steam tender engine named *James*. In Sandham Castle children's play park, a 10¼in gauge railway consisting of a 300-yard continuous loop opened in 1969. A 2-4-2 light green diesel engine *Sandham Castle* built at Shepperton was joined in 1976 by two Co-Bo petrol mechanical engines: D108 *Vanguard* built in about 1962 and 608 *Avenger* three years later. The play park and railway closed in 1989. *Sandham Castle* was sold to the Vanstone Woodland Railway, Codicote, Herts, on 31 May 1991; the others went for scrap.[67]

At Yafford Mill, a historic water mill and agricultural museum, there was a full-size, passenger-carrying, narrow-gauge railway. In June 1992 engines, rolling stock and track were purchased and by August 1995 about 300 yards of 2ft 6in gauge line was in operation; by December 1997 it had grown to a length of ¾ mile. Motive power consisted of two Hunslet diesels (maker's Nos 2250 and 2252) built in 1940 with Gardner 50hp diesel engines and Hunslet 4-speed gearboxes. Designed for use in locations close to flammable and explosive material, they had enclosed electrical equipment, air-operated brakes, spark-arresting exhaust filters and a large water tank to reduce emissions. The railway closed on 11 November 2000 after the mill changed ownership. Two years later the engines and stock were sold to the Sunshine Peat Co., Annaghmore, Co. Armagh.[78]

Several other engines were brought to the Isle of Wight for use on pleasure lines that were never built. In each case they were sold back to the mainland.

The Ruston & Hornsby four-wheel diesel, Works number 186318, at Rookley Brickworks on 30 July 1972. *Collection John Maskell*

Appendix 1: Locomotive Summary

				ISLE OF WIGHT RAILWAY				
No.	Name	Built	Maker	Maker's No.		To IW	To mainland	Withdrawn
W13	*Ryde*	6.1864	Beyer, Peacock & Co.	400		6.1864	13.6.1934	9.7.1932
	Sandown	6.1864	Beyer, Peacock & Co.	401		6.1864	4.5.1923	6.1923
W14	*Shanklin*	6.1864	Beyer, Peacock & Co.	403		6.1864		11.1927
	Brading	1.1841	Edward Bury & Co.		(1)	5.1863		Sold 1872
W15	*Ventnor*	10.1868	Beyer, Peacock & Co.	848		10.1868		7.1925
W16	*Wroxall*	4.1872	Beyer, Peacock & Co.	1141		4.1872	23.6.1933	25.3.1933
W17	*Brading*	12.1876	Beyer, Peacock & Co.	1638		12.1876		4.1926
	St Helens	1.1841	Edward Bury & Co.		(2) (3)	5.1863		Sold 9.1893 (4)
	Bembridge	3.1875	Manning, Wardle & Co.	517	(3) (5)	3.1879	Sold 6.1916	
W18	*Bonchurch*	3.1883	Beyer, Peacock & Co.	2376		4.1883		5.1928

(1) Contractor's engine *Stuart* bought 12.1867. (2) Originally *Stuart*. (3) Bought by BHIR 1879–80. (4) Became contractor's engine *St Lawrence*, scrapped June 1898. (5) Bought by IWR 10.1898.

				ISLE OF WIGHT CENTRAL RAILWAY				
No.	Name	Built	Maker	Maker's No.		To IW	To mainland	Withdrawn
1	*Pioneer*	7.1861	Slaughter, Gruning & Co.	453	(1)	9.1861		30.8.1901
2	*Precursor*	8.1861	Slaughter, Gruning & Co.	454	(1)	9.1861		17.1.1900
3	*Mill Hill*	1.1870	Black, Hawthorn & Co.	116	(1)	3.1870	Sold 2.1918	
	Comet	6.1852	LSWR		(2)	6.1872	12.1872	
4	*Cowes*	5.1876	Beyer, Peacock & Co.	1583	(3)	6.1876		7.1925
5	*Osborne*	5.1876	Beyer, Peacock & Co.	1584	(3)	6.1876		4.1926
6	*Bee*	1870s	Henry Hughes		(4)		Sold 6.1888	
	Newport	1.1861	R. & W. Hawthorn & Co.	1128	(5)	6.1874		4.1890
7	*Whippingham*	10.1861	Slaughter, Gruning & Co.	443	(1)	3.1880		8.1906
6		6.1890	Black, Hawthorn & Co.	999		6.1890		11.1925
7		7.1882	Beyer, Peacock & Co.	2231		12.1906		4.1926
8	(*Bembridge*)	5.1898	Beyer, Peacock & Co.	3942	(6)	5.1898		28.12.1929
9		12.1872	LBSCR as No. 75 *Blackwall*			3.1899		5.1927
10	*Cowes*	8.1874	LBSCR as No. 69 *Peckham*			4.1900	19.5.1936	12.1936
11	*Newport*	3.1878	LBSCR as No. 40 *Brighton*			1.1902	22.2.1947 (7)	28.9.1963
12	*Ventnor*	9.1880	LBSCR as No. 84 *Crowborough*			11.1903	5.5.1936	12.1936
1		9.1906	Hawthorn, Leslie & Co.	2663		10.1906	Sold 2.1918	
2		4.1895	Seaham Works, Londonderry Railway			7.1909	Sold 7.1917	

(1) Owned by Henry Martin. (2) Hired by IWNJR. (3) Purchased by RNR. (4) Believed owned by Henry Martin. (5) Purchased by IWNJR. (6) No. 8 was withdrawn before the nameplates were fitted. (7) No. 11 was renumbered 2640 in 7.1947 and 32640 in 3.1951.

FRESHWATER, YARMOUTH & NEWPORT RAILWAY

No.	Name	Built	Maker	Maker's No.	To IW	To mainland	Withdrawn
1	*Medina*	2.1902	Manning, Wardle & Co.	1555	6.1913	23.6.1933	9.7.1932
2	*Freshwater*	12.1876	LBSCR as 46 Newington		25.6.1913	4.5.1949 (1)	4.11.1963
Rail motor car		26.6.1913	Drewry Car Co.	479	6.1913		31.12.1924

No. 2 was previously LSWR 734. It became W8 *Freshwater* on 9.4.1932 and 32646 on 5.8.1949. (1) Official date 7.5.1949. The rail motor car was allocated SR No. 2462, then 437S.

RYDE PIER TRAMWAY

No.	Built	Maker	Maker's No.	To IW	To mainland	Withdrawn
Vectis	3.1864	Manning, Wardle & Co.	111	3.1864	5.1864	On loan
Steam tram	9.1876	Merryweather & Co.		9.1876	12.1876	On loan
Steam tram No. 1	1880	F. Bradley & Co.		1.1881		10.1884
Steam tram No. 2	1880	F. Bradley & Co.		1.1881		10.1884

CONTRACTOR'S ENGINES

Name	Built	Maker	Used on	To IW	To mainland
Stuart			See Isle of Wight Railway		
Grafton	rebuilt 8.1858	Edward Bury & Co.?	IWR	5.1863	5.1866
Bee			See Isle of Wight Central Railway		
Godshill	1863 or 1865	Worcester Engine Co.	NGSTLR	5.1897	1900
Weaste	6.1888	Hudswell Clarke & Co.	NGSTLR	1895?	1900
Freshwater	1885	Robert Stephenson & Co.	FYNR	6.1897	10.1891

SOUTHERN RAILWAY CLASS A1X

Nos.	IW name	Built	LBSCR No.	LBSCR name	To IW	To mainland	Withdrawn
W3	*Carisbrooke*	7.1880	77	*Wonersh*	5.1927	4.5.1949 (1)	9.1959
W4	*Bembridge*	7.1880	78	*Knowle*	9.6.1929	19.5.1936	10.1963
W9	*Fishbourne*	12.1876	50	*Whitechapel*	28.5.1930	19.5.1936	11.1963

W3 was renumbered W13 *Carisbrooke* in 1932 and 32677 on 5.8.1949. (1) Official date 7.5.1949.
W4 was renumbered W14 *Bembridge* in 1932, 2678 in 7.1937 and 32678 in 9.1949.
W9 was renumbered 515S in 4.1937, DS515 in 2.1952 and 32650 in 11.1953.

SOUTHERN RAILWAY CLASS O2							
No.	IW name	Built	LSWR No.	Nine Elms Works No.	To IW	To mainland	Withdrawn
W14	Fishbourne	12.1889	178	290	5.5.1936		2.1.1967
W15	Cowes	12.1890	195	316	19.5.1936		12.5.1956
W16	Ventnor	6.1892	217	357	5.5.1936		2.1.1967
W17	Seaview	12.1891	208	339	28.5.1930		2.1.1967
W18	Ningwood	9.1892	220	360	28.5.1930		5.12.1965
W19	Osborne	9.1891	206	333	4.5.1923		5.11.1955
W20	Shanklin	2.1892	211	347	4.5.1923		2.1.1967
W21	Sandown	9.1891	205	332	7.1924		1.5.1966
W22	Brading	6.1892	215	355	7.1924		2.1.1967
W23	Totland	10.1890	188	306	26.4.1925		13.8.1955
W24	Calbourne	12.1891	209	341	26.4.1925		14.3.1967
W25	Godshill	11.1890	190	308	25.6.1925		30.12.1962
W26	Whitwell	12.1891	210	342	25.6.1925		1.5.1966
W27	Merstone	6.1890	184	298	17.3.1926		2.1.1967
W28	Ashey	7.1890	186	301	17.3.1926		2.1.1967
W29	Alverstone	8.1891	202	329	20.4.1926	22.2.1947	1.5.1966
W30	Shorwell	9.1892	219	359	20.4.1926		12.9.1965
W31	Chale	4.1890	180	292	5.1927		14.3.1967
W32	Bonchurch	11.1892	226	369	24.5.1928		31.10.1964
W33	Bembridge	8.1892	218	358	19.5.1936		2.1.1967
W34	Newport	7.1891	201	328	20.5.1947		13.8.1955
W35	Freshwater	5.1890	181	294	13.4.1949 (1)		2.10.1966
W36	Carisbrooke	6.1891	198	325	13.4.1949 (1)		20.6.1964
W29 was sent to Eastleigh Works for overhaul and returned to the Island 20.5.1947. (1) Transferred by British Railways; Official date 16.4.1949.							

SOUTHERN RAILWAY CLASSES E1 AND E4							
No.	IW name	Built	LBSCR No.	LBSCR name	To IW	To mainland	Withdrawn
W1	Medina	1.1879	136	Brindisi	4.7.1932		30.3.1957
W2	Yarmouth	10.1880	152	Hungary	4.7.1932		15.9.1956
W3	Ryde	3.1881	154	Madrid	4.7.1932		13.6.1959
W4	Wroxall	11.1878	131	Gournay	23.6.1933		22.10.1960
2510		12.1900	510	Twineham	22.2.1947	5.4.1949	9.1962
No. 2510 was renumbered 32510 upon return to the mainland.							

BRITISH RAILWAYS DIESEL ENGINES						
No.	Built	Maker	Maker's No.	To IW	To mainland	Withdrawn
D2554, 05 001	1956	Hunslet Engine Co.		7.10.1966		Sold 1984
03 079	1959	BR Doncaster		22.10.1983	Sold 5.6.1998	3.6.1996
03 179	1962	BR Swindon		30.6.1988	Sold 8.6.1998	29.10.1993
DS72	1955	Matisa	48588	10.1966		Sold 5.1975
DS3320	1953	D. Wickham & Co.	6645	1973–74		Sold 1976
68809	1986	Permaquip	PER010	1997		Sold 1.2005
68810	1986	Permaquip	PER011	11.1995		Sold 1.2005

ISLE OF WIGHT STEAM RAILWAY						
No.	Name	Built	Maker	Maker's No.	To IW	To mainland
W37	*Invincible*	1915	Hawthorn, Leslie & Co.	3135	3.6.1971	
W38	*Ajax*	1918	Andrew Barclay & Co.	1605	30.11.1972	
W39	*Spitfire*	1946	Ruston & Hornsby	242868	6.6.1972	4.11.1988
	Tiger	1954	North British Locomotive Co.	27415	9.1980	Sold 6.1991
D2059, 03 059	*Edward*	1959	BR Doncaster		4.11.1988	
198	*Royal Engineer*	1953	Hunslet Engine Co.	3798	12.2.1992	
235	*Mavis*	1945	Andrew Barclay & Co.	371	14.2.1992	
192	*Waggoner*	1953	Hunslet Engine Co.	3792	26.2.2005	
41313		1952	BR Crewe		3.8.2006	
46447		1950	BR Crewe		10.2008	31.10.2012
41298		1951	BR Crewe		28.11.2008	
	Juno	1958	Hunslet Engine Co.	3850	5.2009	10.2010
W2	*Yarmouth*	1877	LBSCR as 110 *Burgundy*		30.10.2012	
68800		1985	Permaquip	PER001	26.1.2017	
DS3327		1955	D. Wickham & Co.	6944	25.3.2017	

No. 46447 is on loan to the East Somerset Railway. *Juno* is on display at Locomotion, Shildon.

Appendix 2: Principal Dimensions

These dimensions record measurements taken on the dates quoted and ignore changes of boiler, etc. (For example, by 1900 the cabs and replacement boilers on the older IWR 2-4-0Ts added about 4 tons.) Every source of information differed to some degree.

	ISLE OF WIGHT RAILWAY				
	Ryde, Sandown, Shanklin & Ventnor	*Wroxall*	*Brading*	*Bembridge*	*Bonchurch*
Wheel arrangement	2-4-0T	2-4-0T	2-4-0T	0-6-0ST	2-4-0T
Cylinder diameter and stroke	15in x 20in	15in x 20in	16in x 24in	13in x 18in	17in x 24in
	inside	inside	inside	inside	inside
Leading wheels diameter	3ft 6in	3ft 6½in	3ft 6½in	n/a	3ft 6½in
Driving wheels diameter	5ft 0½in	5ft 0½in	5ft 0½in	3ft 0in	5ft 0½in
Wheelbase	6ft 9in	6ft 9in	7ft 4in	5ft 10in	7ft 4in
	7ft 0in	7ft 0in	7ft 2in	5ft 8in	7ft 2in
Total	13ft 9in	13ft 9in	14ft 6in	11ft 6in	14ft 6in
Boiler diameter	3ft 11¼in	3ft 11¼in	4ft 0in	3ft 4in	4ft 0in
Boiler length	9ft 6in	9ft 6in	9ft 10in	8ft 4in	9ft 10in
Firebox length	4ft 4in	4ft 4in	4ft 4in	3ft 3½in	4ft 4in
Heating surfaces:					
Number of tubes	168 x 2in	168 x 2in	168 x 2in	no data	166 x 2in
Tubes	861sq ft	861sq ft	891sq ft	500sq ft	880sq ft
Firebox	71sq ft	66sq ft	70sq ft	50sq ft	70½sq.ft
Total	932sq ft	927sq ft	961sq ft	550sq ft	950½sq ft
Working pressure	120psi	120psi	120psi	120psi	120psi
Grate area	13.1sq ft	13.1sq ft	13.2sq ft	8sq ft	13.2sq ft
Water capacity	820 gallons	820 gallons	1,000 gallons	550 gallons	1,000 gallons
Coal capacity	1¼ ton	1¼ ton	1¼ ton	1 ton	1¾ ton
Weight in working order:					
Leading wheels	7 ton 10cwt	7 ton 9cwt	8 ton 5cwt	no data	7 ton 6cwt
Driving wheels	11 ton 13cwt	11 ton 13cwt	13 ton 7cwt	no data	15 ton 2cwt
	11 ton 5cwt	11 ton 5cwt	12 ton 15cwt	no data	13 ton 6cwt
Total	30 ton 8cwt	30 ton 8cwt	34 ton 7cwt	22 ton 10cwt	35 ton 14cwt
Tractive effort	7,587lb	7,587lb	10,358lb	8,619lb	11,694lb
Driving position	right-hand	right-hand	right-hand		right-hand
Date & origin of information	1864[14]	1872[14]	1876[14]	1875[20]	1883[14]

COWES & NEWPORT, RYDE & NEWPORT AND IW (NEWPORT JUNCTION) RAILWAYS					
	Nos. 1 & 2	**No. 3**	**Nos. 4 & 5**	*Newport*	**No. 7**
Wheel arrangement	2-2-2WT	0-4-2ST	2-4-0T	2-2-2WT	4-4-0T
Cylinder diameter and stroke	13½in x 16in	10in x 17in	14in x 20in	14in x 20in	15½in x 22in
	outside	outside	inside	inside	inside
Leading or bogie wheels diameter	3ft 2in	n/a	3ft 3in	3ft 6in	3ft 2in
Driving wheels diameter	5ft 0in	3ft 3in	5ft 0in	5ft 6in	5ft 3in
Trailing wheels diameter	3ft 2in	2ft 4in	n/a	3ft 6in	n/a
Wheelbase	5ft 6in	5ft 3in	5ft 10in	no data	(bogie) 4ft 8in
	5ft 9in	5ft 0in	6ft 4in	no data	7ft 11½in
					7ft 2in
Total	11ft 3in	10ft 3in	12ft 2in	no data	19ft 9½in
Boiler diameter	3ft 4½in	3ft 0in	3ft 6in	no data	4ft 1½in
Boiler length	8ft 3in	8ft 0in	8ft 9½in	no data	9ft 9in
Firebox length	3ft 6in	2ft 6in	3ft 7in	no data	4ft 6in
Heating surfaces:					
Number of tubes	119 x 1⅞in	67 x 1⅞in	116 x 2in	no data	162 x 2in
Tubes	496sq ft	272sq ft	552sq ft	no data	888sq ft
Firebox	53sq ft	32sq ft	53sq ft	no data	81sq ft
Total	549sq ft	304sq ft	605sq ft	no data	969sq ft
Working pressure	120psi	140psi	140psi	120psi	120psi
Grate area	8.75sq ft	6sq ft	10.5sq ft	no data	14sq ft
Water capacity	400 gallons	400 gallons	480 gallons	no data	800 gallons
Coal capacity	6cwt	10cwt	15cwt	no data	14cwt
Weight in working order:					
Leading or bogie wheels	5 ton 10cwt	n/a	7 ton 0cwt	no data	11 ton 5cwt
Driving wheels	8 ton 10cwt	5 ton 10cwt	9 ton 15cwt	no data	13 ton 0cwt
		6 ton 0cwt	9 ton 13cwt	n/a	10 ton 5cwt
Trailing wheels	5 ton 5cwt	4 ton 0cwt	n/a	no data	
Total	19 ton 5cwt	15 ton 10cwt	26 ton 8cwt	26¾ ton	34 ton 10cwt
Tractive effort	4,957lb	5,187lb	7,775lb	6,058lb	8,557lb
Driving position	right-hand	no data	left-hand	no data	no data
Date & origin of information	*circa* 1900[35]	*circa* 1900[35]	1876[14]	*circa* 1900?[35]	*circa* 1900[35]

ISLE OF WIGHT CENTRAL RAILWAY (1)					
	No. 6	**No. 8**	**No. 1 Motor**	**No. 7**	**No. 2**
Wheel arrangement	4-4-0T	2-4-0T	0-4-0T	2-4-0T	0-4-4T
Cylinder diameter and stroke	16in x 24in	14in x 20in	9in x 14in	16in x 24in	17in x 24in
	outside	inside	outside	inside	inside
Leading wheels diameter	3ft 0in	3ft 4in	n/a	4ft 0in	
Driving wheels diameter	5ft 3in	5ft 1in	3ft 6in	5ft 6in	5ft 4½in
Bogie wheels diameter					3ft 0in
Wheelbase	(bogie) 5ft 3in	5ft 10in	8ft 0in	7ft 4in	7ft 0in
	5ft 6in	6ft 4in		7ft 2in	9ft 9in
	7ft 0in				(bogie) 5ft 6in
Total	17ft 9in	12ft 2in	8ft 0in	14ft 6in	22ft 3in
Boiler diameter	4ft 0in	3ft 6in	3ft 6in	4ft 0⅞in	4ft 1in
Boiler length	10ft 6in	8ft 9½in	4ft 6in	9ft 10in	10ft 0in
Firebox length	5ft 0⅜in	3ft 7in	2ft 6in	4ft 10in	4ft 9in
Heating surfaces:					
Number of tubes	151 x 1⅞in	116 x 2in	no data	166 x 2in	168 x 1¾in
Tubes	800sq ft	552sq ft	296sq ft	880sq ft	810sq ft
Firebox	80sq ft	53sq ft	32½sq ft	72sq ft	85sq ft
Total	880sq ft	605sq ft	328½sq ft	952sq ft	895sq ft
Working pressure	140psi	150psi	160psi	140psi	130psi
Grate area	14.5sq ft	10.5sq ft	7.5sq ft	14.8sq ft	13sq ft
Water capacity	700 gallons	520 gallons	400 gallons	1,000 gallons	1,075 gallons (2)
Coal capacity	1 ton	16cwt	12cwt	1½ ton	2½ ton (2)
Weight in working order:					
Bogie or leading wheels	10 ton 5cwt	7 ton 8cwt	n/a	7 ton 5cwt	n/a
Driving wheels	14 ton 18cwt	11 ton 18cwt	15 ton 12cwt (3)	14 ton 10cwt	15 ton 10cwt
	14 ton 17cwt	11 ton 11cwt	16 ton 11cwt (4)	13 ton 10cwt	16 ton 5cwt
Bogie	n/a	n/a	n/a	n/a	14 ton 0cwt
Total	40 ton 0cwt	30 ton 17cwt	32 ton 3cwt	35 ton 5cwt	(1) 45 ton 15cwt
Tractive effort	11,605lb	8,193lb	3,672lb	11,078lb	11,883lb
Driving position	right-hand	left-hand	no data	left-hand	no data
Date & origin of information	*circa* 1900[35]	1898[14]	1906[47]	*circa* 1912[35]	*circa* 1912[35]

(1) For details of Nos 9–12 see under Southern Railway
(2) The IWCR restricted capacities to 600 gallons and 1½ tons. The weight in working order was reduced to 40 tons.
(3) Engine weight.
(4) Carriage weight.

FYNR, CONTRACTORS AND HIRED ENGINES						
	FYNR No. 1	FYNR No. 2(1)	Godshill	Freshwater	Comet	Vectis
Wheel arrangement	0-6-0ST	0-6-0T	0-6-0ST	0-6-0T	2-2-2WT	0-4-0T
Cylinder diameter and stroke	14in x 20in	13in x 20in	14in x 18in	14in x 18in	14½in x 20in	6in x 12in
	inside	inside	inside	inside	outside	outside
Leading & trailing wheels dia.					3ft 6in	
Driving wheels diameter	3ft 6in	3ft 11½in	3ft 3in	3ft 8½in	5ft 6in	2ft 6in
Wheelbase	5ft 11in	6ft 0in	5ft 4½in	no data	no data	no data
	6ft 1in	6ft 0in	5ft 10in			
Total	12ft 0in	12ft 0in	11ft 2½in			4ft 7in
Boiler diameter	3ft 6in	3ft 4½in	no data	no data	3ft 6in	1ft 11in
Boiler length	8ft 8in	7ft 9½in	no data	no data	9ft 11in	6ft 9in
Firebox length	3ft 8in	4ft 1in	no data	no data	4ft 0in	
Heating surfaces:						
Number of tubes	no data	113 x 1¾in	124 x 1¾in	101 x 1⅞in	no data	no data
Tubes	600sq ft	424sq ft	468sq ft	470sq ft	674sq ft	no data
Firebox	60sq ft	53sq ft	58sq ft	50sq ft	76sq ft	no data
Total	688½sq ft	477sq ft	526sq ft	520sq ft	750sq ft	100sq ft
Working pressure	140psi	150psi	140psi	100psi	120psi	no data
Grate area	8½sq ft	11.25sq ft	10.25sq ft	10.5sq ft	8.9sq ft	no data
Water capacity	600 gallons	500 gallons	660 gallons	560 gallons	550 gallons	200 gallons
Coal capacity	1ton	13cwt	18cwt	no data	no data	no data
Weight in working order	25 ton 14cwt	24 ton 7cwt	no data	21 ton	27 ton 2cwt	6 ton 10cwt
Tractive effort	11,900lb	9,073lb	10,765lb	6.739lb	6,499lb	no data
Driving position	right-hand	left-hand				
Date & origin of information	1902[20]	1911[33]	1893[40]	1885[51]	1852[35]	1864[20]

(1) With Drummond boiler
Details of other contractors' locomotives are scanty and such as are known are included in the appropriate sections of the main text.

	IWCR Nos 9–12	W8–14	W14–36	W1–4	No. 2510
SOUTHERN RAILWAY					
	Class A1 (1)	Class A1X	Class O2	Class E1	Class E4
Wheel arrangement	0-6-0T	0-6-0T	0-4-4T	0-6-0T	0-6-2T
Cylinder diameter and stroke	13in x 20in	12–14in x 20in	17½in x 24in	17in x 24in	18in x 26in
	inside	inside	inside	inside	inside
Driving wheels diameter	3ft 11½in	3ft 11½in	4ft 10in	4ft 6in	5ft 0in
Bogie or trailing wheels diameter			3ft 0in	n/a	4ft 0in
Wheelbase	6ft 0in	6ft 0in	6ft 10in	7ft 6in	7ft 9in
	6ft 0in	6ft 0in	8ft 6in	7ft 9in	7ft 6in
			(bogie) 5ft 0in		6ft 3in
Total	12ft 0in	12ft 0in	20ft 4in	15ft 3in	21ft 6in
Boiler diameter	3ft 6in	3ft 6in	4ft 2in	4ft 0in	4ft 3in
Boiler length	7ft 10in	8ft 1¼in	9ft 5in	10ft 2in	10ft 7½in
Firebox length	4ft 1in	4ft 1in	5ft 0in	5ft 2¼in	5ft 8¼in
Heating surfaces:					
Number of tubes	121 x 1¾in	119 x 1¾in	201 x 1¾in	174 x 1¾in	242 x 1¾in
Tubes	453sq ft	433sq ft	898sq ft	841sq ft	1,106½sq ft
Firebox	53sq ft	55½sq ft	89sq ft	83sq ft	93sq ft
Total	506sq ft	488½sq ft	987sq ft	924sq ft	1,199½sq ft
Working pressure	140psi	150psi	160psi	170psi	170psi
Grate area	10sq ft	10sq ft	13.8sq ft	15.5sq ft	14.43sq ft
Water capacity	500 gallons	500 gallons	800 gallons	900 gallons	1,408 gallons
Coal capacity	13cwt	1¼ ton	2¼ ton (2)	2¼ ton	3 ton
Weight in working order:			(3)	(4)	
Driving wheels	8 ton 5cwt	8 ton 0cwt	15 ton 1cwt	12 ton 15cwt	13 ton 0cwt
	8 ton 1cwt	10 ton 5cwt	15 ton 9cwt	15 ton 10cwt	14 ton 15cwt
	8 ton 0cwt	10 ton 0cwt		15 ton 18cwt	11 ton 14cwt
Bogie or trailing wheels			16 ton 8cwt		13 ton 3cwt
Total	24 ton 6cwt	28 ton 5cwt	46 ton 18cwt	44 ton 3cwt	52 ton 12cwt
Tractive effort	8,468lb	(5)	17,234lb	18,560lb	20,288lb
Driving position	left-hand	left-hand	right-hand	left-hand	left-hand
Length overall		26ft 0½in	30ft 10¾in	32ft 4½in	
Height over chimney (6)		11ft 0¾in	12ft 3⁹⁄₁₆in	12ft 4⁹⁄₁₆in	
Height over cab		10ft 1½in	11ft 4¹¹⁄₁₆in	11ft 0¾in	
Width over tanks		6ft 7in	8ft 11in	7ft 7in	
Width over cab roof		6ft 1in	8ft 11in	6ft 3¼in	
Width over footplate		7ft 2in	8ft 3in	8ft 0in	
Width over footsteps		8ft 3in	8ft 5¾in	8ft 6in	
Date and origin of information	1872[45]	1911[61]	1889[61]	1932[61]	1900[65]

(1) Also FYNR No. 2 as built.
(2) Original bunker with three coal rails
(3) With Adams boiler.
(4) With Marsh boiler.
(5) 9.073lb (13in cylinders); 10,522lb (14in cylinders).
(6) The height varied by a few inches depending on the chimney carried.

VARIATIONS TO O2 STATISTICS	
O2 SR Drummond boiler	
Boiler diameter	4ft 2in
Boiler length	9ft 4½in
Firebox length	5ft 0in
Heating surfaces:	
Number of tubes	180 x 1¾in
Tubes	811sq ft
Firebox	89sq ft
Total	900sq ft
Working pressure	160psi
Grate area	13.83sq ft
Date and origin of information	1926[12]
O2 with MacLeod bunker	
Coal capacity	3 ton
Weight in working order:	
Driving wheels	15 ton 0cwt
	15 ton 0cwt
Bogie wheels	18 ton 8cwt
Total	48 ton 8cwt
Date and origin of information 1932[61]	

BR DIESEL ENGINES		
	Class 05	Class 03
Wheel arrangement	0-6-0	0-6-0
Wheel diameter	3ft 4in	3ft 7in
Wheelbase	4ft 6in	4ft 6in
	4ft 6in	4ft 6in
Total	9ft 0in	9ft 0in
Fuel capacity	300 gallons	300 gallons
Weight in working order	30 ton 18cwt	30 ton 4cwt
Top speed	18½mph	29mph
Length overall	25ft 4in	26ft 0in
Width overall	8ft 3in	8ft 6in
Height overall	11ft 0in (1)	12ft 2⁷⁄₁₆in
Date and origin of information	1956[72]	1959[72]
Wheelbase	4ft 6in	4ft 6in

(1) Many members of the class had a 1ft higher roof

ISLE OF WIGHT STEAM RAILWAY					
	Invincible	*Ajax*	*Royal Engineer, Waggoner, Juno*	**Nos. 41298, 41313**	**No. 46447**
Wheel arrangement	0-4-0ST	0-6-0T	0-6-0ST	2-6-2T	2-6-0
Cylinder diameter and stroke	14in x 22in	16in x 24in	18in x 26in	16½in x 24in	16in x 24in
	outside	outside	inside	inside	inside
Leading wheels diameter	n/a	n/a	n/a	3ft 0in	3ft 0in
Driving wheels diameter	3ft 6in	3ft 7in	4ft 3in	5ft 0in	5ft 0in
Trailing wheels diameter	n/a	n/a	na	3ft 0in	3ft 0in
Wheelbase	5ft 6in	6ft 0in	5ft 9in	8ft 6in	8ft 6in
		5ft 0in	5ft 3in	6ft 9in	6ft 9in
				7ft 0in	7ft 0in
				8ft 0in	
Total	5ft 6in	11ft 0in	11ft 0in	30ft 3in	22ft 3in
Boiler diameter	3ft 6in	3ft 10in	4ft 3in	4ft 3in–4ft 8in	4ft 3in–4ft 8in
Boiler length	8ft 10½in	9ft 10⁹⁄₁₆in	10ft 2in	10ft 7⅞in	10ft 7⅞in
Firebox length	3ft 0in	4ft 0in	5ft 6in	5ft 11in	5ft 11in
Heating surfaces:					
Number of tubes	126 x 1⅝in	166 x 1¾in	181 x 1¾in	162 x 1⅝n	162 x 1⅝n
Superheater tubes				12 x 5⅛n	12 x 5⅛in
Tubes	487sq ft	737sq ft	872½sq ft	924sq ft	924sq ft
Superheated tubes				134sq ft	134sq ft
Firebox	57sq ft	90sq ft	87½sq ft	101sq ft	101sq ft
Total	544sq ft	827sq ft	960sq ft	1,159sq ft	1,159sq ft
Working pressure	160psi	160psi	170psi	200psi	200psi
Grate area	9sq ft	11.7sq ft	16.8sq ft	17.5sq ft	17.5sq ft
Water capacity	660 gallons	788 gallons	1,200 gallons	1,350 gallons	3,000 gallons
Coal capacity	8cwt	1½ ton	2¼ ton	3 ton	4 ton
Weight in working order:					
Leading wheels	n/a	n/a	n/a	12 ton 10cwt	8 ton 1cwt
Driving wheels	13 ton 5cwt	no data	16 ton 6cwt	13 ton 12cwt	13 ton 7cwt
	13 ton 15cwt	no data	16 ton 0cwt	14 ton 0cwt	13 ton 11cwt
		no data	15 ton 17cwt	13 ton 13cwt	12 ton 0cwt
Trailing wheels	n/a	n/a	n/a	12 ton 10cwt	n/a
Total	27 ton	38 ton	48 ton 3cwt	66 ton 5cwt	47 ton 2cwt (1)
Tractive effort	13,963lb	19,432lb	23,868lb	18,513lb	17,408lb
Driving position	right-hand	right-hand	right-hand	left-hand	left-hand
Date and origin of information	1959[51]	1918[51]	1953[74]	1952[51]	1950[51]
(1) Weight 84 ton 3cwt with tender.					

Tractive effort was calculated using the generally used formula for two-cylinder railway engines and the values were checked against those previously published for a number of the locomotives. The figures provide an imprecise comparison of the relative power of the locomotives. No account is taken of the number of driving wheels and the load bearing down on them (traction). Variation of boiler pressure and changes to cylinder bore (due to wear, reboring or replacement) and wheel diameter (due to tyre wear) will all affect the tractive effort figure.

Appendix 3: Overhaul Dates

This is an incomplete list of overhauls for the years 1923 to 1966 using information from boiler registers, Ryde Works' returns, record cards, etc. Care should be taken as many overhauls have not been traced and some dates are approximate. Eastleigh boiler numbers have been quoted except where indicated.

The overhauls were carried out at Ryde Works except where noted 'A' (Ashford), 'B' (Brighton), 'E' (Eastleigh) or 'N' (Newport). Repairs were classified depending on the amount of work required. During BR days the most extensive was 'General Overhaul', then 'Heavy Intermediate', 'Heavy Casual', 'Light Intermediate', 'Light Casual' and 'Non-classified' but it was quite common to reclassify an overhaul if more or less work was done than planned. Where an entry quotes 'Overhaul' the extent of the repair is unknown, although it was probably a general overhaul. Final mileages have been quoted when known.

FRESHWATER, YARMOUTH & NEWPORT RAILWAY			
No.	**Ex-works**	**Type of repair**	**Notes**
W1	Purchased by FYNR 6.1913, boiler new 12.1902.		
	N 5.1924	Overhaul	Boiler No. 180 allocated.
	2.1929	General	
Withdrawn 9.7.1932 and cut up at Eastleigh Works 29.7.1933			

W2, W8	E 9.1912	General	Loaned 6.1913 and later purchased by FYNR. Boiler new 9.1912.
	N 4.1924	Overhaul	Boiler No. 184 allocated.
	1.1927	General	
	22.3.1932	General	Boiler 1226 fitted, boiler 184 scrapped.
	12.1937	General	Boiler 1014 fitted.
	1940–41	Overhaul	
	5.1945	Overhaul	
	8.1948	General	Wheels turned.
To mainland 4.5.1949. Withdrawn 4.11.1963 with boiler 1012 fitted 2.1958. Final mileage: LBSCR 574,266, IW unknown, 1949–63 116,094. Sold for preservation.			

ISLE OF WIGHT CENTRAL RAILWAY			
No.	**Ex-works**	**Type of repair**	**Notes**
W4	New to RNR 5.1876, new boiler 1904		
Withdrawn 7.1925. Final mileage 893,617. Sold for scrap to Mr Ball, Ryde.			

W5	New to RNR 5.1876, new boiler 1899		
Withdrawn 4.1926. Final mileage 931,309. Sold for scrap to Mr Hunt.			

W6	New to IWCR 6.1890		
Withdrawn 11.1925. Final mileage 663,841. Sold for scrap to Mr Ball, Ryde.			

W7	Purchased by IWCR 12.1906, boiler new 12.1882		
Withdrawn 4.1926. Final mileage: MSWJR 463,928, IW 247,675, total 711,603. Sold for scrap to Mr Hunt.			

W8	New to IWCR 5.1898.		Boiler No. 202 allocated.
Withdrawn 28.12.1929. Final mileage 639,994. Sold for scrap to Messrs W. Hurst & Son, Newport 1.1930.			

ISLE OF WIGHT CENTRAL RAILWAY			
No.	Ex-works	Type of repair	Notes
W9	Purchased by IWCR 3.1899, boiler from No. 12 fitted 3.1917, new cylinders.		
	N 5.1924	Overhaul.	
	1.1927	Overhaul	Boiler condemned, engine beyond economic repair.
Withdrawn 5.1927 (one register stated 1926). Final mileage: LBSCR 580,982, IW 321,669, total 902,651. Sold to Mr Ball for scrap at St Helens Quay.			

W10	Purchased by IWCR 4.1900, new cylinders 6.1915.		
	N 1925	Overhaul	Boiler No. 205 allocated.
	5.1930	General	Boiler 1094 (renumbered from 209) fitted, boiler 205 scrapped.
To mainland 19.5.1936 and withdrawn. Cut up at Eastleigh Works 2.4.1949.*			

W11	Purchased by IWCR 1.1902, new boiler and cylinders 7.1918.		
	N 5.1924	Overhaul	Boiler No. 206 allocated.
	12.1927	General	Boiler 1014 fitted.
	6.1930	Overhaul.	
	7.1933	General	Boiler 186 fitted.
	1936	Overhaul.	
	6.1939	General	Boiler 1226 fitted.
To mainland 22.2.1947. Withdrawn 28.9.1963 with boiler 967 fitted 11.1958.			
Final mileage: LBSCR 522,583, IWCR 198,746, 1923–47 294,601, 1947–63 148,794, total 1,164,724.			
Sold for preservation.			

W12	Purchased by IWCR 11.1903, new boiler and cylinders 7.1916.		
	N 5.1925	Overhaul	Boiler No. 209 allocated. Last engine overhauled at Newport.
	8.1927	Overhaul.	
	12.1929	General	Boiler 1111 (renumbered from 206) fitted.
To mainland 5.5.1936 and withdrawn. Cut up at Eastleigh Works 2.4.1949.*			

No.	Ex-works	Type of repair	Notes
ISLE OF WIGHT RAILWAY			
W13	*Ryde* new to IWR 6.1864, new boiler 12.1900, *Shanklin*'s boiler 5.1921.		
	5.1924	Not known	Boiler No. 210 allocated. Axle problems.
	2.1930	General.	
Withdrawn 9.7.1932. Final mileage 1,566,846. Cut up at Eastleigh Works 14.8.1940.			
Sandown	new to IWR 6.1864, new boiler 5.1897.		
To mainland 4.5.1923 and withdrawn. Final mileage 1,374,751. Cut up at Eastleigh Works 9.1923.			
W14	*Shanklin* new to IWR 6.1864, new boiler 12.1895, boiler ex *Ryde* 7.1921. SR boiler No. 211 allocated.		
Withdrawn 11.1927. Final mileage 1,492,067.			
W15	*Ventnor* new to IWR 10.1868, new boiler 6.1896.		
Withdrawn 7.1925, boiler to *Wroxall*. Final mileage 1,348,548. Sold for scrap to Mr Ball, Ryde.			
W16	*Wroxall* new to IWR 4.1872, new boiler 6.1900. SR boiler No. 215 believed allocated.		
	1925	Boiler transferred from *Ventnor*, original scrapped.	
	3.1931	General.	
Withdrawn 25.3.1933, boiler 'barrel for storage of fuel oil'. Final mileage 1,350,674. Cut up at Eastleigh Works 22.7.1933.			
W17	*Brading* new to IWR 12.1876, new boiler 12.1902.		
Withdrawn 4.1926. Final mileage 1,212,753. Sold for scrap to Mr Hunt.			
W18	*Bonchurch* new to IWR 4.1883, new boiler 12.1921. SR boiler No. 219 allocated.		
Withdrawn 5.1928. Final mileage 1,326,067. Sold to Messrs Jolliffe 8.1928 for scrap at Gasworks siding, Cowes.			
SOUTHERN RAILWAY CLASS A1X			
W3, W13	B 2.1927	General	To IW 5.1927 with boiler 186 (ex Brighton 934).
	7.1929	Overhaul	
	5.1932	General	Boiler 1128 fitted.
	1935	Overhaul	
	1940–41	Overhaul	
	11.1945	General	
To mainland 4.5.1949 with boiler 1128. Withdrawn 9.1959. Final mileage 1,301,612. Cut up for scrap 4.1960.			
W4, W14	B 2.1929	General	To IW 9.6.1929 with boiler 965.
To mainland 19.5.1936. Withdrawn 10.1963. Final mileage 1,389,447, also quoted as 1,411,436. Sold for preservation.			
W9	B 5.1930	General	To IW 28.5.1930 with boiler 1008 (ex Brighton 986).
	10.1931	Not known.	
To mainland 19.5.1936 with boiler 1008. Withdrawn 11.1963. Final mileage 1,271,019. Sold for preservation.			

SOUTHERN RAILWAY CLASS O2			
No.	Ex-works	Type of repair	Notes
W14	E 29.4.1936	General	To IW 5.5.1936 with new Adams boiler 1045
	6.1939	Overhaul	
	12.1948	General	Wheels turned
	4.1951	Not known	Wheels turned
	11.6.1954	Light casual	Wheels changed
	14.9.1954	General	New cylinders
	14.12.1956	Heavy casual	
	6.5.1960	General	Boiler changed, wheels turned
	24.5.1963	Light intermediate	
	10.1.1966	Not known	Wheels changed
Withdrawn 2.1.1967 with boiler 272. Final mileage 1,411,809. Cut up at Newport by H. B. Jolliffe & Co. by 27.7.1967			

W15	E 13.5.1936	General	To IW 19.5.1936 with Adams boiler 373 and new cylinders
	8.4.1948	General	Cylinders rebored, wheels turned
	10.1950	Not known	Wheels turned
	13.5.1953	General	Wheels turned
	24.6.1955	Light casual	Wheels removed for fitting to W16, replacements from W28
Withdrawn 12.5.1956. Cut up in stores road beside Ryde shed by 29.9.1956*			

W16	E 29.4.1936	General	To IW 5.5.1936 with Adams boiler 265 and new cylinders
	by 6.1941	Overhaul	Boiler 265 removed
	1944	Overhaul	
	8.1946	Not known	Wheels turned
	4.1947	Not known	Wheels changed
	2.1949	General	Cylinders rebored, wheels turned
	11.1951	Not known	Wheels turned
	1.2.1954	General	Wheels turned
	30.6.1955	Light Casual	
	19.10.1956	General	Frame welded, new cylinders?, fitted with wheels previously on W15
	17.10.1958	Light casual	
	17.3.1961	General	Wheels turned
	24.7.1964	Light casual	
	11.9.1965	Not known	
	22.2.1966	Not known	
Withdrawn 2.1.1967 with boiler 162. Cut up at Newport by H. B. Jolliffe & Co. by 12.6.1967			

No.	Ex-works	Type of repair	Notes
SOUTHERN RAILWAY CLASS O2			
W17	E 24.5.1930	General	To IW 28.5.1930 with new Adams boiler 843
	by 4.1946	Overhaul	
	4.1949	General	New cylinders, wheels changed
	2.1952	General	Wheels turned
	30.6.1955	Light casual	Wheels turned
	25.5.1956	General	Wheels turned
	16.1.1959	General	Wheels changed
	2.2.1962	General	Wheels turned
	1.5.1965	Intermediate	Wheels changed
Withdrawn 2.1.1967 with boiler 373. Cut up at Newport by H. B. Jolliffe & Co. by 1.7.1967			

No.	Ex-works	Type of repair	Notes
W18	E 24.5.1930	General	To IW 28.5.1930 with new Adams boiler 844
	8.1936	Overhaul	
	1940–41	Overhaul	
	28.2.1947	General	New cylinders, wheels changed
	3.12.1949	Heavy casual	Boiler 183 fitted, wheels turned
	4.1.1952	Intermediate	Wheels turned
	18.4.1954	General	Boiler 196 fitted, wheels turned
	6.4.1956	Light intermediate	Wheels changed
	5.4.1957	Casual	Frame welded
	30.5.1958	General	Drummond boiler 194 fitted, wheels changed
	10.2.1961	Light casual	Tubes (did not enter works)
	29.6.1962	General	Drummond boiler replaced by Adams boiler 212
	31.12.1964	Light casual	Crank pins
Withdrawn 5.12.1965 with boiler 212. Cut up at Cement Mills by H. B. Jolliffe & Co. by mid-1.1967			

No.	Ex-works	Type of repair	Notes
W19	E 10.3.1923	General	To IW 4.5.1923 with Adams boiler 205/369 †
	4.1925	Overhaul	
	5.1930	Overhaul	Boiler 193 fitted, previous boiler scrapped
	10.1933	Overhaul	New cylinders
	by 3.1939	Overhaul	Boiler 193 removed
	12.1947	Overhaul	Cylinders rebored, wheels changed
	12.1949	General	
	1.1951	Not known	Wheels turned
	30.5.1953	Casual	
	10.1953	Not known	Wheels turned
Withdrawn 5.11.1955. Cut up at Ryde by 25.2.1956.*			

SOUTHERN RAILWAY CLASS O2			
No.	Ex-works	Type of repair	Notes
W20	E 24.3.1923	General	To IW 4.5.1923 with Adams boiler 211/370 †
	8.1927	Overhaul	
	3.1929	Overhaul	
	2.1931	Overhaul	New boiler 847 fitted, previous boiler scrapped
	9.1946	Overhaul	New cylinders
	1.5.1948	General	Wheels changed
	3.1951	Not known	Wheels turned
	12.1953	General	Wheels changed
	27.10.1955	Light casual	Wheels previously on W23 turned and fitted
	17.7.1956	General	
	20.6.1958	Light casual	Wheels turned
	11.11.1960	General	Wheels changed
	10.8.1962	Light casual	
	9.5.1963	Light casual	
	12.1964	Light casual	
	4.7.1965	Not known	
	4.11.1965	Not known	
	2.12.1965	Not known	
Withdrawn 2.1.1967 with boiler 197. Cut up at Newport by H. B. Jolliffe & Co. by 20.5.1967			

W21	E 5.4.1924	General	To IW 7.1924 with Adams boiler 179/371 †
	10.1926	Overhaul	
	6.1929	Overhaul	
	4.1935	Overhaul	Boiler 228 fitted
	4.1946	Overhaul	
	1.1949	General	New cylinders, wheels turned, wheels changed on bogie
	31.12.1949	Intermediate	Boiler 187 fitted, bogie wheels turned
	9.1950	Not known	Wheels changed
	16.12.1952	General	Boiler 195 fitted, wheels turned
	25.5.1955	General	Boiler 162 fitted, wheels turned
	2.11.1957	Intermediate	Retubed
	28.11.1958	Light casual	Frame patched
	28.8.1960	General	Boiler 1003 fitted, wheels turned
	14.12.1963	Light casual	Wheels turned
	9.1.1965	Light casual	Frame weld
Withdrawn 1.5.1966 with boiler 1003. Final mileage 1,334,965. Cut up in Ryde goods yard by H. B. Jolliffe & Co. by late 8.1966			

No.	Ex-works	Type of repair	Notes
		SOUTHERN RAILWAY CLASS O2	
W22	E 5.4.1924	General	To IW 7.1924 with Adams boiler 197/372 †
	1.1929	Overhaul	Boiler 989 fitted
	1940–41	Overhaul	
	20.12.1946	General	New cylinders, wheels changed
	3.1950	Not known	Wheels turned
	27.2.1953	General	Wheels turned
	22.4.1955	General	Wheels turned
	5.7.1957	Light casual	
	1.2.1958	Light intermediate	Wheels changed
	4.12.1959	Heavy casual	
	17.3.1962	Light casual	
	22.3.1963	Heavy casual	Drummond boiler 932 fitted
	13.7.1964	Light casual	
	2.12.1964	Light casual	Broken crank pin, damaged tank, wheels changed
	2.10.1965	Not known	
	13.7.1966	Not known	
Withdrawn 2.1.1967 with boiler 932. Cut up at Newport by H. B. Jolliffe & Co. by 8.8.1967			

No.	Ex-works	Type of repair	Notes
W23	E 7.3.1925	General	To IW 26.4.1925 with Adams boiler 231/373 †
	10.1926	Overhaul	
	2.1931	Overhaul	Boiler 720 fitted, pull-push gear removed
	4.1936	Overhaul	Boiler 198 fitted
	12.1936	Overhaul	New cylinders
	17.7.1945	General	Cylinders rebored 5.1945
	2.1948	Intermediate	Boiler changed
	6.1948	Not known	New leading and driving wheels
	6.1951	Not known	Wheels turned
Withdrawn 13.8.1955, wheels transferred to W20. Final mileage 1,599,647. Cut up in stores road beside Ryde shed by 5.11.1955.*			

No.	Ex-works	Type of repair	Notes
W24	E 21.3.1925	General	To IW 26.4.1925 with Adams boiler 216/525 †
	6.1930	Overhaul	Boiler 373 fitted, previous boiler scrapped, pull-push gear removed
	5.1936	Overhaul	Boiler 224 fitted
	10.1939	Overhaul	
	14.5.1947	General	Wheels changed
	4.1950	General	Wheels turned
	3.1953	Not known	Wheels turned
	4.2.1955	General	New cylinders, wheels turned
	8.9.1955	Light casual	Wheels previously on W34 turned and fitted
	5.1957	Light casual	Wheels turned
	21.3.1958	General	Boiler 192 fitted, wheels turned
	3.11.1961	Light intermediate	Wheels changed
	17.4.1964	Light casual	
	29.5.1965	General	Boiler 208 fitted, previous boiler 192 scrapped, wheels turned
Withdrawn 14.3.1967 with boiler 208. Final mileage 1,639,478. Sold for preservation			

SOUTHERN RAILWAY CLASS O2			
No.	Ex-works	Type of repair	Notes
W25	E 20.6.1925	General	To IW 25.6.1925 with Adams boiler 201/720 †
	5.1929	Overhaul	Boiler 372 fitted
	10.1932	Overhaul	Boiler 179 fitted
	4.1940	Overhaul	New cylinders
	1.1942	Overhaul	Boiler 290 fitted
	27.1.1948	General	Drummond boiler 223 fitted, wheels turned
	3.1950	Not known	Wheels changed
	23.11.1951	General	Drummond boiler replaced by Adams boiler 1045, wheels turned
	1.3.1954	General	Boiler 1006 fitted, wheels turned
	8.11.1955	Light casual	Frame welded
	12.7.1957	General	Boiler 847 fitted
	8.4.1960	Light casual	Tubes (did not enter works)
	24.5.1961	Heavy casual	Wheels turned
Withdrawn 30.12.1962 with boiler 847. Final mileage 1,477,096. Cut up in Ryde Works yard by 5.11.1963.*			

W26	E 13.6.1925	General	To IW 25.6.1925 with Adams boiler 188/861 †
	10.1926	Overhaul	
	4.1930	Overhaul	Boiler 179 fitted
	9.1932	Overhaul	New boiler 1004 fitted
	by 3.1940	Overhaul	Boiler 1004 removed
	29.3.1946	General	
	5.1948	Not known	Part worn wheels transferred from W20
	12.4.1949	Intermediate	Part worn wheels transferred from W17
	10.1950	Overhaul	New cylinders, wheels turned
	1953	Not known	Wheels changed
	15.6.1956	Heavy intermediate	Wheels turned
	19.9.1957	Light casual	
	26.6.1959	General	Boiler changed, wheels turned
	15.12.1961	Heavy intermediate	Wheels changed
	7.11.1964	Light casual	Broken crank pin, wheels changed
Withdrawn 1.5.1966 with boiler 946. Cut up in Ryde goods yard by H. B. Jolliffe & Co. by mid-7.1966			

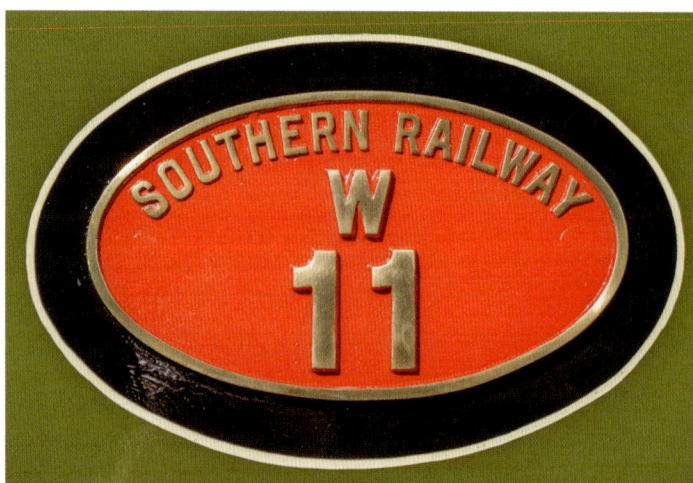

No.	Ex-works	Type of repair	Notes
		SOUTHERN RAILWAY CLASS O2	
W27	E 20.2.1926	General	To IW 17.3.1926 with new Drummond boiler 862
	3.1930	Overhaul	New Drummond boiler 933 fitted
	6.1935	Overhaul	Drummond boiler 864 fitted
	6.1938	Overhaul	Adams boiler fitted
	12.1942	Overhaul	New cylinders
	3.8.1946	Heavy casual	Wheels turned
	8.11.1948	Intermediate	Wheels changed
	2.1951	Not known	Wheels turned
	5.1952	General	Wheels turned
	17.6.1954	Light casual	Wheels turned
	1.3.1956	General	Drummond boiler fitted, wheels changed
	20.8.1957	Light casual	
	26.9.1958	Light intermediate	Wheels turned
	22.9.1961	General	Drummond boiler replaced by Adams boiler, wheels turned
	21.3.1964	Light casual	
	28.9.1964	Light casual	Wheels turned or changed, replacement cylinders
	22.8.1965	Not known	
	30.7.1966	Light casual	Last O2 to visit Ryde Works
Withdrawn 2.1.1967 with boiler 846. Cut up at Newport by H. B. Jolliffe & Co. by 20.4.1967			

No.	Ex-works	Type of repair	Notes
W28	E 13.3.1926	General	To IW 17.3.1926 with new Drummond boiler 863
	7.1932	Overhaul	Drummond boiler 191 fitted
	6.1936	Overhaul	Drummond boiler replaced by Adams boiler
	12.1936	Not known	New cylinders
	4.1937	Not known	Boiler 197 fitted
	1940–41	Overhaul	
	8.7.1947	General	Cylinders rebored
	12.1949	Not known	Wheels turned
	10.1953	Not known	Wheels changed
	29.7.1955	General	Wheels changed, old wheels transferred to W15
	19.9.1957	Light casual	
	2.5.1958	Light casual	
	12.2.1960	General	Wheels turned
	4.8.1961	Heavy casual	
	8.11.1963	Light casual	
	1.8.1965	Not known	
	4.6.1966	Not known	Wheels changed?
Withdrawn 2.1.1967 with boiler 198. Cut up at Newport by H. B. Jolliffe & Co. by 19.6.1967			

SOUTHERN RAILWAY CLASS O2			
No.	Ex-works	Type of repair	Notes
W29	E 26.3.1926	General	To IW 20.4.1926 with new Drummond boiler 864
	4.1931	Overhaul	Drummond boiler 862 fitted
	6.1935	Overhaul	Drummond boiler 934 fitted
	6.1937	Overhaul	Drummond boiler replaced by Adams boiler 371
	4.1941	Overhaul	To mainland 22.2.1947
	E 19.4.1947	Intermediate	Adams boiler fitted, new cylinders. To IW 20.5.1947
	20.12.1948	Intermediate	Wheels turned
	2.1950	Overhaul	Drummond boiler fitted, wheels turned
	5.1952	Not known	Wheels changed
	9.1952	General	Drummond boiler replaced by Adams boiler
	5.11.1954	Heavy intermediate	Wheels turned
	26.4.1957	General	Frame welded, wheels turned
	3.1959	Not known	Fractured piston head
	21.12.1960	General	Wheels turned
	23.8.1963	Light casual	
	9.1.1965	Light casual	
Withdrawn 1.5.1966 with boiler 1044. Cut up in Ryde goods yard by H. B. Jolliffe & Co. by early 8.1966			

W30	E 3.4.1926	General	To IW 20.4.1926 with new Drummond boiler 865
	6.1931	Overhaul	Drummond boiler 864 fitted
	6.1935	Overhaul	Drummond boiler 862 fitted
	9.1938	Overhaul	Drummond boiler replaced by Adams boiler
	8.1945	Overhaul	Boiler 376 fitted
	29.8.1947	General	Boiler 192 fitted, new cylinders, wheels turned
	5.1.1949	Intermediate	Wheels changed
	27.4.1951	General	Boiler 207 fitted, wheels turned
	7.5.1954	General	Drummond boiler 862 fitted, wheels turned
	17.3.1955	Light casual	
	16.1.1957	General	Adams boiler 846 fitted, frame welded, wheels turned
	17.7.1959	Light casual	
	14.2.1961	General	Boiler 207 fitted, wheels changed
	19.7.1962	Light casual	
	9.7.1963	Light casual	Tyres turned
Withdrawn 12.9.1965 with boiler 207. Final mileage 1,611,232. Cut up in Ryde Works yard by 26.11.1965			

		SOUTHERN RAILWAY CLASS O2	
No.	**Ex-works**	**Type of repair**	**Notes**
W31	E 19.3.1927	General	To IW 5.1927 with new Drummond boiler 866
	6.1931	Overhaul	Drummond boiler 863 fitted
	7.1935	Overhaul	
	12.1935	Not known	Drummond boiler replaced by new Adams boiler 1044
	3.1946	General	Boiler 1003 fitted
	27.9.1948	General	Boiler changed, new cylinders, wheels turned
	1.1952	General	Wheels turned
	2.7.1954	General	Frame welded, wheels turned
	8.3.1957	General	Wheels turned
	10.5.1961	Light intermediate	Wheels changed
	5.1.1963	Heavy casual	Drummond boiler 194 fitted
	22.7.1964	Light casual	New cylinders
	13.6.1965	Light casual	New cylinders
Withdrawn 14.3.1967 with boiler 194. Cut up in Ryde goods yard by A. King & Sons by end 9.1967			

W32	E 24.3.1928	General	To IW 24.5.1928 with new Drummond boiler 934
	2.1934	Overhaul	Drummond boiler 866 fitted
	9.1937	Overhaul	Drummond boiler replaced by Adams boiler
	30.10.1947	General	New cylinders, wheels changed
	1.1949	Intermediate	
	5.1950	Not known	Wheels turned
	8.1952	Not known	Wheels turned, bogie changed
	5.6.1953	General	
	6.1.1956	Light intermediate	Wheels changed
	4.1.1958	General	Wheels turned
	7.4.1961	Light intermediate	Wheels turned
	5.6.1964	Light casual	
Withdrawn 31.10.1964 with boiler 1006. Final mileage 1,641,874. Cut up in Ryde Works yard by 8.11.1965			

W33	E 13.5.1936	General	To IW 19.5.1936 with new Adams boiler
	10.4.1948	General	Drummond boiler fitted, new cylinders, wheels turned
	4.1950	Not known	Wheels turned
	12.1950	Overhaul	Drummond boiler replaced by Adams boiler, wheels changed
	4.1953	General	Wheels turned
	10.6.1955	Light casual	Wheels turned
	9.12.1955	General	Wheels turned
	3.4.1959	General	Wheels changed
	12.2.1962	Light casual	
	12.10.1962	Heavy casual	Wheels turned
	29.3.1963	Light casual	
	22.2.1964	Light casual	
	27.6.1965	Not known	
	8.1966	Not known	Repairs (did not enter works)
Withdrawn 2.1.1967 with boiler 1045. Cut up at Newport by H. B. Jolliffe & Co. by 14.7.1967			

SOUTHERN RAILWAY CLASS O2			
No.	Ex-works	Type of repair	Notes
W34	E 19.4.1947	General	To IW 20.5.1947 with Adams boiler, cylinders new in 7.1926
	18.3.1949	Intermediate	Wheels turned
	4.1950	Not known	
	7.1952	Not known	Wheels turned, bogie wheels changed
	1.1953	General	Wheels changed, boiler changed
	3.4.1955	General	Released as 'no repair'
Withdrawn 13.8.1955, wheels transferred to W24. Cut up at Ryde by 8.10.1955.*			

W35	E 19.3.1949	General	To IW 13.4.1949 with Adams boiler, cylinders new in 6.1946
	5.1952	General	Wheels turned
	18.3.1955	General	Frame welded, wheels turned, pull-push gear removed
	12.9.1955	Light casual	Wheels changed
	18.7.1958	Light casual	Wheels turned
	30.10.1959	General	Wheels turned
	12.4.1962	Light intermediate	
	1.1965	Light casual	
	23.10.1965	Not known	
Withdrawn 2.10.1966 with boiler 196. Cut up at Newport by H. B. Jolliffe & Co. by 7.6.1967			

W36	E 19.3.1949	General	To IW 13.4.1949 with Adams boiler 231, cylinders new in 12.1936
	7.1951	Not known	Wheels turned
	24.7.1952	General	Boiler 947 fitted, wheels changed
	3.12.1954	General	Boiler 229 fitted, frame welded, wheels turned, pull-push gear removed
	31.5.1957	Light casual	Wheels turned, retubed
	3.6.1960	General	Boiler 199 fitted
	14.6.1963	Light casual	Tyres turned
Withdrawn 20.6.1964 with boiler 199. Final mileage 1,599,478. Cut up in Ryde Works by 6.11.1965 (boiler 7.1966)			

SOUTHERN RAILWAY CLASSES E1 AND E4			
No.	Ex-works	Type of repair	Notes
W1	E 26.6.1932	General	To IW 4.7.1932 with boiler 814
	4.1936	Overhaul	
	4.1937	Not known	Cylinders rebored
	17.1.1946	General	
	8.1951	Not known	Wheels turned
	2.1954	Not known	Wheels turned
	9.1954	Light casual	
	19.1.1956	Light casual	Wheels changed
Withdrawn 30.3.1957. Final mileage 1,481,664. Cut up on No. 1 coaling road at Ryde by 17.8.1957*			

W2	E 28.6.1932	General	To IW 4.7.1932 with boiler 943, cylinders new 1926
	1.8.1942	General	
	8.1949	General	
	20.10.1952	General	Wheels turned
Withdrawn 15.9.1956. Cut up at Ryde by 2.2.1957*			

\multicolumn{4}{c}{**SOUTHERN RAILWAY CLASSES E1 AND E4**}			
No.	**Ex-works**	**Type of repair**	**Notes**
W3	E 29.6.1932	General	To IW 4.7.1932 with boiler 1162, cylinders new 1923
	21.12.1944	General	Boiler 943 fitted
	14.9.1950	Intermediate	Wheels turned
	6.11.1953	General	Wheels turned
	26.8.1955	Heavy casual	
	16.11.1956	Light intermediate	Tubes
	3.2.1958	Light casual	
\multicolumn{4}{l}{Withdrawn 13.6.1959 with boiler 943. Final mileage 1,505,919. Cut up in stores road beside Ryde shed by 28.11.1959*}			

No.	**Ex-works**	**Type of repair**	**Notes**
W4	E 16.6.1933	General	To IW 23.6.1933 with boiler 1112
	10.1939	Overhaul	
	1943	Overhaul	New cylinders
	22.1.1947	General	Wheels turned
	5.10.1951	General	Boiler 790 fitted, wheels turned
	1.9.1956	General	Boiler 888 fitted, wheels changed
	24.5.1960	Light casual	Tubes (did not enter works)
\multicolumn{4}{l}{Withdrawn 22.10.1960 with boiler 888. Cut up on No. 1 coaling road at Ryde by 14.10.1961*}			

No.	**Ex-works**	**Type of repair**	**Notes**
2510	A 23.11.1946	Overhaul	
	E 17.1.1947		To IW 22.2.1947
\multicolumn{4}{l}{To mainland 5.4.1949. Withdrawn 9.1962.}			

\multicolumn{6}{c}{***CALBOURNE*, *NEWPORT* AND *FRESHWATER* CARRIED THE FOLLOWING BOILERS INTO PRESERVATION** [80]}					
\multicolumn{2}{c}{O2 W24 *Calbourne*}	\multicolumn{2}{c}{A1X W11 *Newport*}	\multicolumn{2}{c}{A1X W8 *Freshwater*}		
Boiler 208 fitted	to engine No.	Boiler 967 fitted	to engine No.	Boiler 1012 fitted	to engine No.
12.1889	178 (later W14)	7.1912	653	5.1913	Fenchurch
9.1915	184 (later W27)	17.7.1937	2678	1.1927	B636 (ex-Fenchurch)
21.10.1926	208 (later W17)	20.2.1954	32661	27.2.1958	32646
15.11.1930	277	22.11.1958	32640		
18.5.1935	232				
19.10.1938	228				
14.9.1946	221				
12.2.1949	30225				
5.1.1955	DS3152				
29.5.1965	W24				

*Week ending date. † Boiler renumbered after transfer to the Island

Appendix 4: Locomotive Liveries

The following descriptions of the more significant liveries are based on the best available information but should not be relied upon as applying to all engines throughout the periods concerned. Any dimensions quoted are approximate. A comprehensive analysis of LSWR, SR and BR colours can be found in various Historical Model Railway Society publications.[15]

	Isle of Wight Railway
From 1864	**Dark chocolate**
Chocolate	Boiler, firebox, tank side, weatherboard, bunker side and rear, wheel spokes and rim.
Black	Smokebox, door, chimney, tank front and top, brake gear, tyres and centres.
Vermilion	Buffer beam.
Brass	Beading to spectacle plates, whistle, dome. Name and maker's plates with green background attached to boiler and tank side. Copper-capped chimney.
Lining	Black edged in yellow to tank side, boiler bands, bunker side and rear.
Lettering	None.
Carried by	*Ryde*, *Sandown*, *Shanklin*, *Ventnor*, probably *Brading* ex *Stuart*.

1872	**Furness red**
	Change of colour.
Red	Boiler, firebox, tank side, bunker side and rear, weatherboard, cab front, rear and side, wheel spokes and rim.
Black	Smokebox, door, chimney, tank front and top, cab roof, footstep treads, brake gear, tyres and centres.
Vermilion	Buffer beam.
Brass	Beading to spectacle plates, whistle, dome (except *Bonchurch*). Copper-capped chimney.
Lining	Black edged in yellow to tank side, bunker side and rear, boiler bands, arranged on the tank in three panels with the corners reversed on tank side.
Lettering	None.
Carried by	*Ryde*, *Sandown*, *Shanklin*, *Ventnor*, *Wroxall*, *Brading*, *Bonchurch*, *Bembridge*, probably *St Helens*.

1880s	Tank side lining simplified to one panel with rounded corners. Name and maker's plates moved to tank and bunker side.
1890s	Westinghouse compressor and reservoir fitted, painted black.

1916	**Midland red**
	Change of colour.[24]
Red	Boiler, firebox, dome, tank side, bunker side and rear, cab front, rear and side, wheel spokes and rim.
Black	Smokebox, door, chimney, Westinghouse compressor and reservoir, tank front and top, cab roof, footstep treads, brake gear, tyres and centres.
Light brown	Cab interior.
Bright red	Buffer beam and inside of the frames.
Brass	Beading to spectacle plates, whistle. Dome painted over. Nameplates on tank side. Maker's plate removed.
Green	Background to nameplates.
Blue	Pipework and handrails (burnished post-war).
Lining	Black edged in yellow to tank side, boiler bands, bunker side and rear.
Lettering	None.
Carried by	*Ryde*, *Sandown*, *Shanklin*, *Ventnor*, *Wroxall*, *Brading*, *Bonchurch*.

c 11.1917	*Sandown*, *Shanklin*, *Bonchurch* finished in unvarnished red/brown, copper and brass painted over. Reverted to Midland red post-war.

Isle of Wight Central Railway

1887	Metallic crimson lake
Crimson	Boiler, firebox, dome, tank side, cab front, rear and side, splasher, toolbox, footstep backplate, bunker side and rear, outside cylinders, wheel spokes and rim.
Black	Smokebox, door, chimney, tank top, cab roof, footstep treads, brake gear, tyres and centres.
Vermilion	Buffer beam.
Brass	Beading to spectacle plates, whistle and dome on some engines. Maker's plates on bunker side when carried (background colour not known). Copper-capped chimney on most when new.
Lining	Black edged in yellow to tank side, bunker side and rear, boiler bands, footstep backplate and toolbox. Cab front and buffer beams on Nos 6 and 8 when new.
Lettering	None.
Carried by	1/2/4–7.

1893	Garter device
	Colours and lining unchanged.
	Garter transfer on tank side. Running number in matching gilt shaded black 4in high inside the garter.
Carried by	1, 3, 4, 6–9.

1890s	Westinghouse compressor and reservoir fitted, painted black.

1900	'Isle of Wight Central Railway.'
	Colours and lining unchanged.
Lettering	Unshaded 'gold' on tank side, matching number on bunker side. Buffer beams lettered, e.g. 'Nº (coupling) 10'.
Carried by	3, 9–12 (lettering in two lines); 4, 5, 6, 7, 8 (lettering in one line).

1906	'I. W. C. R.'
	Colours and lining unchanged.
Lettering	Gilt with brown shading on tank side, matching number on bunker side. Running number on front buffer beam repeated in centre of rear bunker, e.g. 'Nº 7'. No. 1 Motor had the number on buffer beams at both ends. No. 3 Motor carried the number '3' inside a garter on the cab side.
Carried by	2, 5–7, 9, 11, No. 1 Motor, No. 3 Motor.

1912	'I. W. C.' lined black
Black	Applied to previously crimson and black areas.[24]
Vermilion	Buffer beam. Coupling rods on at least Nos 2, 4, 5, 7, 8, 11, 12. Footplate valance on No. 2, possibly others.[24]
Brass	Beading to spectacle plates, whistle. Any remaining brass domes were painted over.
Lining	Red with white edging to tank and cab side, bunker side and rear, boiler bands and wooden buffer beam ends.
Lettering	Gilt with brown shading on tank side, matching running number on bunker side; numerals in yellow shaded black on buffer beams.
Carried by	2, 4–12.

Southern Railway

1923	Olive green[15]
Green	Boiler, firebox, dome, tank side, cab front, side and rear, bunker side and rear, running plate, splasher side, footstep backplate, sandbox, toolbox, wheel spokes and rim.
Black	Smokebox, door, chimney, Westinghouse compressor and reservoir, tank and splasher top, cab roof, coal rails, footstep treads, brake gear, guard irons, tyres and centres. Background to name and maker's plates.
Brass	Beading to spectacle plates, whistle, splasher trim. Nameplate on tank side, if carried. FYNR W1 carried a maker's plate on the cab side.
Red	Buffer beam.
Lining	Black 3in wide edged in yellow to tank side, cab front, side and rear, bunker side and rear, running plate, footstep backplate, splasher, sandbox, toolbox. Black boiler bands edged in yellow. No discernible lining visible to cab front or rear on some Island repaints.

Lettering	Maunsell 'SOUTHERN' in primrose yellow 6½in high on tank side above a 3in 'W' prefix and 18in running number. Buffer beams 5in shaded numerals, e.g. 'Nº (coupling) 22'. The first four O2s briefly carried LSWR-style numerals on buffer beams. Pull-push connections identified on buffer beams of W2, 3, 9–12, 23–24.
Carried by	FYNR W1–2, IWCR W5, 8–12, IWR W13–18, O2 W19, 21–24 (possibly not W20).[10]
1924–25	Number plate with green background fitted to rear of bunker.[10]

1925 **Dark green**
Different colour. Lining changed to black edged in white.

Carried by	FYNR W1–2, IWCR W10–12, IWR W13, 16, A1X W3, 4, 9, O2 W14–33, E1 W1–4.
1928	Brass nameplates with red background on tank side one third from bottom, prefix and 9in-high running number on bunker side. Number and maker's plate backgrounds painted red to match.
1929	'SOUTHERN' lettering repositioned one third below top of tank side; smaller lettering on IWR and A1X engines. Lining to splashers, sandboxes, wheel spokes, rims, boss, name and number plates. Westinghouse compressor painted green and lined on FYNR W1 and A1X 0-6-0s – discontinued *circa* 1934.
1930s	Prefix and number on front buffer beam, e.g. 'W (coupling) 17". Number on rear beam.
1932	Cab doors painted green and lined. Power classification letter added to front of running plate. Larger bunkers fitted to class O2, painted in green and lined; running number repositioned. Three engines, A1X W2, W3, W4, renumbered as W8, W13, W14.
1936	O2 W15 arrived with no brass splasher trim.

1939 **Unlined dark green**
Unchanged apart from a lack of lining.

Carried by	O2 W24, E1 W4.

1940 **Unlined malachite green**
Green	Boiler, firebox, dome, tank front and side, cab front and side, bunker side and rear, running plate, footstep backplate, splasher, sandbox, toolbox, wheel spokes and rims.
Black	Smokebox, door, chimney, Westinghouse compressor and reservoir, tank and splasher top, cab roof, cab rear, coal rails, footstep tread, brake gear, tyres and centres.
Red	Buffer beam, backgrounds to name and number plates.
Brass	Beading to spectacle plates, whistle, splasher trim, name and number plates.
Lettering	Maunsell 'SOUTHERN' and numerals; number on front buffer beam (and rear on W23). Pull-push connections identified on buffer beams of W8, 13.
Carried by	A1X W8, 13, O2 W17, 18, 22, 28–29 (known examples).

1941 **Unlined black**
Black	Applied to previously green and black areas.
Red	Buffer beam, backgrounds to name and number plates.
Brass	Beading to spectacle plates, whistle, splasher trim, name and number plates. No splasher trim on W15.
Lettering	Maunsell 'SOUTHERN' and numerals. Later, 'Sunshine' yellow with a black interior line, green shading and highlights picked out in yellow. The 9in-high bunker side running number lacked the internal line (6in on W8), as did the 4½in numerals on buffer beams. Pull-push lettering on W8. No buffer beam numerals on 2510. Red-painted coupling rods on W16.
Carried by	A1X W8, O2 W14–16, 19–20, 23, 25, 30, 32–33, E1 W2–3, E4 2510.

1945 **Lined malachite green**
Green	Boiler, firebox, dome, tank front and side, cab front and side, bunker side and rear, running plate, footstep backplate, splasher, sandbox, toolbox, wheel spokes and rims. No splasher trim on W15.
Black	Smokebox, door, chimney, Westinghouse compressor and reservoir, tank and splasher top, cab roof, cab rear, coal rails, footstep tread, brake gear, tyres and centres.
Red	Buffer beam, backgrounds to name and number plates.
Brass	Beading to spectacle plates, whistle, name and number plates.

Lining	Black 2½in wide edged in yellow ¼in to tank front and side, cab front and side, bunker side and rear, running plate, splasher, sandbox, toolbox. Black boiler bands edged in yellow. Some O2s, including W18, 21, 22, 24, 27, 28, 31, had yellow and black lining to the front buffer beam. Minor differences on W29.
Lettering	'Sunshine' yellow with a black interior line, black shading and highlights picked out in yellow. The 9in-high bunker side running number lacked the internal line (6in on W13), as did the 4½in numerals on front buffer beam (and rear on W19), 'W' prefix on W29, pull-push lettering on W13.
Carried by	A1X W13, O2 W17–19, 21–22, 24–32, E1 W1, 4.

1947 **Lined light green**
Unchanged from lined malachite green except for a lighter shade of green, lined black edged in yellow.
The running number was repeated on the bunker rear in place of number plate (possibly 6in high). 'W' prefix and numerals on front buffer beam.

Carried by	O2 W34.
9.1948	Tank side repainted in malachite green, lined and lettered 'BRITISH RAILWAYS' (as below).

British Railways
1948 **Transitional lined malachite green**
Unchanged from SR lined malachite green except:

Lettering	'BRITISH RAILWAYS' 6in high in yellow and black without highlights and internal lines. Unchanged bunker side running number and buffer beam numerals. 'SOUTHERN RAILWAY' chipped away from number plates.
Smaller matching 6in bunker side running number on W33 and (by October) on W15.
Carried by	O2 W15, 20, 31, 33.
Partial repaints	A1X W13, O2 W17–19, 21–22, 24–30, 32, E1 W1, 4.

1948 **Transitional unlined black**
Unchanged from SR unlined black except:

Lettering	'BRITISH RAILWAYS' 6in high in yellow and green without highlights and internal lines. Unchanged bunker side running number and buffer beam numerals. 'SOUTHERN RAILWAY' chipped away from number plates.
Carried by	E1 W3.
Partial repaints	A1X W8, O2 W14, 16, 23, E1 W2.

1948 **Transitional lined black**
Unchanged from SR unlined black except:

Brass	Splasher trim painted over.
Lining	Grey, yellow and red applied to the running plate, tank and bunker side.
The bunker lining was at the same height as the tank panel and did not reach the top of the bunker; that on the running plate was not curved downwards at ends. Grey ⅝in wide edged in yellow ⅛in outside a 1⅝in gap in black and a ¼in red line on the inside. That on the tank side had curved corners 4in in radius and were inset about 3in from the edge. Boiler bands had ¼in-wide red lines.[15]
Lettering	W14 had 'BRITISH RAILWAYS' in Gill Sans yellow 8 in high. On W16–17, 21 the tank side was left bare. Yellow 10 in running number above a 2 in SR classification letter on bunker side; shaded numerals on front buffer beam.
Carried by	O2 W14, 16–17, 21.

From late 1949	W16–17, 21: nameplates lowered when emblem attached to tank side.
By 4.1950	W14: nameplates lowered, tank partially repainted and emblem attached. Lining on the running plate had been standardised by 9.1952 but tank and bunker side lining were unchanged until a repaint in 1954.

1949	Standard lined black
Black	Applied to previously green and black areas.
Red	Buffer beam, backgrounds to name and number plates.
Brass	Beading to spectacle plates, whistle, name and number plates; splasher trim painted over (missing from W15).
Lining	Grey, cream and red applied to the running plate, tank, bunker and cab side. Grey ⅝in wide edged in cream ⅛in outside a 1⅝in gap in black and a ¼in red line on the inside. That on the tank side had curved corners of 4in radius and were inset about 3in from the edge. It curved downwards at each end of the running plate. Boiler bands had ¼in-wide red lines.[15]
Lettering	Gill Sans 10in-high cream running number above a 2in SR classification letter on bunker side.
	W35–36 had cream buffer beam numerals until their first overhauls. Other engines had shaded numbers on front buffer beam; W34–36 carried numerals on the rear beam for several years.
	Pull-push lettering on W35–36 until 3.1955 and 12.1954 respectively.
Carried by	O2 W14–36.
From late 1949	Left- and right-facing emblem attached to tank side. Nameplates lowered when the standard size was applied.
	W18 and W28 briefly had a smaller-size emblem and W36 ran without one until 1952.

1949	Standard unlined black
	As for lined black apart from the absence of lining.
	W2 ran without an emblem until 1952.
Carried by	O2 W24, 36, E1 W1–4.

1951	Shed plates fitted to smokebox door.
1954	BR power classification letter placed above running number on bunker side.
1957	New left- and right-facing emblem.
1960	SR classification letter removed from bunker side.
From 12.1960	Left-facing emblem applied following repaints to W16–18, 24, 27–30.[15]

Colourised Photographs

This book includes several black and white images that have been colourised. All manner of factors hamper the creation of accurate colour representations. Nobody alive today will have seen the earlier liveries and the memory can play tricks on those who can remember the later ones. Another problem is that names given to some colours bore little resemblance to what they purported to represent, 'Stroudley Improved Engine Green' being a classic example – it was officially gamboge. Paint pigments were mixed by hand so consistency was difficult to achieve, a slight problem that remains to the present day. Once paint is applied, colours can fade or change in tone for a variety of reasons. The ambient light will also affect how colours appear and reflections from glossy surfaces present a further problem to overcome. Colour cards in various books on liveries sometimes give different tones for supposedly the same colour, but they could easily be more accurate than old colour photos, which can suffer from their own multitude of problems. The SR colours have been sourced from colour cards accompanying the various HMRS publications[15] but those for the Island companies proved more problematical. The 'Furness red' in the image of IWR *Sandown* was cloned from a colour card in a book by Ernest F. Carter entitled *Britain's Railway Liveries, 1825 to 1948*. However, there is no guarantee that this was the precise shade used by the IWR and similar reservations apply to the other images.

Appendix 5: SR Locomotive Restrictions

Timetable beginning	Ryde to Ventnor	Newport to Sandown	Ryde to Cowes	Brading to Bembridge	Newport to Freshwater	Medina Wharf	Merstone to Ventnor West	Shide pit & Cement Mills siding
7.1923	None			Only *Ryde, Shanklin, Wroxall* ‡		Only W9-12	None	None
1.10.1923			Not 206 211*		Not W6 7			
14.7.1924		Not W6 21 22 206 211	Not W6 21 22 206 211	Only W4 5 8 *Ryde Shanklin Wroxall* ‡	Not W7 ‡	Only W1 2 9-12		
22.9.1924		Not W6						
12.7.1925			Not W6 †					
21.9.1925				Only W4 5 8 13-16				
11.7.1926	None		†	Only W8 13-16				
10.7.1927			None	Only W1 2 8 10-14 16	Only W1 2 10-12			
17.6.1928				Only W1-3 8 10-13 16	Only W1-3 10-12		Only W1-3 10-12 §	
7.7.1929								
6.7.1930				Only W1-4 9-13 16	Only W1-4 9-12			
5.7.1931								
18.6.1932					Only W1-4 9-13 16	Only W1-4 9-12		
1933 onwards				Not class E1	None	None	None	Not classes E1 O2

* = Over Newport Drawbridge and Cement Mills viaduct. † = Class O2 limited to 10 mph over Cement Mills viaduct.
‡ = No engines weighing 35 tons or more. § = Also W8 one day a week for relief purposes. None = No weight restrictions.
Details obtained from SR Working Timetables.

Ryde to Ventnor
Newport to Freshwater

Ryde to Newport and Cowes

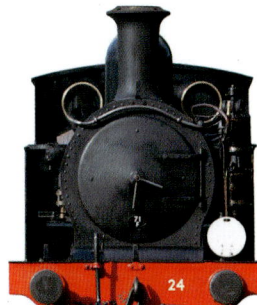

Newport to Sandown
Cowes to Ventnor via Sandown
Brading to Bembridge (1)

Newport to Cowes (2)

Ryde to Ventnor limited stop (3)

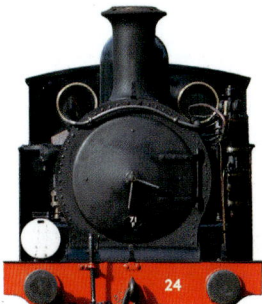

Newport to Ventnor West

Brading to Bembridge (4)

These disc codes applied to passenger trains from 1930 except:
(1) from 1936
(2) observed in BR days
(3) from 1931
(4) until 1936

Route Indication Discs

Appendix 6: Locomotive Shed allocations 1922–66

Year	Ryde shed	Newport shed(s)	To IW	Withdrawn	To mainland	Total
1922	IWR *Ryde, Sandown, Shanklin, Ventnor, Wroxall, Brading, Bonchurch*	FYNR 1-2	IWCR 4-12			18
1923	W13-18 206 211	W1-2 4-12	206 211		*Sandown*	19
1924	W5-6 16 18 19-22	W1-2 4 7-15 17	W21-22			21
1925	W5-6 19-26	W1-2 7-14 17-18	W23-26	W4 6 15		22
1926	W13-14 16 19-26	W2 8-12 18 27-30	W27-30	W5-7 17		23
1927	W13 16 19-24 27	W1-2 3 8 10-12 18 25-26 28-31	W3 31	W9 14		23
1928	W13 16 19-26	W1-2 3 8 10-12 27-32	W32	W18		23
1929	W13 16 19-26	W1-2 3-4 10-12 27-32	W4	W8		23
1930	W13 16 17-24	W1-2 3-4 9 10-12 25-32	W9 17-18			26
1931	W3 9 17-24	W1-2 4 10-12 13 16 25-32				26
1932	W9 13* 17-26	W1-3 8* 10-12 14* 16 27-32	W1-3	W1 13		27
1933	W9 13 17-26	W1-4 8 10-12 14 27-32	W4	W16	W1 16	27
1934	W9 13 17-26	W1-4 8 10-12 14 27-32			W13	27
1935	W9 W13 W17-26	W1-4 8 10-12 14 27-32				27
1936	W14-24	W1-4 8 11 13 25-33	W14-16 33		W9 10 12 14	27
1947	W14-24	W1-4 8 13 25-34 2510	W29 34 2510		W11 29	28
1949	W14-24	W1-4 25-36	W35-36		W8 13 2510	27
1955*	W14 16-18 20-22 24	W1-4 25-33 35-36		W15 19 23 24		23
1956*	W14 16-18 20-22 24 26-27 29-30 35-36	W1 3-4 25 28 31-33		W2		22
1957	W3-4 14 16-18 20-22 24-33 35-36			W1		21
1959	W4 14 16-18 20-22 24-33 35-36			W3		20
1960	W14 16-18 20-22 24-33 35-36			W4		19
1962	W14 16-18 20-22 24 26-33 35-36			W25		18
1964	W14 16-18 20-22 24 26-31 33 35			W32 36		16
1965	W14 16-17 20-22 24 26-29 31 33 35			W18 30		14
1966	W14 16-17 20 22 24 27-28 31 33 D2554		D2554	W21 26 29 35		11

Allocations and totals as at 31 December. * Official allocations uncertain. There were other temporary transfers that have not been recorded. Class A1X W8, 13 & 14 (noted *) were renumbered from W2, 3 & 4 in 1932. The BR shed codes were Ryde 71F, later 70H; Newport 71E, later 70G.

References

1. *The Isle of Wight Railway* by R. Maycock & R. Silsbury. The Oakwood Press, 1999.
2. *The Isle of Wight Central Railway* by R. Maycock & R. Silsbury. The Oakwood Press, 2001.
3. *The Freshwater, Yarmouth & Newport Railway* by R. Maycock & R. Silsbury. The Oakwood Press, 2003.
4. *The Piers, Tramways and Railways at Ryde* by R. Maycock & R. Silsbury. The Oakwood Press, 2005.
5. *The Isle of Wight Railways From 1923 Onwards* by R. Maycock & R. Silsbury. The Oakwood Press, 2006.
6. *Once Upon a Line* by A. Britton, four volumes. Oxford Publishing Co., 1983–94.
7. Newspapers and periodicals in the British Museum Newspaper library, Colindale, London, and locally.
8. Minutes, accounts and related documents of the Isle of Wight Railway. National Archives, Kew.
9. *Locomotives of the Glasgow & South Western Railway* by D. L. Smith. David & Charles, 1976.
10. The MacLeod papers and P. C. Allen's notes. Isle of Wight Railway archives, Havenstreet.
11. Board of Trade inspections and correspondence. National Archives, Kew.
12. *A Locomotive History of the Railways of the Isle of Wight* by D. L. Bradley. Railway Correspondence & Travel Society, 1982.
13. *Chronicles of Boulton's Siding* by A. R. Bennett. Locomotive Publishing Co., 1927.
14. Beyer, Peacock & Co. collection. Museum of Science & Industry, Manchester.
15. *Southern Style, London & South Western Railway, London, Brighton & South Coast Railway, Southern Railway* and *After Nationalisation 1948–1964* by J. Harvey and P. J. Wisdom. Historical Model Railway Society, 2014–20.
16. Name and maker's plates. Isle of Wight Railway museum, Havenstreet.
17. *The Railways and Tramways of Ryde* by A. Blackburn & J. Mackett. Town and Country Press, 1971.
18. *Nameplates of the Big Four* by F. Burridge. Oxford Publishing Co., 1975.
19. Board of Trade accident reports. National Archives, Kew.
20. *Locomotives built by Manning, Wardle & Co.* by F. W. Harman. Century Locoprints, 2005.
21. *The Railways of the Isle of Wight* by P. C. Allen, 1928.
22. *The South Western Railway* by C. Hamilton Ellis. George Allen & Unwin, 1956.
23. Letter from F. Birch October 2003 and article *The Fovant Military Camp line* by N. Pattenden, July 2016. Both in *South Western Circular*, magazine of the South Western Circle.
24. Island companies' liveries. Contemporary paintings by C. Hamilton Ellis.
25. LSWR and SR registers of locomotive stock and boilers. National Archives, Kew.
26. *SR Locomotives 1923–1935* and *The Railways of the Isle of Wight,* articles by C. G. Woodnutt. *Railway Observer*, 1931, 1936.
27. Eastleigh Works drawings register. National Railway Museum, York.
28. Minutes of SR and BR Traffic Managers' meetings. National Archives, Kew.
29. Diaries kept by Thomas Smeaton 1928–1934. Isle of Wight Railway archives, Havenstreet.
30. SR Isle of Wight working timetables and appendices. National Archives, Kew.
31. Locomotive notes in *Railway Observer*, magazine of the Railway Correspondence & Travel Society, 1927–65.
32. Minutes of the Cowes & Newport Railway, Ryde & Newport Railway, Isle of Wight (Newport Junction) Railway and Ryde, Newport & Cowes Joint Committee. National Archives, Kew.
33. *Locomotives of the London & South Western Railway* parts 1 & 2 by D. L. Bradley. Railway Correspondence & Travel Society 1965–1967. Also, *LSWR Locomotives,* four volumes, by D. L. Bradley. Oxford Publishing Co., 1985–89.
34. Unpublished notes on IWCR and FYNR locomotives by G. R. Barrett and H. W. Miller covering the period c. 1875 to c. 1900.
35. Articles in *The Locomotive* magazine, 1900–43.
36. Minutes of the London & South Western Railway and related documents. National Archives, Kew.
37. Board of Trade Company records. National Archives, Kew.
38. Minutes, accounts and related documents of the Isle of Wight Central Railway. National Archives, Kew.
39. Articles and news items in *Wight Report* and *Island Rail News,* magazines of The Isle of Wight Railway Co., 1967 onwards.
40. *'Godshill' A Contractor's engine in the Isle of Wight,* article by S. H. P. Higgins. Stephenson Locomotive Society Journal December 1953.
41. *Rails in the Isle of Wight* by P. C. Allen & A. B. MacLeod. George Allen & Unwin, 1967.
42. *The Ventnor West Branch* by P. Paye. Wild Swan Publications, 1992.
43. Articles and news items in *Railway Magazine*, 1897 onwards.
44. *Railway Heraldry* by G. Dow. David & Charles, 1973.
45. *William Stroudley Craftsman of Steam* by H. J. Campbell Cornwell. David & Charles, 1968.

46. IWCR locomotive reports dated 1901 and 1911. Isle of Wight Railway archives, Havenstreet.
47. Correspondence with Hurst, Nelson & Co. Isle of Wight Railway archives, Havenstreet.
48. *West Medina Cement Mill, Dodnor, Isle of Wight: a History* by A. Dinnis 2016.
49. Appendix to the IWCR working timetable 1919. Isle of Wight Railway archives, Havenstreet.
50. Minutes, accounts and related documents of the Freshwater, Yarmouth & Newport Railway. National Archives, Kew.
51. Locomotive drawings and other documents, Isle of Wight Railway archives, Havenstreet.
52. *The Railway Products of Baguley-Drewry Ltd* by A. Civil & R. Etherington. Industrial Railway Society 2008.
53. Locomotive notes and articles in *Southern Railway Magazine*, 1923–48.
54. *The Island Terriers* by M. Reed. Kingfisher Railway Publications, 1989.
55. Minutes of the Ryde Pier Company and related documents. National Archives, Kew.
56. Obituaries as reported on the Institution of Mechanical Engineers website and in original proceedings.
57. Southern Railway inspection reports. National Archives, Kew.
58. *MacLeod's Other Island* by T. Hastings & R. Silsbury. The Isle of Wight Railway Co., 2011.
59. Files relating to SR Floating Crane No. 1, Associated British Ports archive, Southampton.
60. *Special traffic on the Isle of Wight* and *Branch Line Closures,* articles by M. Brinton. *Island Rail News,* magazine of The Isle of Wight Railway Co., 2010 and 2013.
61. Eastleigh and Brighton Works drawings in *A Locomotive History of Southern Locomotives* by J. H. Russell. Oxford Publishing Co., 1991.
62. *An Illustrated History of Southern Pull-push Stock* by M. King. Oxford Publishing Co., 2006.
63. *The Isle of Wight E1 class 0-6-0Ts*, article by P. Paye. *Back Track* magazine, April 2002.
64. Diaries kept by C. G. Woodnutt 1947–68. Isle of Wight Railway archives, Havenstreet.
65. *Locomotives of the London, Brighton & South Coast Railway*, Part 3 by D. L. Bradley. Railway Correspondence & Travel Society 1974.
66. BR (S) General Manager's correspondence and other documents concerning Isle of Wight closures. National Archives, Kew.
67. Information from M. Birkin, M. Downer, R. Francis, D. Gawn, P. Hayward, J. Maskell, R. Newman, S. Plowman, A. Summers, R. Thorneycroft, J. Woodhams and others.
68. BR (S) register of locomotive stock, record cards, returns and related correspondence. National Archives, Kew.
69. *Ryde Works* by C. G. Woodnutt. Article in *Railway World* January, 1967.
70. *Tube trains on the Isle of Wight* by B. Hardy. Capital Transport Publishing, 2003.
71. *Underground News*, the magazine of the London Underground Railway Society.
72. *BR Shunters* by C. W. Judge. Oxford Publishing Co., 1979.
73. *Rail, Rail Enthusiast* and *Railways Illustrated* magazines, various issues.
74. *The Bicester Military Railway* by E. R. Lawton & M. W. Sackett. Oxford Publishing Co., 1992.
75. *Locomotive Magazine*, magazine of the Industrial Locomotive Society, issue 17. 1980, and the Society's handbook.
76. Correspondence with Cheek Bros. Ltd, 1985. Isle of Wight Railway archives, Havenstreet.
77. Saro Laminated Wood Products Ltd, descriptive brochure 1948. Isle of Wight Railway archives, Havenstreet.
78. *The Terrier*, newsletter of the Sandown Railway Enthusiasts Club.
79. *Sandown Isle of Wight 'Nostalgia'* by D. & L. Bamborough, 2014.
80. *LSWR Stock Book* and *LBSCR Stock Book* by P. Cooper. Kingfisher Publications. 1986, 1990.

Index

The numbers in **bold italics** refer to images.